PREFACE

1916 was one of the bloodiest war-torn years in human history. It was a year .... in Ireland an event which helped change the future of Ireland as W.B. Yeats wrote 'All changed, changed utterly: A terrible beauty is born' [Easter 1916] but in terms of bloodletting the Easter Rising was a miniscule event compared to the Battle of the Somme when gigantic armies battled it out killing and maiming in our first all-out industrial war. It was one of the largest battles of World War I, in which more than 1,000,000 men were wounded or killed, making it one of the bloodiest battles in human history. The Germans disposed of many of their dead by sending trainloads of corpses to be incinerated in a blast furnace. Many on all sides were obliterated as if they had never been on earth. Heroism was unbounded but as in every war others took advantage such as those who avoided conscription while others made profiteering a career and millions of women and children became widows and orphans. And the stay-at-homes safely cheered from the side-lines.

And all of it for what? The glory of Kings and Emperors, politicians and generals and in the main they found their petty kingdoms and grandiose plans crumble to dust around them. Revolution was soon to rage across Europe and sweep away most of the old regimes. This book deals with events local, national and international for despite everything life still goes on. Mundane or the seemingly mundane sits cheek by jowl with seemingly momentous. The excerpts in this book are taken from the three local Fermanagh newspapers of the time – the Fermanagh Herald, Fermanagh Times and Impartial Reporter who all included copy from the British and Irish national papers. Their origin is indicated as IM (Impartial Reporter) FT (Fermanagh Times or Fermanagh Herald.

John B. Cunningham 19-5-2015.

January 1916

Fermanagh Herald January 1st 1916. Obiter Dicta, (Ed. It means by the way) Christmas Day 1915. How will it dawn? How will it dawn on the coming Christmas Day? It was Charles Kingsley's question in 1868. My question is: How will it dawn the coming New Year's Day? It should be a question deeply vital to the interests of everyone today. Writing, as I am on Christmas day, I cannot help casting back to the optimistic days of last spring the days of illusionment, when many of us walked in a fool's paradise. We were saying to one another: It will be over by Christmas! We dare to dream beautiful dreams of peace on earth. Today we are wiser and sadder, though no jot less determined. And now we're about to enter on a new year, commencing with bloodshed and slaughter. How will it dawn for on the coming New Year's Day?

Today the merry boisterous spirits of Charles Dickens is out in the cold. We have little heart for frivolity, merriment, and even the boy at home for his holidays is unnaturally subdued. Many homes, alas, are no longer homes. They are just walls and roofs; places where many a mother or father are eating their Christmas dinner and stealing around the house like ghosts. Poor Jack, I wonder how my boy is today. Perhaps somewhere in Gallipoli is the little grave of him who a year ago was the bread-winner. Somewhere in France the elder brother leapt the golden stile. We know that father or son or brother is telling us from beyond the stars that all is well. But we want him; without him home is not home; Christmas is not Christmas. Today and on New Year's Day both Hall and Cottage rejoice together or mourn together.

IN THE TRENCHES. But today - Christ Day - how did it dawn; what picture unfolded itself as the sun rose in the high heavens, and cast its translucent gaze over the bloody plains of France; over the pinnacle heights of Gallipoli, where so many sons of Patrick have breathed their last. Did it disclose a scene of awful carnage, or what? We know that on this day last year the better instinct was, for a few hours, triumphant. Men forgot to they were out to kill and maim; they remembered they were of the same flesh and blood. They laid aside their instruments of death; they exchanged cigarettes; they talked no doubt of homes in Saxony or Bethnal Green, or sunny, picturesque Fermanagh. Then the circle of military discipline waved her wand. Men sought for their burrows, and once more their sole aim in life was to make death. Christmas came and went. For a short space there was between the trenches peace and goodwill among men. Then the dogs of war were let loose. What was it like out there in France today? Had the poor fellows plum pudding? Hardly. Was the ground damp and odiferous? How was that ghastly wound; did it cause some brave Irishman untold agony - agony on a day like this! Discipline probably made it impossible for friends and foe to meet as brothers. Yet in the rival trenches there was surely much in common - the same great heartache for home - the same hunger for the little children's arms - the same longing to look into the eyes of the girl, of the mother, who writes so bravely, who prays so unceasingly, and cries just at times like Christmas, so heartbrokenly.

Fermanagh Herald January 1st 1916. JOTTINGS. The Statistical Branch of the Department of Agriculture has informed the Armagh Chamber of Commerce that the whole of the wheat grown in Ireland would only feed the population of the country for three weeks.

The death has occurred of Mr. William Quinn, Lisnarick, Irvinestown, who for many years had charge of the Archdale Estate office. Deceased who had reached his 54th year, was deputy vice-chairman of the Irvinestown Guardians, and was connected with various other bodies.

Captain E. J. King, 6th Inniskillings, who has been wounded in Serbia, is a son of the Rev. E. J. King, Kildallen Rectory, Belturbet, County Cavan. He received his commission from the O. T. C. at Dublin University on September 12th 1914 and was promoted captain on May 24, 1915. He was with his regiment at the Suvla Bay landing and subsequently accompanied the 10th Division to Serbia.

The wages earned on munitions by many women and girls without any previous knowledge or experience are surprisingly large, says the *Daily News*. It would be very interesting to know what is the biggest average weekly earnings of a female "hand" who can be legitimately classed as an amateur. The managing director of a munitions factory told the writer recently that he had several girls who, without any training before they came to him, were each receiving nearly £4 a week after a month at his works. "They beat heaps of men hollow," he added "naturally there are men who don't like it. But that's their lookout. The labourer is worthy of his or her hire in war time or in peace."

The purchase of a new anatomical skeleton by the Farnham (Surrey) Guardians for use in the training of nurses in the infirmary was again discussed at a meeting of the Board, says the *Aldershot News*. The House Committee recommended the purchase of a new skeleton at a cost of £8 10 shillings. An amendment that the purchase be postponed until after the war, because the skeleton was not absolutely necessary, was defeated.

An Ashford, Kent, ferret dealer has during the past few months sent no fewer than 600 ferrets to the British front in Flanders and France to assist in hunting out the hordes of rats which infest the trenches. Rat hunting has become quite a sport with the troops and owing to the abnormal demand for ferrets the price of these intrepid little fighters has risen in the Ashford district from one shilling to five shillings each.

Private John Cheevers, 2nd Battalion Royal Inniskilling Fusiliers, a native of Cookstown, who has been 16 months at the front, recently had a short furlough. He had some narrow escapes in 16 months fighting and had no serious injury. He says that the Inniskillings met the famous Prussian Guards on more than one bayonet encounter, and had the better of them. The Prussian Guards, he adds are big men, but the Inniskillings were more than a match for them with the bayonet.

The year 1915 was one of great activity in the Belfast shipbuilding yards, and the war brought much diversified work, which necessitated night shifts. Harland and Wolff's did not launch a merchant vessel during the war, but six small steamers were built by Workman and Clark's for the fruit carrying trade. Employment is plentiful and the scarcity of skilled labour is manifest.

An extraordinary discovery is reported by an American farmer, who it states to have found that feeding pigs on snakes imparts a delicious flavour to the pork. The farm concerned, it appears was infested with snakes which defied all efforts at extermination. Several specimens of a breed of small black pigs were bought and turned loose on the farm. Some time later the farmer received a surprise in the form of a letter from a New York restaurant, which after several weeks had succeeded in tracing to the farmer a shipment of pork which had caused much favourable comment by patrons. It appeared that the pork had gained a particularly rich gamey flavor, and the restaurant proprietor contracted with the farmer for all the pork he could raise.

"HANDS OFF, BOYS!"—Christmas Morning in the Trenches.

Describing the delivery of the Christmas mail to the British troops at the front a correspondent says that during Christmas week the heaviest daily mail consisted of 18,500 bags of letters and parcels. By a conservative estimate the Army postal authorities reckon this to have represented about three million letters and half a million parcels.

Fermanagh Herald January 1st 1916. BOXING DAY CUSTOM. The principal feature of the observance of Boxing Day in the Isle of Man consisted of the ancient custom of celebrating the hunt of the wren. Children bearing a Holly bush decorated with ribbons paraded the streets singing a curious folk-song. The bush formerly contained the body of a wren stoned to death on Christmas Day, but in these days this cruel portion is omitted. The children are rewarded with pence.

Fermanagh Herald January 1st 1916. BRIGADIER-GENERAL L. J. LIPSETT HONOURED. Brigadier General Lewis James Lipsett, a member of the well-known Ballyshannon family of that name, had the honour of being received by the King at Buckingham Palace on the 22nd of December, when his Majesty invested him with the insignia of a Companion of the Order of St. Michael and St. George. The only surviving son of the late Mr. Richard Lipsett, the Brigadier-General was educated at Bedford Grammar School and the Royal Military College. He entered the Royal Irish Regiment there in 1894 and wears the medals with two clasps for the operations in at the north-west frontier of India in 1897/8 and the medal issued for the suppression of the native rising in Natal in 1906. Brigadier-General Lipsett has served with distinction on the Western front being in command of a Canadian brigade, and has been mentioned in dispatches by Field Marshall Viscount French, in addition to being appointed Companion of the Order of Saint Michael and Saint George on the occasion of the King's birthday. It may be recalled that Brigadier-General Lipsett had behaved with great gallantry in the severe fighting at Hill 60, where his cousin, Private W. A. Lipsett – a former member of the Irish Bar – fell in action.

Fermanagh Herald January 1st 1916. MARKING CATTLE. A case of some importance to stock breeders was heard at the Navan Petty Sessions last week. A farmer and his son were charged with ill-treating cattle by marking them with a knife. A police sergeant deposed that the son marked three cattle in his presence. The cut was 1½ inches long and from 1/16th to 1/8 inch deep the skin being cut through into the flesh. The senior defendant stated that he was 40 years in the cattle trade and marked his cattle that way with a knife. He had no alternative method of marking them efficiently. He used to mark them with scissors but there was confusion. The Department's Veterinary Inspector held such a practice was unnecessarily cruel. Cattle could always be marked with the scissors sufficiently to identify them. 20,000 cattle were shipped from Dublin Port every week, and they hardly ever got cattle marked with a knife. The magistrates fined each of the defendants 20 shillings.

Fermanagh Herald January 1st 1916. SCHOOLING AND BOY LABOUR IN ENGLAND. They are coming to think in England that too much schooling – by which is meant too long schooling – is bad for skilled labour in manual work says the *Freeman*. The difficulties in the way of agriculture have brought this conviction home. There is a shortage of agricultural labour and if the farmers are to maintain their normal rate of production they must make up the deficiency by employing inexperienced town labour, or women, or boys under 15 years. The employment of boys is contrary to the school regulations in most districts. There is a strong demand for the abolition of these regulations. It is pointed out that only boys that begin agricultural work early in life are skilled beyond the work of mere labourers, and, since compulsory education took them away from the fields agriculturalists have lost their old cunning in ploughing, draining, ditching, thatching, and hedging, not to speak of dairying and stock grazing. Schooling, say advocates of boy labour on the land, when prolonged beyond the ages of 11 or 12, destroys the boys' chances of advancement in agricultural work, and is bad for the boys and bad for the country. Labour is scarce and will become scarcer. F.H.

Fermanagh Herald January 1st 1916. NEWS IN BRIEF. MAN DROWNED IN FLAXHOLE. The body of Joseph Martin, a servant in the employment of Mr. Peter McArdle, Moraghy, near Castleblaney, was found in a flaxhole late on Sunday night. The deceased who was a native of Donaghmoyne, near Carrickmacross, was 29 years of age.

ALLEGED GAMING HOUSE. The Glasgow police raided an alleged gambling house in Oxford Street, Glasgow, and took into custody 72 men, who were marched off to the Police Court and brought before the magistrates. Six were liberated on bail of £5 each, and the remainder was set free on bail of one guinea. All the money was paid. Lively scenes followed the arrests but there was no disturbance, the men's submitting quietly to the police instructions.

January 6th 1916. HOW OUR MEN SAVED THE DAY. THE RETREAT FROM SERBIA. THE ROYAL INNISKILLINGS. In a vivid and thrilling story of the heroism of the Irish troops in the retreat from Serbia, 'F' in the *Weekly Dispatch* says:- Nothing finer can be imagined than the heroic stand of the depleted 10th division who rallied under the attacks of overwhelming forces to the cry of – 'Stick it, jolly boys; give 'em hell, Connaughts.' A few thousand Irishman and a few hundred Englishmen turned what might have been a disaster into a successful retreat just as surely as the artillery of the Second Corps at daybreak on August 26, 1914, 'the most critical date of all,' turned what might have been an annihilating attack into a successful retirement. In the first trenches were the Connaughts, the Munsters, the Dublin Fusiliers, the Hampshires and the Inniskillings, the latter – to a large extent Ulstermen – holding the extreme right wing. Dawn had scarcely broken when the enemy made his expected attack. The conditions wholly favoured him for a fairly dense fog prevailed and under its cover the Bulgars were able to get within 300 yards of parts of our line without being observed.

The Inniskillings were the first to be attacked; about 5.00 a.m. their outposts were driven in, and then a great mass of the enemy swooped down on the trenches, but were driven back by the fire of our Maxim guns and by the steady magazine fire which came from the trenches. Scarcely had the attack on the extreme right of the line had time to develop the main body of Bulgarians were seen running down a defile leading to the centre of our front. As they reached the end of the defile they spread out as from a bottleneck and with wild cheers flung themselves on our line. But before they had got so far our guns smashed and battered the procession of men leaping out of the narrow gorge. It was impossible to miss them. British artillery has never had such a target since the first battle of Ypres, when the guns literally mowed down the half trained German soldiers who attacked on the Yser.

The brave Irish regiments were pouring lead into them as fast as they could load their rifles. They poured into the oncoming masses as much as 175 rounds at point blank range. This will give an idea of the slaughter that went on this December morning as the dawn slowly beat the mist away. Mingling with the roar of the artillery and the clatter-clatter of the machine guns and the sharp snap of the rifles were the hoarse cries of the half-maddened volunteers whose officers ever drove them on to the death that came quick and hot from the British trenches. Men of splendid physique they were who faced the hail of lead, cheering in a sort of wild enthusiasm of battle with bugles and trumpets blowing defiant challenges, as in the knightly days of the tourney. They did not know many of them whether they were attacking French, British or Turks, but unquestioning, unthinking he came on with the fearlessness of life deserving of a better cause, leaping into a trenches and falling dead with a bullet in their throat or bayonet wound in their breast, or with head blown off by one of our shells. I.R.

10th Battalion, 'C' Company of the Inniskilling Fusiliers - circa 1916

But it was, for all our grim resistance, a hopeless kind of struggle. Sooner or later that unceasing stream of men issuing out of the narrow defile must sweep us back. Always the enemy returned to the charge, undeterred by heavy losses, undismayed by our deadly gun and magazine fire. The line held and to their cheers we gave back answer and to their cries we gave answer with our own cries and if sometimes the line faltered the shouts of officers and men: "Stick it, jolly boys, give them hell, Connaughts" brought new life and new strength. They outnumbered the 10th division in the proportion of at least 8 to 1 and they were obstinately bent on its destruction at whatever cost to themselves. Their artillery far exceeded ours in weight of metal but in effectiveness there was not a comparison. Almost all of our shells told when many of theirs did no more than splinter rocks yards away. The division never lost its cohesion and it gave ground only at the rate of 2 miles a day, which is a proof, if any were needed, of the splendid rearguard action that this so much outnumbered force fought.

In the two days battle the 10th Division inflicted on the enemy at least four times their own number of casualties and what is possibly equally important they taught him the temper and moral of British infantry. The 10th division saved the situation by a display of courage and dogged heroism that cannot be too highly praised. It is hard to explain how the 10th division, encompassed as it was, won through, and perhaps the most satisfactory thing to do is to fall back on the explanation of the Connaught Ranger whose only grumble was that he was kept 12 hours fighting without food; "They beat us with numbers. We couldn't hope to hold up against the crowd they sent against us, a daft, clumsy gang of men. We gave them hell but their numbers beat us." I.R.

January 6th 1916. THE DARDANELLES. THE WITHDRAWAL. THE TURKS OUTWITTED IN A BRILLIANT OPERATION. The withdrawal in the Dardanelles was the most difficult and dangerous work that has yet been undertaken in this campaign. It was completed in the small hours of the 28th Inst. The entire reserve of ammunition and nearly all the stores were removed from the beaches under the eyes and guns of a powerful Turkish army which had never realized that the operation had begun until some hours after the last officers of the naval beach parties had shipped us to their packet boats and steamed away. Lord Kitchener in November brought the fact home to most of us that the whole position here was under review by the highest authorities. That the withdrawal could be done without a loss at all entered into no one's calculation.

The problem was to withdraw divisions and their gear occupying a front of roughly 20,000 yards in length, which was hardly anywhere more than 500 yards, and at some places not more than 50 yards from the enemies trenches, and embark them from beaches which were nowhere beyond field gun range of the enemy positions, and in places actually not more than 50 yards from the enemies

2nd Mounted Brigade concentrating on the banks of Suvla Bay on 18 August 1915.

trenches and embark them from beaches which were nowhere beyond field gun range of the enemy positions and in places actually within rifle range of them. The Turks occupied higher ground and nearly all of the Suvla Bay area was visible to them. The suffering of the men from cold, wet and exposure had been so severe that thousands had to be sent away to recover and frostbite became for a while as bad as it had been last year in Flanders. The sufferings of the Turks were at least as bad. I.R.

January 6th 1916. DISPATCH ABOUT SUVLA BAY. HOW THE LANDING WAS EFFECTED. DESCRIPTION OF A SPLENDID FAILURE. WHY OPERATIONS DID NOT SUCCEED. General Sir Ian Hamilton's dispatch dealing with the Suvla Bay operations and the historic part played by the 10th (Irish) division has been issued. The dispatch deals in much detail with the operations leading up to and following the landing of the 10th Division, and gives special praise to the great gallantry of the Irish regiments. Having described the brilliant work of the 10th Division and mentioned the incomparable 29th Division he explained that he cabled to the War Office for reinforcements at once which were not sent him. "It seemed humanly speaking," he adds "a certainty that if this help would have been sent at once we could have cleared a passage for our fleet to Constantinople. I.R.

January 6th 1916. OLD FERMANAGH ROADS. Perhaps the oldest in all the Lough Erne country was one discovered 6 feet deep overgrown with peat a few years ago in a bog near Abohill in the barony of Glenawley, near Mullaghdun. There was laid bare a distinct roadway of trees cut in two, as if to carry traffic through a soft portion of an ancient track. Mr. Jason Coulter, of Brockagh Bridge and others saw it, and the purpose of the blocks of timber was only too plainly visible, as they rested on other blocks. The roadway was also seen in Rossmacawinny bog further on. In the ancient times travellers or marauding bands made their way from one prominent object in the landscape to the other; and the direction of this road seem to indicate that it had led from Belmore Mountain to Benaughlin. The townland of Tents is elevated and the word Tents signifies a light, and a light on Tents hill would guide a wayfarer by night along this road towards Belmore. For so far it is the only primitive road of the kind which has been laid bare in the country. I.R.
(Ed. This is a Togher (Irish: An Tochar, meaning "causeway or level place")

Fermanagh Herald January 8th 1916. OBITER DICTA, (ED. BY THE WAY). JOTTINGS. The attempt of the Enniskillen Guardians to amalgamate the Unions in Fermanagh was discussed by the Lisnaskea Guardians on Saturday. The proposition was opposed at this meeting on the grounds that no facts or figures were produced by the proposers of the scheme to show that saving would be affected by the proposal. On a vote it was decided to postpone the question of sending delegates on hold until such time as figures would be shown that would go to prove that the proposal would be a financial success. At the same meeting Dr. Annesley, medical officer, Derrylin, applied for and obtained one year's leave of absence as he had obtained a commission in the R.A.M.C. He suggested that Dr. Knox, Lisnaskea should be appointed as a successor at the same salary.

An enthusiastic meeting of the South Fermanagh Executive of the U. I. L. was held in Enniskillen on last Thursday. In his speech to the meeting Mr. Crumley, MP, dealt with the conscription topic and said that the people of Ireland had won the hearts of the British democracy through the acts of Irishmen on the battlefields. He said that the Irish Party would oppose conscription by every means in their power. Resolutions were passed expressing renewed confidence in Mr. Redmond and his colleagues and expressing approval at the action of the party; also expressing satisfaction at the establishment of the new paper *Ireland* in New York.

On last Thursday evening the Enniskillen Catholic Ladies' Society regaled the children of the Enniskillen Workhouse to a splendid an evening's amusement, consisting of singing, dancing, and games. The thoughtfulness of this estimable society is deserving of the highest commendation at the hands of the townspeople

On Monday evening the Ballyshannon hurlers gave a farewell dance to one of the members, Mr. Patrick Daly, son of Mister P. Daly, contractor, Ballyshannon. The club also presented Mr. Daly with a handsome dressing case as a token of their esteem. Mr. Daly left on Tuesday morning for Cahirciveen, where he is going to study wireless telegraphy.

Fermanagh Herald January 8th 1916. THE CONSCRIPTION BILL. IRELAND TO BE UNAFFECTED. ULSTER UNIONISTS PROTEST. The Press Association says the Nationalists members received today definite assurances that there is no intention of applying compulsory military service to Ireland. The Government Bill in its original draft was applicable to all of the United Kingdom. The reference to Ireland was struck out at one of the Cabinet meetings of last week. Irish Unionists are raising a vigorous protest against the exclusion of Ireland. At a meeting of the Irish Unionist members held this evening in the House of Commons, Sir Edward Carson presiding, it was decided to forward to the Prime Minister and to Mr. Bonar Law, copies of a resolution declaring that the Government's intention to exclude Ireland from the scope of the Bill constituted "an insult and humiliation to the loyal and patriotic population, and an abandonment of the principles of equality and sacrifice at times of war on the part of his Majesty's subjects."

January 13th 1916. ENNISKILLEN YACHT CLUB. MEMBERS IN THE ARMY. It transpired at the annual meeting of the Enniskillen Yacht Club that eighteen of its members have joined the army since the outbreak of the war. As a gesture of appreciation the Club recently decided to send each of them a gift of cigarettes and tobacco at Christmas. The club has invested £200 in the War Loan. They have received lengthy replies from many of the recipients such as Major C. F. Falls, M.A. and Lieutenant H. C. Gordon. F.T.

January 13th 1916. COMING ULSTER LAWSUITS FOR THE FOUR COURTS. In the court of Mr. Justice Barton a very interesting litigation arising out of the will of the late Mr. Jeremiah Jordan M.P. for South Fermanagh (who died possessed of considerable property principally in the town of Enniskillen) may develop. The short title of the case is Buchanan vs. Hamilton and it was only opened last sitting to be adjourned for argument this month on the supplemental or amended list. The testator left a number of charitable bequests, chiefly to Methodist institutions and he also left an annuity to the North and South Fermanagh National Registration Committee. The will was a very lengthy and peculiar document in which the testator gives directions as to his mode of burial and the kind of grave in which he should be interred. He directed that it should be built in brick that no clay was to go on his coffin but only in the smallest quantity consistent with sanitation. A very large Bar is engaged but it was hinted when the case was mentioned last December that efforts might be made to arrange a settlement. F.T.

Mr. J. Jordan.

January 13th 1916. THE FERMANAGH TIMES CONTAINS OVER SIX COLUMNS OR PRACTICALLY A FULL PAGE MORE OF LOCAL AND GENERAL NEWS THAN ANY OTHER NEWSPAPER PRINTED IN ENNISKILLEN. F.T.

January 13th 1916. ENNISKILLEN POST OFFICE. AN OLD LINK BROKEN. For a period extending for over 60 years the family of Presley have been identified with Enniskillen Post Office but now the link has been broken at least temporarily by the fact that both John Presley and George Presley have joined the Army Service Corps and gone to do their bit in the Great War. Both had considerable service in our local Post Office, the former being there over 25 years, while their father, the late Mr. John Presley acted as postmen in Enniskillen for over 35 years and was exceedingly popular with people of all classes and creeds. F.T.

January 13th 1916. BRITISH FARMERS RED CROSS FUND. FERMANAGH'S CONTRIBUTION A SPLENDID RESPONSE. Dear Sir, The response to this from County Fermanagh has been most satisfactory. At present with approximate returns from three districts not yet complete the amount contributed is upwards of £800 which speaks well for the generosity of our farming community. I have read correspondence regarding Belcoo district in the last issues. The people of that locality are second to none for real hospitality and generosity as is proverbial with all Irishmen. Their failure to respond to this very deserving appeal is simply the want of organisation of the local Committee. F.T.

January 13th 1916. January 13th 1916. LOUGH ERNE DRAINAGE BOARD AND THE BELLEEK POTTERY. The following letter was read at a meeting of the Drainage Board from Mr. Michael Maguire, solicitor, Ballyshannon. January 1, 1916 – I have received instructions from the directors of the Belleek Pottery Works Company Limited to inform you that in consequence of the action of the Lough Erne Drainage Board and their servants on Monday last the 27th ult in refusing to alter the level of the lake to such an extent their works were then and still are rendered idle. I am to point out that this is a serious matter for my clients' company and for the entire hands employed at the Pottery Works. I am instructed to ask your Board to have the proper water level to the pottery wheel immediately restored otherwise I am to take the necessary steps for an injunction. F.T.

Fermanagh Herald January 15th 1916. WAR NEWS. THE ALLIES HAVE EVACUATED GALLIPOLI AND WITHDRAWN WITHOUT LOSS. The following statement was issued by the War Office on Sunday night: - General Sir Charles Monroe reports that the complete evacuation of the Gallipoli Peninsula has now been successfully carried out. All guns and howitzers were got away with the exception of 17 worn-out guns which were blown up by us before leaving. The casualties amounted to one British rank and file wounded. There were no casualties among the French troops. General C. Monroe states that the successful accomplishment of this difficult task is due to Generals Birdwood and Davies and to the invaluable assistance rendered in an operation of the highest difficulty by Admiral de Robeck and the Royal Navy.

Fermanagh Herald January 15th 1916. THE TURKISH VERSION. A Constantinople telegram of today states that during the night, as the result of a violent battle the British completely evacuated Sedd-El-Bahr, with great losses. Not a single soldier remained behind. The Gallipoli Peninsula is now clear of the enemy. All Constantinople is bedecked with flags to celebrate this victory. Everywhere demonstrations of joy are evident. In the mosques and churches thanksgiving services are being held. During the evening the city was illuminated.

Fermanagh Herald January 15th 1916. THE OPERATIONS. The Dardanelles operations began on February 19, 1915 when a general attack by the Allied squadrons was delivered. The combined land and sea operations did not begin until April, 25th, following the failure of the naval operations to force the Dardanelles. The memorable landing of troops took place in the early morning when the Irish regiments suffered terrible losses on what was known as "V" beach.

Fermanagh Herald January 15th 1916. SIR IAN HAMILTON'S FINAL SENSATIONAL DISPATCH ON THE DARDANELLES EXPEDITION. Sir Ian Hamilton had to deal with operations which began in April, and ended, for him, in the second week of October; with a desperate six months campaign, practically every day of which had its full tale of achievements and disappointment; with a prolonged but hopeless contest in which the British lost 4,915 officers and 108,600 men killed and wounded, beside suffering 96,613 casualties from sickness. Hearty optimism as to the success of this or that plan marks Sir Ian Hamilton's narrative, but always – or nearly always – something occurred to defeat his expectations. On August 15th he could have cleared (he writes) a passage for the fleet to Constantinople if he had been sent reinforcements. His wants were not small. The British divisions alone were 45,000 under establishment strength, and he needed 50,000 fresh rifles. The required help was not sent him, "the reason given being one which prevented me from further insistence."

January 20th 1916. THE FERMANAGH COUNTY SURVEYOR WRITES ABOUT LOCOMOTION AND THE NEED FOR IMPROVEMENT. Mr. Burkett in a report to the County Council says: - I feel it my duty to put in writing the matter of my own locomotion. I see more and more each day that it is exceedingly bad business your County Surveyor having no speedier means of locomotion than a common bicycle or occasional horse car. It is nothing to me personally, but it is utterly foolish, I think as regards the public. I am quite satisfied to go on as I am, but with all the increasing supervision needed by new methods of work, by the almost hopeless task of trying to get unskilled men to do skilful work, by the increasing difficulty in getting farmers to work at all at their roads, and the gradual breakup of the contract system which is quickly spreading all over Ireland, and by the steadily increasing numbers of roads and works in our own charge about 50 at present - for all these reasons I must tell you straight bad business is going on in not providing me with better means of supervising the 17 or 20,000 pounds that you spend each year.

Of course I know this is a time of strict economy but that is rather the reason I mention the matter. I am asking for no compliment. It is nothing to me, though after 17 years a complement might not be out of place. I am the only Surveyor in Ireland of 17 years standing, who has not had his position very largely improved. Even before the war I was in every penny of £100 a year worse off than when I came here owing to changing times. I have had to cut down my way of living by that amount and more since the war. I have about 150 more miles to manage and about quadruple the work. I.R.

(Ed. Mr. James Parsons Burkett achieved fame in the field of ornithology in the 1920s. He pioneered the ringing of birds and astonished the subject by capturing a robin that he had ringed 13 years previously – 'the oldest robin in the world.')

January 20th 1916. NOTES. Shop assistants are receiving great criticism and indeed odium for staying at home doing the work of girls and measuring tape or selling ribbon instead of joining the army. At Athy and other Rural Councils they were pointedly referred to. I.R.

The command of battalions at the front is now not to be given to any officer whose age exceeds 40, according to new decision of the military authorities, as the exertions of trench warfare demand useful physical powers. Half of Armagh L.O. Lodge No 109 has joined the army having given 45 out of 90 members. An Armagh paper gives the names of all the clerks in local branches of the Belfast and Ulster Banks which have joined the army, and says that the local branches of the Provincial, Hibernian, and Northern Banks did not supply one. I.R.

January 20th 1916. A RELIC OF 1821. An interesting relic, commemorative of the visit of George 1V to Ireland in 1821 has been found in Lisnaskea. When digging in the garden belonging to Mr. William Richardson, at the rear of the market house, a large medal was found. On the front side was the head of George 1V, and on the reverse side the words "Ireland hails with joy the visit of her Sovereign August 1821." The medal has been secured by Mr. Peter Costello, Lisnaskea, who is a collector of old and rare coins. Mr. Costello has also a large municipal medal struck to commemorate the erection of a statue to Napoleon 111. It was taken from a German captured in Lille. I.R.

January 20th 1916. AN ORANGE HALL OPENED IN IRVINESTOWN. SPEECH BY MR. E. M. ARCHDALE. It is questionable if any town for its size in Ireland is as well off for public halls as Irvinestown. There is the Concert Hall, a new Townhall, Mr. Lee's Hall, and now there is the new Orange Hall, the opening of which took place on Thursday evening last. The need for an Orange Hall has long been felt, as the local brethren of L.O.L. 1270 had no home of their own. Some years ago the building of a hall was discussed and decided upon, and Mr. F. E. Townsend was appointed the architect. The site is within what was known as the grand entrance to Castle Irvine, which had been disused for a long time. It was granted free of cost through the generosity of the W. M., of the lodge, Major C. C. D'Arcy Irvine, J. P. It has seating accommodation for 300 people, and what is so badly needed in most halls, a built up stage, with stage entrance and ante room. It has cost over £400 and of this sum about £100 is required to clear the building of debt. But for the war this sum would have been raised before the opening and the brethren of Lodge 1270 are hopeful of shortly wiping out this debt and intend to let the hall to theatrical companies and for other purposes, so that it will become a source of income as well as a great benefit to the town. I.R.

January 20th 1916. ON A DEAD MAN'S LAP. AIRMAN'S EXPLOIT AT A HEIGHT OF 10,000 FEET.
This story is related in the Daily News in a letter just received from a young officer attached to the Royal Flying Corps now a prisoner in Germany. Poor B! I was so sorry he was killed, he writes. He was such a nice boy and only 19. I had a fight with two German aeroplanes and then a shell burst very close to us and I heard a large piece whizzing past my head. Then the aeroplane started to come down headfirst spinning all the time. We must have dropped to about 5,000 feet in about 20 seconds. I looked around at once and saw poor B with a terrible wound in his head quite dead. I then realized that the only chance of saving my life was to step over into his seat and sit on his lap where I could reach the controls. I managed to get the machine out of that terrible death plunge, switched off the engine and made a good landing on

terra firma. We were 10,000 feet up when B was killed and luckily it was this tremendous height that gave me time to think and act. I met one of the pilots of the German machines which attacked me. He could speak English quite well and we shook hands after a most thrilling fight. I brought down his aeroplane with my machine gun and he had to land close to where I landed. There was a bullet through his radiator and petrol tank but neither he nor his observer was touched. F.T.

January 27th 1916. INNISKILLING PRISONERS INTERNED IN GERMANY RENDER THANKS FOR THE GIFTS. Our donations towards the prisoners of war have been greatly increased by the generous donations of Irvinestown per Mrs. D'Arcy Irvine of Castle Irvine and we are sending it out to those for whom it is intended. It is 48 lbs of sugar, 10 lbs of tea, 10 tins of Oxo, 12 packets of cocoa, 2 lbs of candles and 16 tins of sardines. I understand that some tins of condensed milk are on their way also, for all of which we are deeply indebted to our loyal friends in Irvinestown. I.R.

January 27th 1916. OUTLOOK FOR FARMERS - ARE THEY MAKING BIG PROFITS? Never since the war began has the industrial community in Ireland reached a graver crisis. Foodstuffs are rising rapidly, Meal is almost at a prohibitive price, and unless the farmers bestir themselves ruin may affect many of them before the war be out. We do not wish to be alarmist, but facts must be faced as they are found. About last October the present crisis really began. There was a serious shortage of shipping to Ireland, and the consequence was that freight rose, with the result that the condition of affairs has steadily been getting worse, and if it continue much longer business will be paralysed and the price of all articles of food be at famine rates.

Farmers, no doubt, have made large sums of money through the war. Cattle have been sold at enhanced prices; milk and butter produced at almost the same cost as before the war, have maintained a steady advance of about 50 per cent; and pork reached the record figure of 82s per cwt in Enniskillen market on Tuesday and on yesterday at Irvinestown 83s per cwt. Against all this, feeding stuffs, through the present shortage of shipping and not through traders inflated profits, as some allege, have advanced enormously. Meal, the staple fattening food for pigs and fowl, which a short time ago could have been purchased for 13s a cwt, is now at 28s. This price has frightened small farmers, and many have disposed of their pigs and ceased keeping them as they feared a loss. Prices are alarming, but more alarming still are the outlook that supplies may almost altogether cease.

In France the women are able to save all crops by the use of machinery. In the Ballinamallard district the great advantage of machinery has been made evident. There some farmers have binders and potatoes diggers and Mr. E. M. Archdale, D. L., addressing a co-operative conference last week said that his binder which cost him £30 paid for itself the first year and did the work of 20 men. Mr. W. H. West told how he saved 20 acres having one and that it would work in any field in which farm machinery, such as the mowing machine is used. No one would expect a small farmer to purchase a binder or potato digger, but Mr. West urged that poor farmers should cooperate and work on this principle and means are now being taken in certain district to carry out this idea.

Plough then is the watchword. Yellow meal will soon be hardly procurable. Sow oats in the upland and rye in the bog land, also catch crops such as rape, hybrid turnips and vetches, which make excellent fattening for cattle and pigs and cost a fraction of the cost of meal. Yellow meal has been the groundwork of all our system. The great fundamental asset to the farmers, beef, pork, eggs and butter, depend on it, and now that it will be scarcer, a substitute must be found. At substitute can only be found by the plough. There is no better manure than lime. 50 years ago every farmer had his own lime kiln. The system of burning line has died out, as artificial manure can be bought so easily and at so low a price. Now prices are up, and recourse is again being had to the burning of lime. The Kesh Co-operative Society has already taken the matter in hand; and in connection with that a Co-operative lime kiln is being organized, to supply the members of the society with burnt lime at a cheap rate. The present state of affairs cannot continue unless disaster is to ensue. Prices of foodstuffs will not decrease: they will increase. I.R.

January 27th 1916. MIGRATING NORTH. PROTESTANT TENANTS COME TO SETTLE IN FERMANAGH. Within recent years a number of Protestant farmers have migrated from the Midlands and west of Ireland to the north. During the period before the war, when the Home Rule crisis was at its height, numbers of these farmers sold their holdings and came to Fermanagh to reside. There is now migration taking place, but not from dread of political warfare. The Estates Commissioners, who have purchased the Clanrickarde Estate under the recent Birrell Land Act, which killed land purchase in Ireland, except in congested districts in the west, have compulsory purchased the tenant right of a number of Protestant tenants on this estate. They must leave by the 1st of March next, and a number of them are providing themselves with holdings in Fermanagh. Already some of them have secured a new place of abode, in the Lisbellaw district and others are negotiating for farms in the same neighbourhood. These farmers of the West cannot understand the high price of land in Fermanagh. The land here is not as good as the

Ulick de Burgh, 1st Marquess of Clanricarde.

fattening lands of Galway, but a peaceful and law abiding county attracts purchasers and there is always keen competition. As an example, Mr. P. R. Brown, F.A.S.I., Auctioneer, a few weeks ago sold six and ¼ Irish acres near Lisbellaw for the sum of £600. Almost 100 pounds per acre! It is an immense price, and if the farm had been situated in the west, it might not have fetched £20 an acre. I.R.

January 27th 1916. NOTES. Two infant children are said to die in the United Kingdom for every man killed in the war.

Mrs Lort, a farmer who lives near Carnarvon, when charged with not having 25 sheep dipped, said that she did not know whether they were sheep or not, as some of them had six horns, others only four, and were said to be descendants of those which had been found on ships of the Spanish Armada.

The Pope has hitherto appointed an Irish-American to the Archbishopric of Chicago and a departure from the understood rule in the appointment of a prelate named Mundelein has been hailed by the German Press with delight. I.R.

January 27th 1916. DUBLIN SENSATION. NIGHT RAID BY POLICE. SEVERAL HOUSES VISITED AND ARMS AND AMMUNITION REMOVED. A wholesale raid was carried out in Dublin on Saturday by the Dublin police on the residences of a large number of people who it is stated had been suspected for some time past of acting in contravention of the provisions of the Defense of the Realm Act. The raids were a complete surprise, and though the persons concerned expostulated, no resistance was offered and no arrests were made. The police removed arms, ammunition, and alleged seditious literature, to the Castle where they were impounded. The only name mentioned in the reports of the affair is that of the Countess Markievicz, from whose residence in Rathmines the police are stated to have removed a printing press, with type and paper. This lady's husband left Dublin at the outbreak of war to join his regiment in the Russian army. I.R.

January 27th 1916. LISNASKEA, A SHOCKING CASE. DRINKING SEPARATION MONEY. MAGISTRATES LENIENT SENTENCE. Shocking revelations as to how a soldier's young wife, with 25 shillings separation allowance, starved her children and drank all the money, was told in Lisnaskea court on Saturday when the NSPCC prosecuted Mary Molloy aged 24 with neglecting her four children the youngest of whom was six months old. Mr. Winslow, solicitor for the complainants, said that the case had been under the supervision of the NSPCC for almost a year past. Inspector Mallon proved to various visits. The children were poorly clad, barefooted, and filthy. They slept on an old paillasse sacking. Her room was dirty and had no furniture in it. She drank all her money, and two days after she took the pledge from the Parish Priest he found her lying drunk in bed. She received several warnings and was fined twice for drunkenness, and eventually the children had to be taken from her and sent to the Workhouse. Two women witnesses told of defendant's drunken habits and also of her immorality. She on occasions slept out at night with the baby. The children were covered with vermin and had scalded ears and sore eyes. Defendant said she did not beat the children which was different from neglect. The chairman Mr. Walker, R.M. said that the case was a bad one and there could be no plea of poverty. Defendant would go to jail for 14 days. I.R.

January 27th 1916. BRITISH DESERTERS FATE. Mr. Tennant, in Parliamentary papers, last week informed Mr. Farrell that Private T. Hope of the 2nd Battalion Leinster regiment was tried by field general courtmartial on February 14th 1915 on a charge of desertion. The evidence showed that he absented himself from the trenches on December 23rd until February, 9th. It is well known to all soldiers, adds Mr. Tennant that desertion in the face of the enemy is liable to be punished by death. Private Hope was informed of his sentence more than 12 hours before it was carried out. I.R.

January 27th 1916. LISNASKEA BOARD OF GUARDIANS. The clerk reported that Patrick McCormick, the porter, was invalided home from the front, and was expected any day in Lisnaskea. A reply was received from the Gaelic League thanking the Guardians for their resolutions of protest against the curtailment of the Government's grants for the teaching of Irish. The reply was in English, but the signature to the letter was in Irish. Chairman (Mr. Kirkpatrick) – How nice it would have been if the letter had been in Irish. Mr. McElgunn – We are a scandal to the country we are living in, Irishmen don't know their own language – for shame! It is not our fault of course for we were prosecuted for it. I.R.

January 27th 1916. INNISKILLING HERO DEAD. SERGEANT JAMES CARNEY. Mr. Edward Carney, Abbey Street, Enniskillen has received word from the War Office that his son, Sergeant James Carney, 1st Inniskillings, was killed during the recent fighting in the Balkans. Sergeant Carney had served in France with the 2nd Battalion and received the Cross of the Order of Saint George fourth class for gallantry on the 28th of October 1914 when he brought in a wounded comrade under heavy machine gun fire, thereby suffering his own wounds. He served through the South African war and at the battle of Colenso brought a wounded comrade from the firing line to the field hospital amid a hail of bullets, and was complemented by his commanding officer. He was specially promoted to Corporal in the Mounted Infantry in which he served two years, for scouting with ability. He has the Queen's Medal with five clasps and the King's Medal with two clasps. He served three years in Egypt under Major Hessey, now Lt. Colonel commanding the 11th Inniskillings. I.R.

January 27th 1916. ENNISKILLEN WORKHOUSE. MORE ABOUT EXTRAVAGANCE. The extravagance alleged in the Enniskillen Workhouse about which the public has heard so much recently was further discussed at a meeting of the Board of Guardians on Tuesday. In reply to a member the Master said that though there were no patients in the Fever Hospital, still 6 cwt of coal was sent up for the week, and added Mr. Meehan, that was only for the nurse and the servant. Mr. Crumley, M.P. (Chairman), said that he had got tired of this question, with its accompaniment of anonymous cards coming to him about the coal and egg question. Mr. W. J. Brown calculated this little hospital burnt three times as much as an ordinary house. The question was also asked – was the coal and oil sent up to the infirmary in excess of the Boards allowance. The clerk replied yes. 12 gallons was the allowance and 15 was used. Mr. Crumley said they must be living on oil. I.R.

January 27th 1916. GERMAN AEROPLANES BEAT BRITISH ENGINES. Although our flying men are the best in the world they are out engined by the new German Fokker which is believed by the French to be fitted with a 200 h.p. water cooled Mercedes engine. The machine gun is fixed so that to aim the monoplane must be maneuvered exactly as the torpedo tubes in a submarine are aimed. It fires directly ahead through the propeller. The bullets which pass between the blades carry straight. Bullets which touch the blades as these revolve are deflected by bulletproof deviators attached to the blades. The toll of the Fokker stands for the past month at 15 British aeroplanes. F.T.

January 27th 1916. MASTER W. H. A. WEST. Seldom has so large or representative cortege been witnessed in Fermanagh at the funeral of a child as that which followed the remains of William Henry A. West, eldest son of Mr. John West, Crocknacrieve, to Enniskillen cemetery on Sunday afternoon. From near and far came members of the Pilgrim sect to express their sympathy with the bereaved parents while the attendance also included large numbers of members of other Churches in the surrounding district. The deceased little chap was only 12½ years of age and had been ailing for about a month. Previous to that he had always enjoyed the best of health and was extremely popular among his schoolmates at Sydare School where he was quick and intelligent at his lessons and gave every promise of developing into a clever youth. The funeral as stated took place on Sunday, the service at the graveside being conducted by Mr. George Beatty and Mr. Edward Armstrong, two members of the Pilgrim Sect. F.T.

Crocknacrieve House

January 27th 1916. WHOLESALE ROBBERY OF WAR STORES. HOW PUBLIC GENEROSITY IS ABUSED. The way in which comforts and other stores for our troops mysteriously disappear occasionally is illustrated by a story told by Lance Corporal Caddick. His platoon he says was billeted upon a farmer who seemed very irritable and who expressly forbade the troops to visit one particular portion of his farm. This naturally excited the curiosity of the troops and one of the privates decided to investigate. He made a startling discovery which he communicated to the officer in command who ordered a raid on the place. The result was the finding of thousands of new shirts sent from Canada and England which had never been unpacked, besides tins of biscuits, jam, condensed milk, etc. Thousands of pairs of gloves, many with little notes attached bearing the names of the girls who had knitted them and the schools they attended. It is shocking of course that such dishonesty should exist and it is particularly mean because of the gifts intended for the personal use of the soldiers. The story can be capped by an even more flagrant case. A major in one of the Canadian regiments was in need of socks and went into a shop in a French town to buy some. The shopkeeper supplied him without any difficulty but when the major came to put the socks on he found something inside one of them. He pulled it out and found a Christmas greeting card from H.R.H. Princess Mary! The socks belonged to her Christmas gift consignment and this proved that some parcels of them at least had got into dishonest hands. The major took the socks and the card straight to his commanding officer and it is hardly necessary to say there was a strict investigation. F.T.

Fermanagh Herald January 29th 1916. MIRACULOUS ESCAPE AT MAGUIRESBRIDGE. CHILD FALLS FROM TRAIN AND IS UNINJURED. A miraculous escape from death occurred on last Tuesday. When the train due from Dublin in Enniskillen at 12.40 arrived at Maguiresbridge, a woman desired to alight at the station, but through a mistake opened a door at the wrong side and discovering her mistake closed back the door but did not turn the handle. Mrs. Cleary and her four children, residing, it is stated, at Abbey Street, Enniskillen, were in the carriage at the time travelling from Lisnaskea. Shortly after the train had left the station at Maguiresbridge, one of Mrs. Cleary's children, a little boy of seven years, went to the apparently closed door in order to look through the window. He leaned against the door, which had the effect of throwing it open, and the young fellow was thrown from the train and on to the permanent way. Mrs. Cleary, we understand, pulled the communication cord in order to stop the train, but evidently did not pull it down far enough, for the train did not stop until its arrival at Lisbellaw, where very much upset she reported the matter to the station master. The latter gentlemen, with some helpers, walked back down the line and found the young fellow close to the place where he had fallen out, quite uninjured, and none the worse of his dangerous fall.

Fermanagh Herald January 29th 1916. OBITER DICTA, (ED. BY THE WAY) I AM ORDERED FROM COURT. Those who left the Enniskillen Petty Sessions Court on last Monday at the termination of the hearing of the cases missed a treat. Had they remained they would have witnessed what was intended for a tragedy, but in reality was so ludicrous that it bore the appearance of a most diverting comedy, and might well have been entitled "The Man who put his foot in it" – with my old friend, Mr. Trimble, in the leading role of "The Man." In order to appreciate the incident which I am going to relate, it is necessary to explain that Mr. Trimble and myself are very old friends, so great that we might have fought in the Boer War, side by side, and might have performed a similar feat in the present conflict but –

"Said I to Cope will you fight any more?
O no says Cope my eyes are too sore."

(Cope – short for Copeland, Mr Trimble's middle name.)

And since then he has studiously avoided me. He has written a good deal in his paper to the detriment of the Nationalists, but since the editor started this column I have watched him and asked him for explanations, facts and figures, concerning many incidents, but he always ran into a corner and put up his hands. This, of course, made him cross, and for some time he has been longing for a "go" at myself but he never had a chance and he never will have a chance. On Monday, however, he thought he had his revenge and he appeared mighty pleased. It happened like this.

The cases in the Petty Sessions had all been heard, and many of the magistrates had left the bench, only three, I think, remained looking at some papers. Mr. Walker, the courteous Resident Magistrate, was just finishing filling in the book, and was about to leave. The public had also departed. The representatives of four newspapers remained writing. One of my colleagues who is always liberal with his cigarettes, very thoughtfully produced his case, and offered one of the reporters a cigarette. He then took one himself and lastly handed the case to me. Our donor struck a match and lighted his cigarette. Mr. Trimble said nothing. The reporter then lighted his friend's cigarettes. And still Mr. Trimble said nothing. Then my cigarette was ignited. And then Mr. Trimble spoke. In infuriated accents he mumbled something about the Court not being over, and added some statement about contempt of Court. At that time I saw visions of 14 days in Sligo jail. But Mr. Trimble got my reply, and on hearing it, immediately exclaimed: "Constable remove that Man!" He directed no particular constable; so he in fact ordered all the constabulary, who were enjoying the joke, to remove me. Then Mr. Trimble left the bench almost frothing, so mad was he that he almost ate a poor woman who addressed him near the Press box. Needless to say, I was not removed; neither did Mr. Trimble's wrath have the effect he wished. On the contrary, I enjoyed the joke, as it showed me in an admirable manner the class of man he is, and if that is the only retaliation he can have of me, he had better throw down his pen and go in for bird catching. I wonder if he is ever heard that little ditty from the Mikado entitled "Tit Willow." It might be altered to the following: -

A pompous J.P. who sat on the bench,
Cried: I'm Trimble! I'm Trimble! I'm Trimble.
He saw Obiter Dicta beginning to smoke,
And cried: smoking! Oh smoking! Oh smoking!
It is weakness of intellect, Trimble, I roared!
Or are you seeking revenge 'cause I've got you floored?
But he up with his finger and pointed right out:
Remove him! Remove him! Remove him!

Fermanagh Herald January 29th 1916. JOTTINGS. Sophia Mercer, writing in a Dublin paper, says: the Arigna coal is most satisfactory; it is not so quick lighting, but is much more lasting than English, and in every way a good all-round coal.

Mrs. Hamilton, Pullnaranny, Ballintra, was killed by lightning while in bed early on Thursday morning, her husband being awakened by the fall of the chimney demolished by the lightning and finding his wife dead beside him, a child being uninjured. The deceased woman's face was blackened and her hair singed. Two head of cattle and a donkey were killed in a byre, a portion of which was also destroyed.

On Tuesday evening a most enjoyable dance was held in the Minor Hall of the Town Hall, Enniskillen under the auspices of the Drapers Association. For many years the Drapers have catered for the enjoyment of the drapers assistants, under the careful supervision of Mr. McKeown, President, and Mr. Fitzpatrick, Secretary. Tuesday night's dance was quite as successful as those held on previous occasions.

We have received a letter from an Arney correspondent which we are unable to publish in full owing to the pressure of space. He takes exception to a reference to Arney in a poem which appeared in a local paper, and points out that over 20 Catholics from the Arney district have joined the colours. He adds that three men from the district have been officially reported killed, one at the Dardanelles, another in France, and the third in Africa. Two more are missing since the period of the early fighting in the Dardanelles. Seven were wounded, four of them have recovered, and went back again in the firing line. One of the soldiers killed leaves a widow and a child, and one of the missing soldiers leaves a wife and five children. On Saturday morning Mrs. L Hegarty, the Back Street, Ballyshannon, received the sad news that her husband Private J. Hegarty, 1st Battalion Royal Irish Rifles had been killed in action. Private Hegarty was a son of Mr. Joseph Hegarty, Donegal town. He was nine months in France, and saw some severe fighting. The Rev. D. Aherne who wrote acquainting Mrs. Hagerty of her husband's death and who administered the last Sacraments to the deceased soldier conducted a retreat in Ballyshannon some five years ago.

Fermanagh Herald January 29th 1916. A CONSTABULARY INQUIRY AT LACK.
A Royal Irish Constabulary inquiry was opened in Lack police barracks on Friday to investigate certain charges – which included that of tippling and making false entries in the barrack books – brought by Constable James Nicholson against Sergeant Cleary, who has been in charge of the Lack barracks for some years. Constable Nicholson, the complainant, swore that Sergeant Cleary had the appearance of having had drink taken on the 30th of November, and he arrived at that conclusion because the Sergeant was untidy and inclined to be unsteady. On the 1st of December witness noticed that about 4.00 the Sergeant had drink taken, and at 10.30 p.m. that he had a lot of drink taken. On the 2nd of December Sergeant Cleary was drunk on parade – his cap was on the back of his head, his tunic was partially open, and he had not had a shave for at least two days. Witness produced a bill given to him by Mrs. Monaghan, who kept a public house in Drumskinny, in the middle of December. The bill was for two shillings due by the sergeant for Bass beer. Witness did not give the bill to the sergeant, but kept it for that inquiry. The Sergeant's name was not on the bill.

February 1916

February 3rd 1916. A GREAT AIR RAID. A ZEPPELIN FLEET. RIGHT ACROSS ENGLAND. The zeppelin raid on England on Monday night was the strongest and most extensive yet attempted. At least six centres are known to have been visited and some 220 bombs dropped doing material damage, the extent of which is not officially stated and casualties were officially given as 54 killed and 67 injured. These figures come second to the casualties in the great raid on the London area on October 13th, when 56 persons were killed and 114 injured. Altogether six or seven zeppelins were employed on the murderous mission, the area covered being the Midlands, North-Eastern and Eastern counties. I.R.

February 3rd 1916. ONE ZEPPELIN LESS. HER CREW LOST. LEFT SINKING IN THE NORTH SEA. The captain of a French vessel which arrived at Hull on Thursday reported having seen a Zeppelin destroyed in the North Sea. Skipper William Martin of the Grimsby trawler Stephen K., says the disabled Zeppelin is L19, that the car was entirely submerged and part of the envelope was floating in the water, the crew being driven to the higher part of the envelope. Although at least 20 Germans came into view there were others on board, as sounds of tapping with a hammer could be distinctly heard. In all probability the Zeppelin would remain afloat for several hours. Owing to the number of Germans it was impossible to attempt their capture. They asked to be taken on board the trawler, but as the trawlers crew only numbered nine hands all told the presence of two dozen Germans on board would have been most inadvisable. I.R.

February 3rd 1916. AN EXPLOSION. GERMANS AT WORK IN OTTAWA PARLIAMENT HOUSE. SIX PEOPLE KILLED. A fire believed to have been caused by a German incendiary, which broke out in the Dominion Parliament Buildings, Ottawa, on Thursday night while the House was in Session, practically demolished the structure, the damage being estimated at considerably over one million. The library building has been saved. Six persons including two nieces of the Speaker lost their lives. Several persons, including the Minister of Agriculture (Mr. Burrell) were injured and others are reported missing. The Speaker's wife and children were saved by a life-net. The King and Boner Law have sent messages of sympathy to the Governor General. I.R. (Ed. An accidental fire and nothing to do with German spies.)

February 3rd 1916. A PLUCKY FIGHT. Describing the brilliant bombing feat by a party of British officers and men about the Kemmell-Wytschaete road, in which the enemy suffered 40 casualties and had two machine guns destroyed, a special correspondent says that the raiders tell of a German sentry with a nasty cough. In the silent blackness an unseen bayonet thrust cured the poor wretch of his crouping for all time. Bombs flashed crimson death to right and left and in the squealing confusion the invaders did their work with grim promptitude. An officer having emptied his revolver, snatched up a Germans rifle and either bayonetted or clubbed scores of foes. They came tumbling out of dugouts falling in panic with blankets wrapped around them. Wild rifle fire broke out all along the enemy front but the only casualties which befell the gallant party were caused by the devotion of a couple of men who were assisting a wounded comrade over the parapet. I.R.

February 3rd 1916. THE INNISKILLINGS COMFORT FUND. WHAT WE HAVE DONE. Our people have risen to the occasion. £926 10s 1d has been supplied to this office in cash and about £500 worth of woollen and other goods altogether, apart from what has been contributed to the Central Depot Fund, the Red Cross and other Funds. I.R.

Fermanagh Herald February 5th 1916. THE DEFENSE. The charges preferred against Sergeant Cleary, R.I.C., Lack, were concluded early last week. The case for the prosecution has already appeared in our columns. The case for the defence was supported by William and Sarah Johnstone, public house keepers in Lack. They swore that Sergeant Cleary had never been drinking in their house to their knowledge. A hotel keeper named Andrew Noble, residing and carrying on business in Lack, swore that the sergeant had only ½ glass in his house on the evening of the 2nd of December. It had been stated by the prosecution that the sergeant was so drunk on the 2nd of December that he had to be assisted home. This was denied by Robert Adams and Joseph Adams. They were with the sergeant on that particular date, and swore that the sergeant did not fall, and was not assisted home by them. Joseph Adams also swore that Constable Nicholson followed him into the house of Mrs. Virtue (witness's sister,) and endeavoured to get him to sign a statement regarding the sergeant, which he had not made. Mrs. Virtue corroborated. Dr. Patten said he attended the sergeant on the 3rd of December, and treated the sergeant for tonsillitis. The patient, he said, had no appearance of drink and did not smell of it. Two men named Owen McCanny and Robert Wilson could not agree. They said the sergeant had a drink with them on the 1st of December, but McCanny was positive it was porter, and Wilson swore it was port which the Sergeant drank on that occasion. Quite sober on the 2nd of December, was also the statement made by the barrack servant. The inquiry concluded as stated above, early last week.

Fermanagh Herald February 5th 1916. WOULD NOT LEAVE THE WORKHOUSE. An interesting discussion arose over an inmate from Killybuggy. It would appear that this woman was in the habit of living with her married daughter and was in receipt of the old age pension. She went away from her daughter's house and sought refuge in the Manorhamilton Union. Her daughter appeared before their Guardians asking that her mother be requested to leave the workhouse and go back to live with her as heretofore. The Guardians could not persuade the woman to leave the house so they allowed her to stay for the present.

Manorhamilton Union

February 10th 1916. THE FAITHFUL HORSE. A remarkable story of a horse's faithfulness is related in the monthly magazine of the Claremont Mission Pentonville N., by one of the Coldstream Guards Regiment. After the fierce fighting at Loos he writes it was noticed that there was a horse standing between the firing lines. For two days he remained there. Then some of our men crawled out and found that he was standing by the dead body of his rider and would not leave the spot. Later on some of our men bravely arranged to get out to the horse again, blindfolded him and brought it back to our lines. By no other means could the faithful beast be persuaded to leave its dead master. F.T.

February 10th 1916. NOTES. Certain areas in the United Kingdom have now been forbidden to aliens. In Ireland these included the counties of Dublin, Cork and Kerry.
The Compulsory Service Order of England comes into force today. Unmarried men from 19 years to 30 are being called up, the last of them to report by March 3.
An old Crimean veteran named Matthew Johnston has died as a pay patient in Enniskillen Workhouse hospital on Tuesday. He had served under the late Col. Johnston of Snowhill and told how he used to carry biscuits from Balaclava to Sebastopol sometimes in his bare feet in the snow. He received a special service pension about 15 years ago. He will be buried today. I. R.

February 10th 1916. SERGEANT J. FYFFE 18TH ROYAL IRISH, rushed home from his regiment in France to see his father in Eden Street, Enniskillen, but before he could reach home his father had passed away. Sergeant Fyffe is a smart young soldier and instructor of athletics in his battalion. He met James and Willie Quinn of the Diamond, Enniskillen of the 5th Royal Irish Rifles near his own battalion in France and says that the Ulster division with the local battalion lay not far off from where his own battalion was located. The Ulster division and other Divisions are on the best of terms. All are comrades out there, no matter from the south or north and all are much superior in physique and in condition to the German soldiers. The German soldiers would desert in numbers but that their own officers tell them that they would be shot at once if taken by the British. One of the prisoners taken by the 18th on Christmas night was so frightened that he begged his captors to leave him his German head: he was led to believe that his head would be cut off. The well-known action at the Brickfields reduced the 18th from 1,100 to about 43 men, they were so decimated. The Germans, Sergeant Fyffe says no longer advance in solid masses as they used to do, but in open formation. They had suffered so much by the former that they were taught a lesson. I.R.

February 10th 1916. THE 12TH INNISKILLINGS. A draft of the 12th Inniskillings stationed at Enniskillen, has gone to the front and received a hearty send off, the whole of the battalion lining up and heartily cheering their departing comrades. The officers of the battalion bade the men farewell at the Railway Station. With the drafts leaving were the following officers – Second Lieutenants Allen, McKinley, Baker, Shannon and Reid. The fine corps of drums played the men off to the tunes of "The girl I left behind me", and to "Keep the home fires burning", while at intervals "Auld Lang Syne" was played. Among the men of the draft are some old soldiers who saw service in South Africa. The order for departure was received only one hour before train time and so the townspeople had not an opportunity of knowing of the departure of the men, and of giving them a fitting send off. I.R.

Fermanagh Herald February 12th 1916. OBITER DICTA. THE CONVENT BELL. There is apparently no limit to the appalling pomposity of a certain set of Protestants, who are unfortunately in Enniskillen. But happily their influence is nil. Nevertheless that little bird known as rumour has just hopped on my table and told me a surprising story concerning the Convent bell. The hint is quite sufficient for this sect. I write the above just to let them know that I am fully conversant with all of the leading facts, and I'm seriously thinking of pulling back the veil in a short time and exposing the bigoted scheme.

Fermanagh Herald February 12th 1916. DROMORE BISHOPRIC. APPOINTMENT OF THE VERY REV. EDWARD CANON MULHERN, D. D., P. P., INISHMACSAINT. A Reuter's cable from Rome of Monday's date intimates that, on the recommendation of the Consistorial Congregation, his Holiness the Pope has appointed the very Rev. Edward Canon Mulhern of Inishmacsaint to be Lord Bishop of Dromore in succession to the late most Rev. Dr. O'Neill. The new Bishop-elect is a native of Ederney, County Fermanagh and received his early education at St. Macartan's Seminary, Monaghan where he ranked among the most successful students of his time.

Fermanagh Herald February 12th 1916. IT WILL BE LEARNED WITH REGRET that Private S. H. Young, of the 8th Highland Light Infantry, and brother of Mr. D. Young, Omagh, was killed by shrapnel in France on the 21st of January. Private Young was a native of Belleek, County Fermanagh and was employed for some time in Messrs. White Bros.' hardware establishment in Omagh. After the outbreak of the war he joined the colours and went on active service about October last. The news of his death was conveyed in a letter from the chaplain of the regiment, who states that he was buried with his Scottish comrades.

Fermanagh Herald February 12th 1916. CAPTAIN D'ARCY IRVINE KILLED. Captain Charles William D'Arcy Irvine 6th Service Battalion, Leinster Regiment, who is reported in Monday's casualty list to have been killed in action at the Dardanelles, was reported wounded and missing,

CAPT. C. W. D'ARCY IRVINE, 6th Leinsters, wounded and missing, believed killed, is the elder son of Major C. C. D'Arcy Irvine, J.P., of Castle Irvine, Irvinestown, and of Fanny Kathleen, daughter of Lieut.-Colonel Jesse Lloyd, of Ballyleck, Co. Monaghan. He was formerly in the 3rd Irish Rifles. His father was an officer of the 3rd Royal Inniskilling Fusiliers and of the North of Ireland Imperial Yeomanry.

believed killed, in September last. He was the eldest son of Major Charles Cockburn D'Arcy Irvine, J.P. of Castle Irvine, Irvinestown, and of Fannie Kathleen, daughter of the late Lt. Colonel Jesse Lloyd, of Ballyleck, County Monaghan. He was a grandson of the late Captain W. D'Arcy Irvine, D. L. of the 67th Regiment now the 2nd Battalion Hampshire Regiment, and his great grandfather, the late Mr. W. D'Arcy Irvine of Castle Irvine served at Waterloo with the 1st Dragoon Guards. Captain C. W. D'Arcy Irvine who was 31 years of age, served for a time in the 3rd Battalion Royal Irish Rifles. He afterwards transferred to the Leinster Regiment, and accompanied the 6th Battalion to the Dardanelles last year, taking part in the Suvla Bay operations. His services were mentioned in dispatches by General Sir Ian Hamilton.

Fermanagh Herald February 12th 1916. AGAINST FEMALE LABOUR AT PIT HEAD. The Executive Committee of the Northumberland Miners have resolved to oppose the introduction of female labour at the pit head, and recommended instead a rearrangement of male labour. Their contention is there are many strong men at the bank who might be better employed underground, and many discarded old men who could be re-employed. There are no pit head woman workers in Northumberland.

UNITED IN DEATH. The deaths have taken place of John Gorman, aged 86, and his wife Mary Gorman, aged 84 of Lismacaffrey, Granard within a few hours of each other.

RECORD PRICE FOR PORK. In Cookstown market on Saturday 87s a hundredweight was paid for pork the highest price known to have been ever reached in the district. Other remarkable prices were: - Dungiven 76s; Omagh 86s; Letterkenny, at 83s to 86s 6d.

Fermanagh Herald February 12th 1916. WHAT OF THE NIGHT? Every day of the war brings to the public mind some fresh and more painful idea of the struggle in which the nations are engaged. People generally are not so light-hearted as they were 12 or six months ago, and it is well that they should begin to think soberly. In the early stages of the conflict the man in the street imagined that, considering the nature of the engines of death with which the combatants were equipped, the formidable opposition with which the Central Empires were confronted and the weakness of Germany's navy compared with those of the Allies that the struggle would be short, sharp, and decisive. The man in the street has been disillusioned, and he will yet be more so. The eating of the Allies Christmas dinner in Berlin was a foolish dream of the lay mind, and nobody now talks of "a holiday trip to the German Capital." The military issue of the war is by no means in doubt, and with truth it can be said that neither is the economic result. For generations to come the nations will eat the black bread of sorrow, and generations yet unborn will say that they were blessed in not being alive in these days. The world will never be the same again, trade and commerce will be revolutionised, jealousy and hatred will exist between nations to a greater degree and for a longer time than ever before, and even man's relations to his fellow man will undergo a radical change. The modern world needed purification, and it is being visited with the greatest affliction that God can send – war. But the world is apt to forget and misapply lessons, and he would be a bold prophet who would say that a nobler, purer, conception of right is about to dawn on the dull consciousness of humanity. Be that as it may, it behoves us to enquire; "Watchman, what of the night?" War is an expensive way of giving vent to human passions, and the peculiar sorrow attached to it is that the innocent as well as the guilt-stained suffer.

February 17th 1916. I.R. MISS CAVELL'S DEATH. THE DEATH OF THE INFORMER. Louis Bril, the waiter who was found guilty of murdering a journalist named Keels, who informed against Nurse Cavell, was executed on Friday. Bril admitted that he assisted Belgians to join the army and gave a Belgian ex-officer named Betrancourt an account of how he followed Keels, accompanied by Maurice Leclerc, through Brussels and shot him dead. Maurice Leclerc was sentenced to 10 years and his father who admitted having assisted Belgians to join their own army, was sentenced to five year's penal servitude.

Fermanagh Herald February 19th 1916. JOTTINGS. Mrs. O'Keefe, the Rectory, Garrison, County Fermanagh, has been informed that her nephew, Trooper Harold Johnston Miles, has died from wounds received in action in the Gallipoli Peninsula.

February 24th 1916. ALL THE DISTILLERIES. A SWEEPING SCHEME. Mr. Lloyd George is carrying out a more ambitious scheme for the acquisition of distilleries than was supposed. It is understood that he has decided to take over as 'controlled' establishments for the production of the alcoholic spirit required for explosives not only the patent-still distillers, but the pot-still distilleries as well – in fact, the whole of the distilleries of the United Kingdom. This will shortly be done under the Munitions Act. The arrangements are in course of completion and then no more whisky will be produced for public consumption until after the war. The public will be confined to the stocks of whiskey at present in hand, and although there is said to be a large stock it is inevitable that prices will rise. The distilleries will be kept fully employed, for the Minister of Munitions requires an enormous output of spirit for war purposes. Arrangement will be made, however, to supply chemical factories, etc., with the spirit they require for necessary purposes. I.R.

February 24th 1916. BELLEEK. THE DEATH OF MRS. DAVID MCBRIEN. The death took place on the 16th of February at Belleek of one of the oldest and most respectable inhabitants of the district. Up to lately Mrs. David McBrien had been in her usual health when she took a slight cold some four weeks ago, when, hoping against hope she gradually grew weaker in spite of medical aid and skilful nursing, bearing her affliction patiently and conscious to the last she passed peacefully away on Tuesday surrounded by her sorrowing children. Deeply regretted not only by her family, but by those outside, she was loved by all who will miss her cheery word and the happy smile with which she greeted everyone.

The funeral took place on Friday and was the largest and most respectable seen in the district for the past 30 years. Evidence was shown of the great esteem in which she was held, all classes and creed being represented, followed the remains to the family burying ground at Slavin. The remains were met at the graveside by the Rev. G. E. O'Keeffe who read the service of the Church of Ireland. The coffin was of polished oak beautifully mounted and bore the inscription 'Margaret McBrien died February 16th' was covered with floral wreaths from her sorrowing family and friends. Just a week previous to her death, her son Private David McBrien of the 2nd battalion first Canadian Contingent, was enabled to get home in time to see his mother. As soon as he received the news of his mother serious illness, he applied for furlough, and although he was in the trenches leave was granted, which was a great consolation to his friends. I.R.

February 24th 1916. THE COMPULSION ACT. DEALING WITH CONSCIENTIOUS OBJECTORS. At the Westminster tribunal under the Military Service Act a man aged 25 employed in a Government office said he had a conscientious objection to taking life. He realised that the country needed his services but he objected to fighting. But he would not object to serving in the Royal Army Medical Corps. 'My views of Christianity condemn killing,' he added. It was decided that he should be put in the non-combatant services.

At the same court a bookkeeper, aged 20 who said he was a Wesleyan pleaded that he had conscientious objections to war. Mr. McMillan – I have not heard before that it is part of the creed of Wesleyans that fighting is a wicked thing. Mr. Davies representing the War Office – 'Would you rather let your mother and sister suffer than you should kill Germans?' The applicant – 'I will protect them, but not kill.' The Chairman said he did not think there was sufficient to satisfy the tribunal that the applicant had a bona fide conscientious objection and the application was refused. I.R.

Fermanagh Herald February 26th 1916. LISNASKEA CATHOLIC DANCING CLASS. A social in connection with the above was held on last Saturday night in Liberty Hall, Lisnaskea, when about 120 members attended, and enjoyed themselves to the early hours of the morning. The event was an extremely pleasant one, and was attended with a full measure of success. The hall was tastefully decorated, and the scene was a most animated one, while the energetic committee left nothing undone to make the night a most enjoyable one, and deserve every congratulation.

Fermanagh Herald February 26th 1916. LOCAL WAR ITEMS. Admiral St. George D'Arcy Irvine, K.C.B., who has been awarded a naval pension of £150 a year from the sixth inst., in the vacancy caused by the death of Admiral C. S. G. Grant is a member of the well-known Fermanagh family. He is a brother of Commander John D'Arcy Irvine, Rathmullan; Co., Donegal, and entered the navy in 1845, serving in Nicaragua, China, Crimea (including Sebastopol,) Turco-Russian war, 1878, and at the bombardment of Alexandria.

Company Quartermaster– Sergeant T. E. Burke, Irish Guards, has been promoted to a commission for services on the field. He was a policeman in Enniskillen prior to the war and is a son of ex-sergeant M. Burke, R.I.C., Cornakinegar, Lurgan.

Second-Lieutenant H. Archdale Porter, who has been wounded, is the second son of Mr. John Porter Porter, Belleisle, Lisbellaw, Co., Fermanagh. He is serving with the 9th Lancers, the regiment of his elder brother, Captain J. G. Porter, who has twice been wounded in the present war, and was awarded the D.S.O. for gallantry at Hooge, in May 1915.

Hit recordings of 1916

"O Sole Mio" by Enrico Caruso
"Santa Lucia" by Enrico Caruso
"Somewhere a Voice is Calling" by John McCormack
"Where Did Robinson Crusoe Go With Friday On Saturday Night?" by Al Jolson
"I Love A Piano" by Billy Murray
"Pretty Baby" by Billy Murray
"I'm Gonna Make Hay While the Sun Shines in Virginia" by Marion Harris
"Keep the Home Fires Burning ('Till the Boys Comes Home)" by James F. Harrison
"There's A Long Long Trail A-Winding" by James F. Harrison
"Ireland Must Be Heaven, For My Mother Came From There" by Charles Harrison

John Francis, Count McCormack (14 June 1884 – 16 September 1945) was a world-famous Irish tenor, celebrated for his performances of the operatic and popular song repertoires, and renowned for his diction and breath control. He was also a Papal Count.

MARCH 1916

March 2nd, 1916. AN ASTONISHING STATEMENT. BRITISH AIRMEN FIGHT EACH OTHER. An astonishing story was told in Parliament by Captain Bennett Goldney, who said that when the enemy aeroplanes dropped bombs over the first class fortress of Dover a month ago, in broad daylight, British aeroplanes were not ready for flight and the officers were not on the spot, being at lunch, and their mess rooms being 2 miles away. An official denial was given by Mr. Tennant to the latter portion of the statement.

One British airman, when he got his machine ready, according to Captain Bennett Goldney, had no arms or ammunition only a Winchester rifle and five rounds of ammunition. Yet he went up, and there soon followed a battle between the British aeroplane and a British seaplane each mistaking the other for the enemy. That was not the end of the blunder. Land gunners, mistaking both were enemy aircraft turned their fire on them, and managed to damage the tower of Walmer Church and injure men in the barrack. I.R.

March 2nd, 1916. NOTES. Nenagh enjoys a record other than a military one. In his 'History of the Ely O'Carroll Territory' Father Gleeson says it is stated that Nenagh and the neighbouring parishes consume monthly £2,000 of Guinness stout in other words 160,000 creamy pints.

A German farm, a German wife, and three marks a day for life is stated to have been the bribe offered to Irish prisoners of war in Germany by Sir Roger Casement, on condition of their forming an German-Irish brigade, according to an account from an Irish soldier of the address delivered by Sir Rodger at Limburg.

Editors who must serve. Under the Derby scheme claims for exemptions of editorial staffs will not be entertained in respect to art editors, photographic staff or darkroom operatives, society, sports, fiction and caption editors. Only one principal sub-editor of military age will be allowed on the staff and six sub-editors will not be exempted from the same staff. I.R.

March 2nd, 1916. EXTRAORDINARY FACTS ABOUT LIQUOR PROHIBITION IN CANADA AND THE STATES. On January 1, 1916, the end of the licensed liquor traffic came in seven American States. There are now 18 States under prohibition, and in Virginia probation will come into force next November, the law having already been voted on. The sweep has been a clean one. 6,800 bar-rooms have been closed. It is the greatest prohibition achievement in the history of the American continent. The seven new prohibitory States are apparently determined to see that the law is enforced. In Arkansas the penalty for liquor selling is a year's imprisonment. In Colorado five breweries and 1,600 licensed premises are out of business. In Idaho the law provides punishment for the possession of drink even by private citizens. Canada is following suit. Every bar in Saskatchewan was closed. 33 Government dispensaries were established, and already some of these have been abolished. Alberta in July adopted prohibition by a 2 to 1 vote. I.R.

March 2nd, 1916. A CORRESPONDENT FROM LISNASKEA writes to complain of the noisy rushing about of motor cars in Lisnaskea Street on Sunday night, when a concert was given, he says, in the Moat School. The tooting of horns, the rushing, the shouting, and the singing disturbed inhabitants, and he alleges that knockers were taken from doors. If this be all true, where were the police? No one is at liberty to disturb his neighbour in that fashion. If the allegations be true there was disorderly conduct of a much worse character than often meets with a sentence of two weeks' imprisonment. Where were the police? I.R.

March 2nd, 1916. THE LATE LIEUTENANT COMMANDER GARTSIDE TIPPING. The Life Boat for February contains a picture and obituary notice of Lieutenant Commander H. T. Gartside –Tipping, R. N., whose death we noticed recently when killed in action while in command of the armoured yacht *Sandra* on the 25th of September, 1915. He was born in 1848 and joined the Navy in 1860 and retired from active service in 1892. But on the outbreak of war, and when 66 years of age, he volunteered again for service; and was mortally wounded when commanding the *Sandra* on the Belgian Coast. Our present King George never forgot the relations between himself and Lieutenant Commander Tipping when His Majesty was a cadet under that officer aboard the *Dagger*. I.R.

March 2nd, 1916. A VAST PUSH IS THE AIM OF THE CROWN PRINCE AGAINST VERDUN. In this greatest of all worlds battles tens of thousands of men are slaughtered in fierce attacks and counterattacks in 10 days of unequalled fighting in the struggle for Verdun. Not since the memorable but ineffective push towards Calais have the Germans attempted so energetic and vast attack as now proceeding to the north of Verdun. Since September 1914 the Crown Prince has been trying to win renown by forcing a way through to the walls of Verdun. Having apparently won his father's consent something like half a million men have been concentrated on a front which stretches from the plains of Champagne to that of the Woevre. So that the Crown Prince might be saved from a repetition of his previous blunders he appointed as his adviser the veteran campaigner, Von Hacteler formerly in command at Metz and therefore well acquainted with the terrain over which the present attack it being made. Adopting the plan which brought success to Hindenburg in Russia, the Kaiser's son assembled 100,000 troops in a narrow front of 7 miles. This works out at about 90 men per yard. I.R.

Fermanagh Herald March 4th 1916. NEWS IN BRIEF. 600 WOUNDED ARRIVED IN DUBLIN. The hospital ship *Oxfordshire* with 600 soldiers from Harve, wounded recently at Ypres, was berthed on Sunday at the North Wall and the cases will be apportioned between Dublin, Belfast, Cork, and Queenstown hospitals. Prior to this trip the *Oxfordshire* brought to Southampton 600 wounded from the Dardanelles.

IRISH LABORERS AND MUNITIONS WORKER. Several hundred Co., Mayo labourers have been engaged for munition workers across the Channel, and have left to take up work, their fares being paid. From the Achill district alone, a Claremorris correspondent says, it is estimated that over 500 men have been engaged. They have been assured that they do not come under the Military Service Act.

TRAGIC FATE OF AUTHOR'S BROTHER. A tragic fate befell Mr. John McManus, brother of Mr. Seamus MacManus, the well-known author, on the night of the 25th. Returning from Donegal to Mountcharles, he proceeded along what is known as the "bank wall," but in the darkness he stumbled and fell a considerable distance to the shore, sustaining a deep cut on the head. Stunned by the fall and unaware of his whereabouts it appears that he walked into the river. He was, however quickly recovered, and a doctor summoned, but restorative methods proved unavailing and life was pronounced extinct.

MARRIED IN THE WORKHOUSE. At the meeting of the Donegal Board of Guardians, the Master reported that during the week a marriage had been celebrated in the institution. The groom, who is in the army, had crossed from England for the ceremony.

Fermanagh Herald March 4th 1916. JOTTINGS. Mr. J. Benson, son of Mr. S. Benson, Dublin Street, Monaghan, who is home from service with the 5th Scottish Regiment in France relates that on a space between the British and German lines he saw standing erect for days two warriors who met death together, each with the other's bayonet sunk deep into his body. One was an Irish Guard and the other a Prussian.

Congratulations to the most Rev. Dr. Mulhern on his elevation to the See of Dromore have been tendered by the Ballyshannon Old Age Pension Committee.

Fermanagh Herald March 4th 1916. GIFTS FOR THE IRISH GUARDS. To the editor of the Fermanagh Herald. Sir – would you be so good as to allow me space in your valuable journal for letters of thanks which I received from the Irish Guards, for a few little presents which I have sent them. I avail myself of this opportunity of appealing in your journal to the many admirers of those gallant Irishmen, for sending me contributions, be they ever so small, and I will feel great pleasure in sending them forward to those gallant sons of Erin who are upholding the traditions of our country. –I am, sir, yours respectfully Lilly Elmes. Kesh February 26, 1916.

31st of January, 1916. Dear Miss Elmes, - On the morning I left England to join their British Expeditionary Force, less than two weeks ago, I received from our Chaplain pretty Rosary beads. On a slip of paper attached to them was written your name and address, and thinking that you might be curious (and some girls are inquisitive) to know where they got to, I am writing to say that I have the beads with the pale blue stones, that I am grateful for them, that they are very much appreciated and valued by me, and that I am particularly happy to know that there is at least one girl in the old country who is interested in the spiritual welfare of those Irishmen who have chanced their fortunes in the present campaign. I repeat that the beads are particularly appreciated by me, for I am one of those who was induced to join the army owing to the sacrileges committed in the convents and churches of Belgium and France.

If you have leisure moments, and you would not consider it a breach of convention to write to a stranger, I would be very happy to hear from you occasionally. My address is: - Sgt J. S. McGuinn, 2nd Battalion Irish Guards, B.E.F., France. A letter only – for I am luxuriously looked after in physical and temporal as well as in spiritual matters – but I would be pleased if I could think that you said an occasional Hail Mary for my safe return to Ireland. I will now say goodbye, dear Miss Elmes and thank you ever so much for your thoughtfulness in sending beads, etc., to our chaplain. This writing is very illegible, but you may understand it. – I am ever, yours very sincerely John F. McGuinn.

R. C. Church, Wardley, Brentwood, 17th of January 1916. Dear Miss Elmes many thanks for your kind parcel of religious objects for the soldiers. Yesterday, at Mass, we prayed for you and your intentions. Had you heard the prayer recited by 1,000 men you would have been truly edified. Two of the Guards are going to acknowledge the gifts. Ambrose McGrath, O.S., C.F.I.G

March 9th, 1916. FOR RECITATION. A BIT OF BUNTING. BY A WOUNDED ANZAC. The rest of this recitation is on my blog www.cunninghamsway@wordpress.com

They have settled the ward for the evening,
And straightened every bed:
We have drunk our bowls of cocoa
And they have covered the lights with red.
We are lying down to the morning –
'Tis a terrible time to wait, when the day seems 24 hours
And the night seems 48;
For the man to the right is restless,
I can hear him mutter and mourn,
And the boy in the bed beside me
Is breaking his heart for home.
I doze a little in moments,
'Till I'm back with the heat and the flies
In the snipers line of fire,
With the sunlight in my eyes.
It's curious lying thinking
When the clock strikes once and again.
How fate has formed us together
In a regiment of pain.
ANZAC. I.R.

March 9th, 1916. DUBLIN LABOUR UNREST. Labour unrest, with demands for increased rates of wages, continues to develop at Dublin port and city. On Friday another steamer, the *Clydebrae*, chartered by the Dublin General Steam Shipping Company to bring in a cargo coal from Ayr, was held up in the Liffey, in company with the steamer which has lain there undischarged since her arrival. About 1,500 tons of coal in these vessels was untouched on Friday, the regular dockers refraining from work till five shillings extra for wet weather was granted. The city of Dublin cross-channel steamer continues unsettled after four months. One steamer with a scratch crew sailed on Thursday. The British and Irish boats Dublin to London have paid off three crews and put new men on two steamers. The builders and joiners also in the Dublin District are stated to be shortly demanding an extra penny per hour for working periods. Labour conditions are much unsettled generally, and much inconvenience is occurring to trade. I.R.

March 9th, 1916. BELLEEK. GOOD TEMPLAR SOIREE IN DRUMBAD. A very successful soiree and concert in connection with the recently established lodge 'Erin's Hope' of Good Templars was held in Drumbad School on Friday, the 25th of February. As the evening was fine many friends came long distances – from Pettigo, Ballyshannon, Churchill and Garrison. After tea, on the motion of Bro. J. W. Noble, seconded by Bro. Jas. Earls, the chair was taken by Bro. W. W. Read, P. C. T. In a neat address he reviewed the history of the Good Templar Order, its constitution and aims and the necessity of combating the drink habit especially at the present time. Bro. Joseph Atkinson, Ballyshannon proposed a resolution calling upon the Government to totally prohibit the drink traffic during the continuance of the war and for at least six months after - which was passed unanimously. I.R.

March 9th 1916. NOTES. The Portsmouth magistrates yesterday imposed fines of £1 each in three cases under the Defence of the Realm Act in which tobacconists were summoned for selling packets of cigarettes containing photographs and descriptions of His Majesty's ships alleged to be information calculated to be of use to the enemy. A defendant pleaded that he did not know the packets, which were supplied by the manufacturer, contained the photographs, but the magistrates held that the selling constituted publication.

A black cow the property of Mr. Moses Maguire, Cashel, near Derrygonnelly, gave birth to three black heifer calves on the 27th ult. The cow and calves are doing well. The cow is now four years old and this is five black calves she has had. The bull the calves are bred from is now owned by Mr. John Cathcart, Tullycreevy, Monea.

The news that Mr. Redmond has arranged for shamrocks to be sent to all the Irishmen in the fleet and to every Irish battalion at the front for St. Patrick's day is welcome for at such a time as the present these little bits of sentiment mean almost everything to our fighting men. F.T.

March 9th 1916. WHISKEY FOR THE HUNS. MR. LLOYD GEORGE AS THE WORLD'S GREATEST DISTILLER. Replying to a deputation from the Temperance Council of the Christian Churches Mr. Lloyd George at the Ministry of Munitions said that through the work of the Central Controlled Board drunkenness had decreased by 40 per cent and that there was no doubt that the diminution of facilities had resulted in the diminution of drinking. 'During the past few weeks', said Mr. Lloyd George, 'I have found it my painful duty to become the greatest distiller in the world. I have taken over the whole of the patent-still distilleries in the kingdom and also as many pot-stills distilleries as I could make any use of so that you will find that there would be very few distilleries during the period of the war available for distilling spirits. In fact I'm doing my best to provide whiskey for the Germans and if the whiskey pellets I am distilling for them will do half as much harm to the Germans has whiskey has done for this country I shall feel very satisfied and so will every good patriot. F.T.

Fermanagh Herald March 11th 1916. DERRYGONNELLY NOTES. About 17 marriages have taken place in the Derrygonnelly parish during the past two weeks.

Fermanagh Herald March 11th 1916. FOUND DEAD NEAR DERRYGONNELLY. WOMAN'S HOARD. LARGE SUM OF MONEY DISCOVERED IN HER ROOM. On Saturday evening an old woman named Anne Hoy, of Scandally, about 3 miles from Derrygonnelly was found dead in bed. A young man named Joseph Magee had occasion to attend his cattle convenient to her house, and seeing no smoke on his second visit in the evening became suspicious that she might be dead. He started off to Derrygonnelly and informed Sergeant Bradley who with Constables Flannigan and Toughy visited the place and immediately broke in the door, and found the old woman dead in bed. There was no food in the house. Constables Flanagan and Toughy began to search her room, and to their surprise found £40 in pound and £5 notes and silver and a bank receipt for £200. The money found in the house by the police was rolled up in old rags and paper, and concealed in holes in the room in which she died. She was aged about 78 years.

Fermanagh Herald March 11th 1916. JOTTINGS. NO MORE PAPER WRAPPERS FOR MEAT. Owing to the difficulty of getting paper, the Belfast butchers have requested their customers to make suitable provision for conveying their meat from the shops to their homes.

RAILWAY FATALITY AT ENNISKILLEN. An inquest was held in Enniskillen on Monday by Mr. Rogers, deputy coroner, on the remains of Mrs. Annie Maguire, aged 75 who were found alongside the railway line at the Drumclay level crossing, close to the town. It appeared from the evidence that deceased who is slightly deaf, was going for water to a well beside the line and was struck down by the 6.35 p.m. train from Enniskillen to Derry on Saturday last. F.H.

March 16th, 1916. SINN FEIN DISLOYALTY. MORE BLATHER. Countess Markievicz addressed a public meeting in the City Hall Cork on Monday night under the auspices of the woman's branch of the Sinn Fein party. She said she was proud that there was today an Irish man in another country who is making treaties for Ireland with England's enemies. (Cheers.) Today the men of Ireland were alive and realized that the only way to speak to England was with guns in their hands. They had not dared to have conscription in Ireland because the volunteers had guns in Ireland today. The authorities knew they were disloyal and they were afraid of them. (Voice. Down with Redmond and cheers.) They had seen the letter in the papers from Mr. Skeffington saying the reason Zeppelins had not dropped bombs on Ireland was because they had an ambassador at the Court in Berlin. Robert Emmet's epitaph could only be written in the blood of England with swords in the hands of Irishmen.

WOOD FOR THE TRENCHES. Farnham Wood, which is situate along the slope of the hills between Newry and Omeath, is at present being cut down by a Glasgow firm, and the timber is being sent to the seat of war for trench making. A saw mill is being erected at the base of the wood, and a large number of huts have been also erected, in which the men with their wives and families are to live. It is stated the work of cutting the timber may last for a couple of years. The wood belonged to the Earl of Kilmorey.

LESSENING DRUNKENNESS. On February 28 there Liquor Control Board closed five public houses in Glasgow. The action had a remarkable effect upon convictions for drunkenness. The weekly average for four weeks before the closing of these houses was 370 convictions. The figure for the following week was 187. I.R.

March 16th, 1916. PARLIAMENT. Colonel Winston Churchill, it is hoped, will accept the advice of Admiral Sir Hedworth Meux to remain in France, that he was not wanted here. He is at present an 'exploded volcano' and may render himself better service in the field than in Parliament.

When Lord Shaughnessy feared that the proposal to raise a Canadian army of half a million men would disturb the agricultural, industrial and financial affairs of Canada, Sir Sam Hughes replied vigorously that they would not suffer if twice a half a million men were sent by the Dominion to the front. Germany had sent one man out of five to the army; and Canada could send a second 500,000 men if necessary. This is splendid! But how poor is the record of Ireland beside it. I.R.

March 16th, 1916. Promotion of Admiral Lowry. British Command Orders intimates that the Admiralty has notified that in future the Admiral whose flag flies at Rosyth Naval Base will have the status of Commander-in-Chief. Admiral Sir Robert Lowry, the present occupant of the post, accordingly becomes Commander-in-Chief at that base. Admiral Lowry is a distinguished Ulsterman, being the eldest son of the late Lieutenant General Robert W. Lowry, C. B., of Aghnablaney, County Fermanagh. (Ed. Near Pettigo.) I.R.

March 16th, 1916. NOTES. A potato famine exists in German towns. In the country districts there is no meat to be had.

The Don't-want-to-Fight Men of England are being formed into a non-combat corps with the ordinary infantry pay but none of the working or proficiency pay. The corps will perhaps generally be known as The Cowards Corps.

Admiral Lowry

Women are appealed to by the Committee for War Savings to avoid elaboration and variety in dress, new clothes, and all forms of luxury, and not to motor for pleasure, to have less elaborate meals, cut down the number of servants and give up hothouses.

Liverpool dockers have refused to work with women. The old-world prejudice of men has to be broken down. Women have as much right to live as men. I.R.

March 16th 1916. THE EXCEPTION TRIBUNALS AND HOW THEY WORK IN SCOTLAND. OF 93 APPEALS; 90 ARE GRANTED. A correspondent sends to *The Times* newspaper a report of the sittings of Aberdeenshire tribunals to show how things are being run there. The tribunal for Huntley District met on Saturday and heard appeals with the above results – only three refused. A farmer asked exemption for his brother, a ploughman. The applicant said he had 320 acres. There were six on the place and himself. This was the only man of military age. The Chairman asked how is your father and was told he is very well. The Chairman said he is a wonderful man and I propose total exemption I know the family and their history. Total exemption was granted. Another farmer asked exemption for a son, a cattle man. The applicant stated that there were 100 acres of arable and 14 of pasture. He had two sons at home. Major Gray said the Advisory Committee had refused his application, because the other son had been granted exemption. The Chairman asked how are they to work the farm with girls? The Chairman said I know the family root and branch. There is not a straighter man in Aberdeenshire than this. A Member said I cannot vote against him I know him so well. Exemption was granted. F.T.

March 16th 1916. AND THE MAN WHO WOULD NOT SERVE ANY COUNTRY. A young man of 21 who applied for total exemption at the Whitehaven tribunal said he was born in England but emigrated to the United States when he was 12. Coming home to recruit his health in 1914, he was not allowed to return to America. The chairman said that as a British subject you ought to be proud to have an opportunity of serving your country. The applicant said I happen not to be proud to serve my country. I would not serve any country. The world is my country and if I do not like the laws of one country I go to another. Application refused. A conscientious objector said he was a Wesleyan and would not join the Army on any consideration. Replying to a question with regard to David being an instrument in God's hands when he slew Goliath in the war with the Philistines the applicant said God commanded that war but he did not command the present war. The Mayor said how dare you sit there and say that? He applicant said I am as certain as I sit here that the war is not a righteous war. War of any kind is against the word of God. 'I suppose you accept the protection of the British Crown?' 'Certainly not. I take my protection from God above.' 'Well? You're not fit to live that's all.' I'm certain I am but there are a lot of people not fit to live. Exemption from combat service only granted. F.T.

Fermanagh Herald March 18th 1916. JOTTINGS. A committee has been formed in Clones and £300 has already been subscribed to promote a memorial to the late Right Rev Monsignor O'Neill, P.P., V. F., Dean of Clogher. The list is to be kept open for one month.

Private Thomas Kelly, Townhall St., Enniskillen, who joined the 8th Battalion Inniskilling Fusiliers, some five or six months ago, has, we regret to say been killed in action. The notification was recently received by his sisters. Private Kelly was previously employed by ex-County Inspector Maguire, and subsequently by the Scottish Corporative Wholesale Society, Enniskillen. His death will cause profound regret among his relatives and friends.

March 23rd 1916. ENNISKILLEN PROSECUTIONS. The practice of depositing ashes and refuse on public thoroughfares in Enniskillen has recently been so greatly on the increase that the Urban Council have been compelled to take legal steps to put an end to it and on Monday they prosecuted three defendants, Mrs. Ann Somers, John Goodwin and James Morrison for having been guilty of this offence. The prosecution said there had been complaints that the roadway at the rear of Ann Street was being obstructed by parties throwing rubbish, ashes and old tin cans on it. Somers was fined 2s 6d and costs, Goodwin five shillings and costs and Morrison two and six and costs.
At Enniskillen Petty Sessions under the Weights and Measures Act Andrew Parker, of Ann St., merchant was charged with having a weighing machine in his shop to one side of which a piece of lead had been attached making in register 1 ½ ounces against the customer. Frederick Carson, a young assistant, in the defendant's shop stated that he had attached the lead without Mr. Parker's knowledge. The chairman said that the Bench

had taken a very lenient view of the case and decided to impose a fine of 10 shillings with three and six costs.

Fermanagh Herald March 25th 1916. AIR RAID ON KENT. Nine people were killed and 31 injured as four German seaplanes flew over East Kent today. As far as we can ascertain 48 bombs were dropped altogether. Three men, one woman and five children were killed and 17 men, five women, and nine children were injured.

Fermanagh Herald March 25th 1916. ARMY ACCOUNTS. NO OFFICIAL RECORDS OF SOME SOLDIERS EXIST. CLOTHING DEALS: UNIFORMS WHICH COST £2,650 WERE RESOLD FOR £400. A report by the Comptroller and Auditor General, which reveals the unsatisfactory condition of certain Army accounts, was issued on Saturday. In all dealings with the Army and supplies, there is a considerable amount of muddle, as these vouchers are not infrequently missing or incomplete. Forage, animals, fuel and light accounts for the period immediately preceding embarkation were not filled. Up to February 12th 1916, no store accounts of transport vehicles had been furnished. This is put down to extreme pressure in the earlier months of the war. Horses arrived by rail at night with no voucher to show who sent them or the station from which they came, or with no identification labels. Units transferred horses to other troops without vouchers, and one unit apparently had failed to keep accounts as no record could be found of receipt or disposal of animals.

The Comptroller refers to large quantities of clothing that had been written off as destroyed on the authority of Courts of Inquiry. The papers showed that in September 1914, a firm offered a supply of part worn clothing for the use of the troops. Purchase was effected, but shortly afterwards complaints were received as to the unsatisfactory condition of jackets and trousers, some being verminous and others threadbare. Large quantities were ultimately condemned as unserviceable and returned to the ordnance officer, and together with the balance unissued from store were resold to the firm for £400 having cost £2,650. Further quantities of the clothing, for which about £4,700 had been paid, were destroyed by units as unserviceable.

A contract was placed "without competition" with a firm for the supply of one million great coats at 30 shillings and 1,000,000 suits at 23 shillings. Arrangements were subsequently made with the Wholesale Clothing Manufacturers' Federation, under which its members supplied great coats at 28 shillings and suits at 21 shillings and nine pence.

Several officers and men, the Auditor-General continues, were paid rewards for inventions, and a Mr. S. W. Hiscocks received £25 for an improved method of constructing dirigibles. A sum of £5 was allowed to Mrs. Angus Shureys, the widow of a storeholder, for an idea for the strengthening of mallet heads by riveting. Captain C. A. Crawley–Boevey, A.S.C. was rewarded with £250 for a non-skid device for motor lorries.

Many men were taken on pay for whom none of the usual attestation documents were forthcoming. This was more particularly noticed in the case of the Army Service Corps, especially the mechanical transport section, many of the men apparently having been clothed and sent abroad without any record of their existence or identity. The total expenditure on billeting included in the accounts to March 31, 1915 was almost £6,250,000. Although instructions indicated that the price payable on impressment for an officer's charger should be £70 it was noticed in the accounts of one command that in three cases £200 per horse was paid in addition to about 20 cases varying from £110 to £160. Although these purchased cannot be said to be contrary to regulations, they seemed to be of an extravagant character says the report.

Fermanagh Herald March 25th 1916. A NATION OR A PROVINCE? I have often thought that sometimes when we speak of Ireland a Nation a great many of us have not the faintest idea of what nation means. In the first place, according to my interpretation, no country can claim to be a nation unless it has a distinct National Life, and this seems impossible without the national language. Once admitted that the national language is necessary – and I hold it to be indispensable – it must make its way into every department of the country's life: it must inspire the village blacksmith as much as the poet, musician, and sculptor; people must think in it, and their actions must be guided by the thought it produces. The whole history of the world confirms this view and I know of no nation that has continued to preserve its national and political integrity in defiance of such a law. I do not know of any nation that allowed its language to decline that continued to be a great and powerful nation.

Fermanagh Herald March 25th 1916. LAST WEEK I DREW ATTENTION TO ERRONEOUS STATEMENTS made by a local Unionist editor concerning our Irish language, which he described in words which were tantamount to stating that it was worthless. I disposed of that statement and proved its falsity. In last week's issue of his paper he quotes a portion of an article written by H de Vere Stackpole, whom he describes as the well-known novelist, and presumably on that account Stackpole must be taken seriously in his statements regarding the Irish language. In this local Unionist organ we have been greeted with quotations from Robert Blatchford, Austin Harrison and, and now Stackpole. Who is Blatchford? He is the most famous of Northcliffe's employees. He has stated in the *Clarion* that he does not believe in God, mysteries, or life after death.

H de Vere Stackpole.

Fermanagh Herald March 25th 1916. £1,000 DAMAGES FOR MRS. ASQUITH. "IRRESPONSIBLE TITLE TATTLE." Mrs. Asquith, wife of the Prime Minister, was given a verdict by consent for £1,000 damages and costs against *The Globe* for libel on Tuesday. The grounds of the action were that the newspaper had made assertions to the effect that she had played lawn tennis with German officers interned at Donnington Hall, and had also sent them gifts.

Mrs. Asquith and her daughter, Miss Elizabeth Asquith, occupied seats next to the Hon Charles Russell at the solicitors table, and in the witness box she gave emphatic replies to the questions put by her leading counsel Mr. Duke, who asked: did you at any time hold any communication with any prisoner at Donnington Hall? - Never. Did you send any kind of present or communication to any prisoner at Donnington Hall? - Never. It was alleged that you sent delicacies from Messrs. Fortnum and Masons. What presents have you ever sent through them? - To my son in the Dardanelles. Did you ever send any other? - Never.

Lieutenant Meyer stated that it was his duty to supervise and inspect all communications and parcels that came to Donnington Hall for German prisoners. He stated that no presents had ever been received from Mrs. Asquith nor any communication or any presents or communications from any member of her family or from the wife of any other Cabinet Minister.

Fermanagh Herald March 25th 1916. TULLAMORE SENSATION. AN AFFRAY WITH THE POLICE IN A SINN FEIN HALL. ONE OFFICER SHOT. THE POLICE SEIZE ARMS AND ARREST FOUR MEN. Scenes of an intensely exciting character were witnessed in Tullamore on Monday night, when the rooms of Sinn Fein Volunteers and Cumann na mBan were besieged by a hostile crowd. About eight or clock considerably over 100 boys carrying Union Jacks paraded the streets, singing and shouting. When opposite the Volunteer rooms they halted and commenced booing and shouting down with the Sinn Feiners. A slight scuffle took place but the police appeared on the scene and cleared the crowd away but they remained on the street and footpath opposite for over an hour. When the besieged began to make their appearance the police had to escort some to their homes, while others remained in the rooms. Stones were then thrown at the windows, and those inside replied to the fusillade by revolver shots. Afterwards the police raided the rooms with the intention of searching the occupants for arms. The Sinn Feiners refused to allow themselves to be searched and turned their revolvers on the police at whom several shots were fired. Sergeant Aherne was shot on the shoulder and side and badly wounded. He was subsequently brought to the Union Hospital where he lies in a precarious condition. Four arrests were made, the prisoners being from Tullamore, namely Joseph Wrafter, Joseph Morris, Henry McNally and Thomas Byrne, all Irish Volunteers. Three revolvers were captured by the police, one of which was an automatic pistol.

Fermanagh Herald March 25th 1916. EACH SHOT OF THE JACK JOHNSTON COSTS £524. *The New Yorker World* prints the following details relative to the famous German 42 cm 16.5 inch howitzer: - the weight of the gun is 9,400 tons, the weight of the platform is 41 ¼ tons, the length of the barrel is 16 feet 5 inches the weight of the shell 805lbs, the length of the shell 4 feet 2 inches, and a number of parts of the gun, 172: the railway cars to transport it 12; depth of the foundation 26 feet.

Liege was shelled from a distance of 14 miles, and the casualties from the first shot were 1,700; the casualties from the second shot 2,300. Namur and Maubeuge held out to two shots. The putting up of the gun takes 25-26 hours, and the adjustment of the range 6 hours. All the windows are broken within a radius of 2 ½ miles. Each shot costs £524 and to serve the gun it takes 200 men. The gun crew proper wear protectors over their mouths, eyes, and ears and lie on their stomachs to keep from being injured by the shock of the discharge. The entire gun emplacement is mined, and the engineer in charge is sworn to blow up the gun if it is in any danger of capture. – *Daily Express*.

(Ed. "A 'Jack Johnson' was the British nickname used to describe the impact of a heavy, black German 15-cm artillery shell. Jack Johnson (1878-1946) was the name of the popular U.S. (born in Texas) world heavyweight boxing champion who held the title from 1908-15.)

Fermanagh Herald March 25th 1916. THE LIGHTING OF BROOKEBOROUGH was again discussed at the meeting of the Lisnaskea Rural Council held last Saturday, when the Brookeborough Lighting Committee reported upon the recent installation of the acetylene gas plant. It was decided to send the report, which stated that the work had been properly and legally carried out, to the local government board, stating that the council approved of the work.

Fermanagh Herald March 25th 1916. MOST REV. DR. MACRORY, BISHOP OF DOWN and Connor, preaching in St. Patrick's Church, Belfast on St. Patrick's Day urges his hearers to remember always, while clinging like leeches to their own faith, to respects, esteem, and love all their fellow countrymen whatever religion they belonged to. They worshipped, continued his Lordship, the same God with us according to their lights. The same motherland has nursed us all, and Ireland needs the cooperation and united energy of all her sons. Let us then always scrupulously avoid any offensive word or act against the religion of others. It is enough for us that we hold fast the faith that St. Patrick brought us.

Fermanagh Herald March 25th 1916. INTERESTING ITEMS FROM ALL QUARTERS. PENSIONER'S HOARD. In the house of an old age pensioner and small farmer named J. Martin, who resided in the townland of Moneygore, near Rathfriland, and who died a few days ago, a box was discovered, which on being opened, was found to contain £540 - £400 in gold, £100 in notes and the balance in silver and copper coins.

PENNY COFFINS. At a meeting of the Athlone Guardians the tender of a local undertaker to supply infant coffins at one penny and for young people at five pennies was accepted.

GREAT EGG ADDLING SCHEME. A committee representing agricultural interests in Western Scotland is appealing to all owners of rookeries to arrange for men in relays to fire guns every quarter of an hour or so for 24 hours when nests are full of eggs and the birds begin to sit. The firing, it is pointed out, would frighten the birds whose absence from the nests would cause the eggs to become addled, and so the next generation of rooks will never materialise.

PRAMS AND LIGHTING. It is explained that the new Lighting order in Great Britain is not applied to perambulators when on the footpaths or crossing the street, but when in the roadway they must bear a light showing white and a red light at the rear.

BANKS AND MILITARY SERVICE. At the London City Military Tribunal assent was given to an arrangement with various London Banks, by which it is proposed to take from them by the beginning of July about 75 per cent of men eligible, single and married.

SWEETS FOR BISCUITS. The Dover Guardians, having discovered that the workhouse children, instead of eating the two biscuits given them for lunch, pooled and sold them, purchasing sweets with the proceeds. They have decided to stop their lunch.

SOAP BUBBLE A MONTH OLD. A soap bubble which is already a month old and is still perfect was exhibited by Dewar at the Royal institution. The bubble was blown on February 17th and its long life was stated to be due to the fact that it was blown with clean air free from motes of solid particles. The bubble, which was on view in the laboratory, is suspended from a tube inside a glass vessel. Those who attended Dr. Aubrey Stratan's lecture inspected it with great interest. Its diameter was said to be about 7 inches.

Fermanagh Herald March 25th 1916. THE ERNE ESTATES. APPLICATION IN DUBLIN. THE EARL MISSING SINCE LAST YEAR. On Tuesday the case of Erne v. Erne was before Mr. Justice Ross in the Land Judge's Court, Dublin, on a report of the receiver–examiner on the estate of Henry William Earl of Erne, who has been missing since early last year when he was engaged with the British Expeditionary Force in France. This suit is of a friendly character.

March 30th 1916. WAR ITEMS AND THE PRICE OF HORSES. In the Irish Command a large number of horses were cast as unsuitable for military purposes and sold at prices which indicated considerable loss. The proportion in the southern circle was especially high being above 12 per cent comparing very unfavourably with 2.12% in the northern circle and two per cent in England and Scotland. It appears that want of knowledge

of military requirements on the part of both military and civilian buyers and unsound advice from their veterinary assistants led to unprofitable purchases whilst carelessness in branding made possible the substitution of inferior horses between purchase and delivery, there being no means of identifying the buyer responsible for any particular animal. F.T.
(Ed. An estimated 8,000,000 horses are said to have died in WW1.)

March 30th 1916. 65 AIRMEN ATTACKED A SEAPLANE STATION AT ZEEBRUGGE and 10,000 pounds of bombs were dropped. The Admiralty announced on Monday a big raid by Allied airmen and 50 airmen formed the attacking squadron accompanied by 15 fighting machines. Each machine carried 200 pounds and considerable damage was done. All machines returned safely. F.T.

March 30th 1916. MILITARY NOTES. CLONES OFFICER KILLED. News has been received from France of the death in action of Captain Frederick J Duggan, Royal Field Artillery, son of Mr. Creighton Duggan, a prominent Clones gentleman. The deceased officer who was in his 34th year had been in the army before the war broke out. The colonel of his battery in conveying the sad news to his widow in London says he was one of the very best and loved by all the officers and men. He leaves two sons. His death is deeply regretted in Clones and district where the deepest sympathy is extended to his father.

Midshipman Humphreys Archdale, RN, HMS *Temeraire*, having passed for the rank of acting sub lieutenant has been appointed to HMS destroyer *Savage*. He is the younger son of Mr. E.M. Archdale of Riversdale, Ballinamallard who was himself a formerly a lieutenant in the Royal Navy. His eldest brother Commander N. E. Archdale commanded HMS *Hazard* in the bombardment of the German army's right wing off the Belgian Coast on 18 October, 1914 and subsequently. Two other brothers are in the Junior service: Captain Audley Quinton Archdale, Royal Field Artillery, and Lieutenant Dominic Mervyn Archdall 1st (Central Africa) Battalion the King's African Rifles. F.T.

March 30th, 1916. MILITARY SERVICE ACT. IMMUNITY OF IRISH LABOURERS. The administration of the Military Service Act was criticised by several members in Parliament on Monday the 22nd and Captain Amory said that the Prime Minister seemed to hate decisions even more than he hated the Germans. Mr. Lloyd George said they had to discriminate between the real conscientious objectors and those who use their conscience as a cloak for cowardice. Instead of criticising they should help the tribunals to solve the difficulty. After further discussion, Mr. Long made it quite clear that Irish labourers coming over for agricultural or other work would not be liable to be called up upon to serve in the Army. The position of these men was absolutely secure and clear, and, if necessary, the Government would make some announcement in a general form which would allay any doubt. I.R.

April 1916

Fermanagh Herald April 1st 1916. JOTTINGS. Private Hazlitt 11th Batt. Royal Inniskilling Fusiliers, the first man of the corps to win the D.C.M., belongs to Roslea. He has been promoted Corporal.

Major C. C. D'Arcy Irvine, Castle Irvine, Irvinestown, has accepted a captaincy in the 20th (R.) Batt., R. I. Rifles. His elder son lost his life at Suvla Bay.

A notice of motion been in the name of Mr. William Elliott, of Florence Court, and which proposed that the children in the Enniskillen Workhouse be sent out to the town schools was at the meeting of the Guardians last Tuesday, defeated by 22 votes to 10.

At Lisnaskea Petty Sessions last Saturday, Mary Ann McFarland, of Lisnaskea, was sent to jail for one month for neglecting her children, aged five, 11, and 14 years. The defendant said she was in gaol before, and "could do it again and again and again."

Mrs. Kelly, Townhall Street, has received official information that her brother, Private Thomas Kelly, of the 8th Battalion Royal Inniskilling Fusiliers, was killed in action at the front on the 6th of March. The sympathy of the townspeople will go out to the deceased's relatives and friends.

The number of men who have crossed over to Ireland to escape military service is anything but negligible says the *Liverpool Echo*. "Careful watch," it says, "is kept for the renegades at the ports." Many of the men, who are classed as deserters, are traced, and an escort is sent to carry them home.

At a public meeting in Ballybay it was unanimously decided to form a unit of the War Time Council calling for the total prohibition of strong drink. Mr. H. Stevens Richardson presided, and said the war had revealed the hideousness of the drink evil. It was evident they could not win the war so long as John Bull carried a beer barrel on his back. Several speakers condemned the Government for not stopping drink during the war, as their Allies had done.

The death has occurred in London of the well-known Irish musician and songwriter, Mrs. Milligan Fox, eldest daughter of Mr. Seton F. Milligan. She was born in Omagh in 1864, studied in Frankfurt and Milan conservatoires and at the Royal College of Music, London and devoted much of her time to the collection of the lost music of Ireland, having the cooperation of her sisters, Mrs. Wheeler and Miss Alice Milligan in her work of composition.

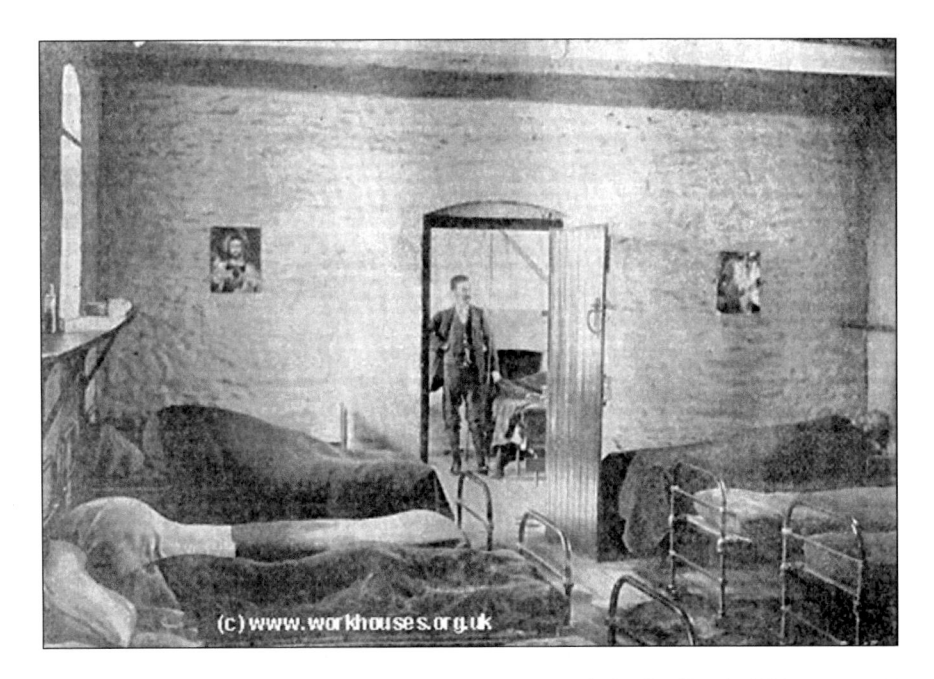

Fermanagh Herald April 1st 1916. IRISH WORKHOUSE EXTRAVAGANCE. One of the greatest curses ever inflicted by the English Government on this country was the Workhouse system, which O'Connell prophesied would be productive of bad moral and financial results. It was the old story of trying to fit a square peg into a round hole, and all-seeing statesmen and politicians who knew practically nothing concerning Ireland's needs, saw no reason why a method of alleviating distress which was considered highly satisfactory for England should not prove a blessing to the step-sister Kingdom also; it was not a question of consulting Ireland but of forcing the English Workhouse down her throat.

From the financial point of view, this means of coping with poverty, disease and infirmity has proved a drag on the country contending against ever increasing battalions of other difficulties; its crudeness has inflicted deep wounds on the susceptibilities of the Irish poor, who like all other sections of the Irish race look with abhorrence on the red tape and benevolence through machinery; it has pandered to the taste of the idle and vicious, and, apart from the legitimate tramp who is the victim of unpreventable, misfortune, it has created a type of men and women of the road who are a menace to our society. We always must have adequate provision for the sick and infirm poor, for the proper upbringing of the child thrown on the mercy of the public, but there seems no need to maintain the present costly Workhouse system for the realization of such ends. In England, where, of course, local rates obtain benefit through Government grants, outdoor relief is given on a much higher scale than in this country, with the result that the feelings of the recipients are not subject to the hurt that is common in Ireland. The Workhouse is the last place in the world where children should be housed or reared, and good results will certainly accrue from the adoption of the boarding-out system, but still further reforms are possible. There is no reason why public charity should be saddled with the duty of providing, as at present, for the professional tramp class, nor reason why labour colonies should not be established, making the despiser of work useful to the community.

Fermanagh Herald April 1st 1916. A CHILD'S BODY FOUND ON THE RAILWAY LINE NEAR MAGUIRESBRIDGE. The police are investigating the mysterious discovery of the body of a three months old male child lying on a bridge on the Great Northern Railway line. James Fagan, a workman of Drumeer, deposed to walking along the line and at 5.30 that morning seeing the body lying on a bridge on the side of the line. He did not touch it nor go near it, nor did he know whether it was dead or alive, but he believed the child was dead. He went and told the police. How the body got to be on the railway bridge, or who left it there, is a mystery. A woman named Rose Ann Boyle, belonging to the Lack district, has been arrested on suspicion.

April 6th 1916. THE LATE MAJOR N. J. ARCHDALL. By command of His Majesty the King his assistant military secretary has written to Mr. E. Hugh Archdall, Drumcoo, Enniskillen, as next of kin of the late Major M. J. Mervyn Archdall, of the Cameron Highlanders, informing him that this officer was mentioned in dispatches from General Sir John French dated 28th November last for gallant and distinguished service, and expressing the King's high appreciation of these services and that his Majesty trusted that this public acknowledgement might be of some consolation in their bereavement. I.R.

April 6th 1916. DUBLIN SINN FEINERS. SCENE AFTER MEETING. REVOLVER SHOTS IN THE STREETS. A meeting was held on Thursday in the Mansion House, Dublin, to protest against the banishment of Irishmen. The chair was occupied by Alderman Corrigan. Speeches of a violent nature were delivered. The proceedings were opened by the reading of a number of telegrams from, amongst others, several priests, one of whom pictured the Nationalist party as walking in the footsteps of Cromwell. The allusion was greeted with enthusiasm and hisses.

One of the speakers was a priest from Ballinasloe, who counselled a day and night vigil round the place where the two Sinn Feiners who have been ordered to leave the country are confined prior to the banishment. The speaker concluded his remarks with the solemn benediction: 'If you are faithful and zealous then I can promise you very confidently God's blessing and success in your work. The singing of 'The felons of our land,' brought the meeting to a close. An exciting incident occurred after the meeting. The crowd headed by a pipe band marched through the principal streets cheering and shouting. In Grafton Street it rose to such a pitch that a youth in the procession smashed the lamps of a motor car. The police attempted to arrest him and instantly a scene of confusion occurred. Revolver shots were fired and there was an ugly rush at the police. Inspector Barrett was struck on the side by a bullet which fortunately lodged in a bundle of papers in his pocket and inflicted no damage. The crowd rapidly dispersed and the streets became quiet in a quarter of an hour. During the procession soldiers were everywhere vigorously hooted. I.R.

April 6th 1916. A SENSATIONAL INCIDENT. AN OFFICER'S CONDUCT IN PARLIAMENT. In the House of Commons on the 28th a powerfully built officer in khaki uniform who was subsequently stated to be Lieut. Turnbull R.A.M.C. arose from a seat in the Ordinary Stranger's Gallery and advance rapidly through the Distinguished Stranger's Gallery to the rail which terminates that space and immediately overhangs the floor just at the bar of the House. Amid loud cries of protest he clambered over the rail and hung suspended by his arms for several seconds ultimately dropping onto the floor on his hands and feet a distance of 20 feet. On rising he attempted to walk up the floor but several members standing near surrounded him and forced him into the lobby. Whilst this was being done the officer who appeared to be in a highly excited condition and was gesticulating wildly shouted out 'I ask you to protect the heads of British soldiers against shrapnel fire.' His object was, it is stated, to draw attention to the use of steel helmets for the forces. I.R.

April 6th 1916. DEPRESSION IN BERLIN OVER THE FAILURE AT VERDUN. A leading Swiss financier who has just returned from Berlin, Hamburg, Dresden and other German centres, says that nothing since the war started has caused more depression and despondency among the German people than the failure of the great Verdun offensive. In the public mind, he says, the attack on Verdun was to have been a quick and decisive affair and the air is now full of speculation as to the cause for the failure. The German people know that something went wrong at Verdun. The German army, German organisation, German science, they say are invincible then why do they not go ahead. It is asserted that German scientists have invented a new invisible scentless gas which renders its victim's unconscious – something like sleeping sickness –for three weeks, but that owing to the 'maudlin humanity' of the Kaiser the German army was not permitted to use this gas at Verdun. Many Germans now accept the French estimate of the German losses where it is stated that 60,000 German soldiers have been killed in a month. I.R.

April 6th 1916. THE TRAITORS. CLYDE MISCHIEF MAKERS. Mr. Robert Blatchford writing in the *Weekly Dispatch* on the Clyde revolt says: - The Government have brought these troubles upon themselves by their weakness. They have tried to compromise and conciliate when they ought to have governed. They have always had the country behind them. They are responsible for the conduct of the war: they are responsible for the supply of guns and shells; they are responsible for the lives of the officers and men in the trenches. The Clyde revolt is due to an attempt by a clique of malignants to dictate to the Government and blackmail the country. The strikers have no real grievance. They have not the sympathy of the people. They are recognized as traitors by the Navy and the Army and all the parents, wives and friends of the sailors and soldiers. These men have made trouble from the beginning of the war, and they have been pampered and deferred to until they imagine the British people will stand tamely by and allow them to hold up the war. These men are holding up important work of guns and munitions. They betray the men at the front. They are playing into the hands of the enemy. Nothing could excuse such conduct. No profits of the employers, however huge, no grievance about hours or wages could justify the action of these men. The Clyde ringleaders have been guilty of mutiny in the face of the enemy and now that they have been deported their workmates are threatening to strike unless they are released. There is no excuse for these ringleaders nor for the dupes who follow them. Such men at such a time must be dealt with sternly. I.R.

April 6th 1916. FERMANAGH MURDER CHARGE. INFANT'S BODY ON THE RAILWAY LINE. A young woman named Rose Ann Boyle, Edinaclaw (Little), near Ederney, County Fermanagh, was arrested by Sergeant Cleary and Constable Molloy, of Lack, in connection with the death of her three months old male child whose body was found on the railway line at Maguiresbridge on Tuesday. She was conveyed to Lisnaskea and brought before Mr. T. Gavin, J.P. on a charge of murder. In a statement to the police she admitted she was the mother of the infant and said she travelled with the child from the Belfast Union on Monday evening. After the train had left Maguiresbridge station the child began to cry and she opened the carriage door and threw him out. District Inspector Gillis applied for a remand, which was granted, the accused being conveyed later to Derry Jail. The child's body was discovered on the morning of the 26th by a work man named James Fagan of Drumeer, lying on a bridge at the side of the Great Northern Railway. An inquest was opened by Mr. James Mulligan and adjourned for a post mortem examination. I.R.

April 6th 1916. EMBEZZLEMENT CHARGES. HORSE DEALER IN THE DOCK. On Thursday, Thomas E. Caldwell, horse dealer, Clones, was arrested on a warrant issued as a result of information sworn by David Levinson, Clones, with whom he had business relations for some time past in connection with the horse trade. He was charged with, while working as a servant of David Levinson, selling horses on behalf of him failing properly to account for the money in question. He sold 41 horses at Perth for the sum of £1,450 and accounted for £1,140 of this amount; two horses at Perth for the sum of £64; four horses at Liverpool for the sum of £120; eight horses at Carlisle for the sum of £270 all of which were the property of the said David Levinson. An adjournment was granted, defendant being allowed out on bail himself in £100 and two sureties of 50 each. The sureties were at once forthcoming in the persons of Mr. Peter Carron, Clones, and Mr. McCullagh, horse dealer, Ballybay. I.R.

April 6th 1916. WORKHOUSES IN ULSTER. Mr. Birrell replying in the Parliamentary papers to Mr. Coote. (U., South Tyrone,) gives unions where the number of inmates were under 100 on the 25th of March, 1916 and also of the numbers that were in these workhouses on the 1st of August, 1908, the date of the passing of the Old Age Pensions Act. In the province of Ulster the unions are (Fermanagh interest) Bawnboy 1916, 47; 1908, 51 Donegal, 1916, 62; 1908, 77. Irvinestown 1916, 31; 1908, 64. Lisnaskea, 1916., 56; 1908, 58. Clones 1916, 86; 1908, 113. Castlederg, 1916, 40; 1908, 55. I.R.

Fermanagh Herald April 8th 1916. A ZEPPELIN RAID ON SCOTLAND. 10 KILLED AND 11 INJURED. It appears that altogether six Zeppelins took part in the raid of last night. Three of them raided the south-eastern counties of Scotland, one the northeast coast of England, and the remaining two the eastern counties of England. In all 36 explosive and 17 incendiary bombs were dropped in various places, damaging some hotels and dwelling houses. The vessels which raided Scotland crossed the coast at 9.00 p.m. and cruised over the south-eastern counties of Scotland until about 1.10 a.m. One vessel visited the north east coast and dropped 22 explosive and 15 incendiary bombs. The two remaining ships crossed the English Coast at about 10.15 p.m. and cruised over the eastern counties until about 1.00 a.m. They were engaged at various times by anti-aircraft artillery, and appeared to have been prevented by this means from selecting any definite locality as their objective. The total casualties caused by Zeppelins since the outbreak of the war now amount to 154 killed, 346 injured.

Fermanagh Herald April 8th 1916. BUDGET PROPOSALS. The new taxes are on matches, amusements, railway tickets, and mineral waters. There are increases on cocoa, sugar, coffee and motors. The total yield of the new taxes is £115,950,000.

FERMANAGH Herald April 8th 1916. FERMANAGH OFFICERS WILL. On Monday in the probate court Dublin an application was made on behalf of Mrs. Margaret Matilda Moore, for a grant of administration with the will annexed of the goods of Major Nicholas James Mervyn Archdall, 3rd Cameron Highlanders as a person supposed to have died. Enquiries made of officers and men of his regiment show that he was wounded at the battle of Loos on that date, and was believed by them to be dead. Among the many letters received by the members of the family was one from Colonel D. W. Cameron of Lochiel, commanding the battalion, to Colonel H. St. George Stewart, an uncle, in which it was stated: - On Saturday the 25th we made an attack and your nephew was commanding the leading company. Needless to say they did splendidly. The last thing that was heard of your nephew was that he had been hit in the legs and that while he was trying to raise himself on his knees to give orders he was shot on the head. Although I return him as missing, I am afraid there is little doubt he is dead. He was a splendid company leader, and I do not know how I shall be able to replace him. If it is any consolation, I have put his name down for a mention in dispatches. I should add his company were absolutely devoted to him, but, alas, only 17 of them, and not an officer came out of the action untouched. The medical officer of the 5th Camerons, referred to the fighting in which Major Archdall took part, reported – I may say that the bombing and shelling were so severe that I fancy a great many officers and men noted as missing were simply blown to pieces, and, of course, the remains are not identified.

Uniform of 5th Camerons.

Before leaving for France, Major Archdale had made his will. It was witnessed by two brother officers and was very concise. This is my only will. I leave everything I am now possessed of in equal shares between my sisters, Maude Olpert, Margaret Matilda Moore, and my brother, Henry Lucas St. George Archdall of Mildina, Victoria, Australia. Mr. Justice Madden said he had no hesitation in granting the application.

April 13th 1916. OBITUARY OF MISS DOLLY ZINGG IMPERIAL HOTEL ENNISKILLEN. All that was mortal of a young life greatly prized and held in remarkable affection by a large number of the outside public was laid to rest in the Cemetery on Sunday afternoon. If there be solace in genuine and abiding sympathy then will Mr. and Mrs. Zingg have much to help them towards resignation at the death of their only daughter? From near and far they have received tributes expressive of sincerest regret at their bereavement, of surprise and sorrow and loss of one who gave rich promise of a long and useful career. She had not yet attained her 18th year. Tall of her age, well-formed and distinctly prepossessing anyone might well have taken a lease of her life. Bright, vivacious and lovable best describe the qualities of her nature. F.T.

April 13th 1916. MOTORING IN FERMANAGH AND THE EFFECT OF NEW TAXES. In Fermanagh as in most other parts of the Kingdom the new and very heavy tax on motors of all kinds has created something approaching consternation amongst the users of such vehicles. The number of people using cars and motor bicycles in this County has increased almost 4 fold during the past six years as is exemplified by the amount paid in motor license duty which was as follows £117 11 6 in 1910 and £424 11 6 in 1915. There are at least 26 cars over 16 horsepower of which license is paid in Enniskillen and on which the duty under the new Budget will be trebled while all other vehicles that duty will be doubled so that theoretically the amount which Fermanagh motorists would have to contribute this year in the shape of taxes would be raised to at least the very substantial sum of from £1,200 to £1409. But will the hopes of the Chancellor of the Exchequer be realised? Here as in other parts of Ireland there are a number of Ford and other cheap but highly powered cars in use and the owners of these will be especially hard hit by the new imposition. Already the excessive price of petrol and all other motor accessories has causing numbers of them to seriously consider the advisability of dispensing with their cars and now that the tax has in so many cases been raised from six guineas to 18 guineas per annum they have definitely decided either to dispose of them or to cease using them until the tax and the cost of running have been reduced. The effect may be the exact opposite to the Government proposals and less money will be received from licenses than formerly. F.T.

April 13th 1916. POLITICAL POINTS. It is said that Mr. Seumas McManus the ex-Irish rebel schoolteacher who gloried in teaching his children to hate the British Government is now in Berlin; and that Sir Rodger Casement has taken steps to become a naturalised German citizen. The latter may become a naturalised German citizen, but that will not save him from the fate he so richly deserves when victory crowns our banners. The traitor must pay the full penalty of his crimes.
President Wilson and his Cabinet have entered upon another expostulatory correspondence with Germany, to the ridicule of the civilised world. While the President uses a pen the Kaiser uses a torpedo and smiles at Mr. Wilson.

Mr. Birrell is one of the 'Wait-and-see' men and therefore we can understand his delay in dealing with the Irish Volunteers. He says he is giving his closest attention to the rebels. Does he shut his eyes and close his ears?

Mr. Asquith.

The need of a strong man to lead the country is being felt more and more. Mr. Asquith is absolutely unreliable and is hopelessly discredited. The country has had to force him from point to point and when he mustered the courage to adopt a Military Service Bill he spoiled it with the provision in it for the conscientious objector. The Newspaper Press had to force the case of unmarried men first, of an adequate Air Service, of air raids on the Zeppelin sheds of the enemy, and the country is weary of forcing a policy on a man who should be strong enough to lead. I.R.

April 13th 1916. THE SINN FEINERS. FR. NEVINS VIEWS ON SOME CLERICAL BRETHREN. Two further meetings to protest against the deportation of Sinn Fein Volunteer organisers, and to obtain recruits, were held on Thursday in Dublin. Councilor Cosgrove declared that the young men of Ireland should train and arm themselves in their own defence. Rev. Father Eugene Nevin, C. P., Mount Argus, who recently was rector of the Passionist Order at the Graan, Enniskillen, said there were many sham movement in Ireland, directing the people the wrong way, leading them to illusory and spurious ends but the only movement in Ireland that directed them in the right way that was sincere and honest and uncorrupted was the Irish Volunteer movement. They had no personal ends to gain; they were actuated by the purest motives, the undying principles of Irish nationality. Proceeding he said he deplored the action of a small section of his brethren in standing upon recruiting platforms and asking young Irishman to lay down their lives for – what? - the rottenest and most unscrupulous empire that never existed. That would never be said of him, and England would never get a recruit through him. His forefather had died for his national principles, and he also, if need be, would die for them. I.R.

April 13th 1916. EXCERPTS FROM 'A DAY IN THE TRENCHES WITH THE 11TH INNISKILLINGS' BY SECOND LIEUTENANT CYRIL FALLS. It is very dark and very quiet. The officer of the watch moves slowly along the trench. Coming round the traverse he encounters a dim figure, monstrous in a grey goatskin coat. 'N.C.O. on trench duty sir. All correct.' 'Any word of the patrol yet, corporal?' 'No sir not yet.' 'Well its 3.45 and they were due back at three. Hope there's nothing wrong.' 'I expect it's all right. There hasn't been any sound.' The officer passes down the line, stopping now and then to speak to a sentry. Then he enters a long narrow listening post, running out through the British wire towards the German lines. One of the two sentries posted at the end meet him halfway down. 'The Bosche train is in again at the station sir. We can hear it quite plain. The brakes of her was cringing a minute since. And there is transport up around her.' 'Right you are! Get back to the post and listen.'

The officer turns and makes his way down the communications trench to the signal office. He scribbles a message on the form handed to him by the telephonist and hurries back to the fire trench. There he waits 5 minutes, 10 minutes, a quarter of an hour, kicking his toes against the fire platform to warm them and bestowing a few extra curses on that oft cursed instrument, the field telephone. At last – oh joy high above his head sounds the wuz-uz-uz-uz of a howitzer shell sailing over and a few seconds later the roar of its explosion a mile in front. 'Right into the - - - station, I do believe.' Says the officer to himself, rubbing his hands. Hope I got a few of the - - - s! It may here be mentioned that there are two words of very frequent occurrence in the trenches, a noun and an adjective. To describe our friend the enemy they are generally used together. If the reader will imagine one or the other, or more frequently both, in every sentence spoken, it will be unnecessary to indicate their presence hereafter.

Now the field guns take up the tale and for the next 5 minutes the station and the whole village is peppered from end to end with shrapnel. The train is heard backing out in a hurry, the clatter of horses at the gallop tells of the transport dispersed, and dimly across the valley, come the shouts of the drivers and their officers. One can imagine blood curdling Bosche curses hurled across at the Irish mercenaries. Our friends have, it would seem, 'got it in the neck.' Their gunners, waking up and apparently taking a serious view of the case proceeded to put about 40 shells of various caliber into the two villages directly behind our lines. As things quiet down, the officers of the watch meets a sergeant passing down the trench and informing each sentry that the patrol is in. He looks at his watch. Its 10 minutes to five.

'And you may pass down right and left, Sergeant, stand two from me.' 'Very good sir!' Then he betakes himself to the dugout where the other three officers of his company are sleeping on their wire beds and pokes his head in. From its recess greets him a delicate scent blended of coke-fumes, goatskin coats, rubber boots slightly heated, tobacco smoke, and moderately well-washed humanity. One man is snoring lustily, another sitting up and extricating his feet from the sandbags he has been wearing in order to keep his boots from dirtying the blankets. 'Stand to, you blighters!' he remarks amiably, then passes on to the mess dugout and breaks opened the box containing the morning's rum. With one jar under his arm and a cup in his hand he returns to the fire-trench. The dawn is reddening the sky as the men pass to their places in the fire bays from their dugouts. They look lovingly on the stone jar as it passes slowly up to them. 'I am a Catch –me–Pal (Ed. Non-drinker) at home, right enough observes one, but out here begob ------------ the rest is a gurgle followed by a cough.

The serving out of rum helps to pass, for officers and men, the chilly and unpleasant hour of morning 'Stand to.' As soon as 'Stand down' has been passed along the line by the Company Commander, the Officer of the Watch, his Watch now over returns to Company headquarters, pours himself a coffee cup full of milk and whiskey – in this sector there are some cows included in 'trench stores' so we luxuriate in fresh milk – and so with the aid of a cigarette and *La Vie Parisian* of the week before last, he endures till he hears the welcome sizzling of bacon from the kitchen opposite. As we sit down to breakfast, the ration men 'the mate-carriers' go past with that of the men, the field kettles full of tea and pans of bacon carried in wooden frames, each on the shoulders of two men.

Between 'Stand down' - say 6.00 at this time of year – and 10.00 is the quietest time in the trenches. It is occupied with breakfast, the cleaning of rifles and bombs and sleep. Unless when the trenches were flooded, when the pumps must be kept going, no other work is done. We always believe that the enemy also takes it easy at this time. Just about 'Stand to' he becomes very energetic and obnoxious; the fire from his rifles fixed on various portions of our line increases five-fold, and his machine guns traverse our parapet. Then smoke begins to ascend from his trenches, and for the next few hours he leaves us more or less alone.

At 10.00 our day's work begins. A throng of men assembles round the Company Sergeant Major's dugout, where he gives out tools and materials and details the various working parties. The 11th pride themselves on their work in the trenches, and boast that they have never yet been in a sector without making a change in that during their stay that the merest tyro could appreciate. Shortly before this the Battalion Bombing Officer, known to the irreverent as 'Bim-Bom' has arrived for breakfast. The great man dwells at Headquarters in a palatial dugout, but deigns to visit his company at mealtimes, or rather to take his meals there at his own times. Beaming after a wash and shave following a good night's sleep, he makes us all feel very haggard and tired and dirty. His mouth full of bacon, he lectures us on not keeping our bombs as they are to be kept and we promise humbly to amend our ways.

The 11th have another boast aside that of working well in the trenches – that they never lose an opportunity to annoy the enemy. Experience has already taught them that if you lie down to the Boche he walks on your stomach. Half a dozen of snipers from each of the companies in the firing line station themselves in well concealed positions. They have telescopic sights on their rifles, and are a terror to any German who dares shows any portion of themselves even if he be 1,000 yards away. Bim-Bom and three or four of his desperadoes go off to fire volleys of rifle grenades into a German sap-head. Another officer takes a powerful telescope to an observation post and rakes the trenches in front of us and the ground behind them, noting where work is in progress, the position of dugouts, paths and trenches to the rear and evidently much used by night; all of which information will eventually reach the artillery and the machine gun company, who will, we hope, take action accordingly.

So the morning and early afternoon pass pleasantly enough. It is fine weather, the trenches are dry, and we look back, as on an ugly dream on the days when rain stopped only to give place to snow, and the pumps ceased never, day nor night, and we were stuck in the mud and had to be pulled out minus our thigh boots. Our artillery is wire cutting and we have observers at the frontline noting where the bosche wire is destroyed so that by night we may harass him with the fire of Lewis guns and rifles as he attempts to repair the damage. Occasionally our aeroplanes cross the German lines, or, more rarely, one of his comes over our own, and then the sky is flecked with the white puffs of shrapnel from the anti-aircraft guns which the airman seem to treat with complete and well merited contempt.

After tea and before 'stand to' the Boche is particularly quiet. Two officers are in Company Headquarters writing home, the rest are up in the line. Presently they strolled into the trench. Though the sun is low it is still warm. 'It'll be 'stand to' in half an hour' he says, 'Let's go and see if we can strafe a few rats in the old trench before….' – The other catches him by the arm. 'Look! Look! Right into the village! Against the sky almost over their heads a little shell shaped projectile is sailing by in a leisurely fashion. It drops beside the house they can see through the trees. A second later stones, bricks, clods of earth are flying through the air and there follows a thunderous grinding explosion. Our old friend, the Boche trench-howitzer perhaps the most deadly weapon in all his armoury, with a range of over 1200 yards, has opening on us. After an interval of 1½ minutes, a second shell follows the first. This appears to land in open ground and the onlookers are relieved. They know that by now every man in the village has had time to take cover. They discuss the direction from which the gun is firing. 'The same old spot, I'll take my oath!' says one. 'That's coming from the very place she was pooping from last time. Just about 50 yards back from – My God! She's shortening! Run for it. The caves!'

It may be explained that the mess dugout faces a high bank out of which is hollowed a cave with several entrances, the abode of a reserve battalion and the Company signal office. Into this haven the two officers dash – just in time. There is a tremendous roar as the bomb explodes on the bank above their heads. Some of the shoring supporting cracks and strains ominously and a shower of chalk falls about the heads of those inside. One of the officers runs out into the trench to watch for the next bomb. The gun evidently takes some time to fire, for there is a regular interval of at least 100 seconds between the shots. He comes back with word that the next is landing almost in the same place. It actually falls into the trench about 20 yards below them and again comes that ear splitting roar and a fresh shower of earth and chalk from the roof of the cave. 'Damn it, I'll try and get the artillery on to the blighters!' says the officer and picks up a block of message forms. The message, giving the point from which the gun is believed to be firing, necessarily takes some time to write, partly because the shock of each bomb exploding puts out all the candles in the cave, and several more have burst, some close at hand, some further down the trench, before it is handed to the telephonist. Then the officer goes back to the mouth of the cave. After three more explosions, he heard the voice of one of the signallers behind him. 'We can't get the artillery sir or Headquarters. The wire is broke.' The officer says that which he considers to be warranted by the occasion. 'And Headquarters won't know what the deuce is happening to us,' he goes on. 'Look here, someone must scoot out as soon as the next bursts and run like blazes for it. I tell them we are all right but that we're getting it pretty warm and that the gun is firing from the old spot.' A volunteer at once steps forward and rushes out while the earth thrown by the next bomb is still pattering down into the trench. In a moment he is back. 'Please, sir, there is no trench at all left below us there. Sure the whole of it is levelled out and filled with lumps that'll take ye half an hour to climb over, I'll try if you like -.' Bang! The next bomb burst just about where the messenger would have been had he carried on his errant. The officer feels that even swearing is no good now. He turns to the telephonist. 'Certain you can't get any of the companies?' He demands. 'All the wires gone?' 'Then, by Jove, someone must try the other way up the trench!' The boy at the telephone slips the receiver-band from his head and hands it to a comrade. 'They are all cut, sir right enough. I will run away up the other way down Dolly's Bray and across the open. I'll not be two minutes.' He waits for the next to burst, and runs up the trench. But he need not have hurried, for this, the 25th shot, is the last, and those in the cave are left to sally forth after a few minutes and survey the damage. The trench for 100 yards down is a trench no more, and all about are holes 10 feet deep and 12 across. Three men, who have run down from the firing line are surveying the mess dugout, the door of which is filled in, horror stricken, and one is calling to his God that the officers are buried in there so they are.

So ends the 'strafe,' for our artillery decides not to retaliate just at present, though a promise is sent from the heavies that in due time they would plough up the whole sector from which the howitzer has been firing. We proceed to count the damage. The casualties are: one man suffering from shock – he was knocked down, stunned, and half buried – one man with a piece of lead the size of a pea in his calf, who returns to duty next day, and one particularly fine buck rat. The officers' dugout takes some time to reopen and repair. Our dinner is an hour late, and the beef is full of grit. That is all. The telephone is working as well as it ever works – which is not saying much – within half an hour. One hundred men from the support company, working nearly all night, dig out the trench, and by morning light there is no sign of the Boche handiwork. A box of detonators, the property of Bim-Bom has disappeared from the shelf in our dugout, and we are left in pleasing uncertainty as to where they now abide. But the Boche trench-howitzer officer probably thinks he has exterminated us and we feel sure he has been awarded the Iron Cross. March 1916 Cyril Falls. I.R.
(Ed. Boche and Bosche are used interchangeably as a derogatory term for German soldiers. It roughly translates as 'Blockhead.')

April 13th 1916. HORSE DEALER'S CASE. In the King's Bench Division, Dublin the cases of Bunting v Levinson & Co., was before Mr. Justice Gibson re an action for final judgment for £422 the price of eight horses alleged to have been sold by the plaintiff, James Bunting, horse dealer of Ballyhenry, County Antrim to the defendants David Levinson and Co., horse dealers, Clones. The horses, plaintiff alleged, were delivered at defendants stables in Liverpool and subsequently sold by them at a sale at Perth. It was alleged in defence that the horses were bought by a former partner of the defendants who had no authority to purchase horses on behalf of the company, which had been dissolved. Mr. Justice Gibson made no rule on the motion. I.R.

April 13th 1916. CLONES MAN'S DEATH. Private Reuben Farrell, son of Mr. C. Farrell, photographer, Clones has been killed in action in France. He had been mentioned in dispatches for bravery in rescuing a wounded officer under fire. Mr. Farrell, senior, has had another son accidentally drowned while on duty in France, and a third wounded and subsequently discharged as unfit for further service. I.R.

Fermanagh Herald April 15th 1916. INTERESTING ITEMS FROM ALL QUARTERS. BELFAST DRINK BILL £1,000 PER HOUR. In Belfast 138 persons per hour went into each of the 600 public houses there, said Mr. Mercier Clements. That meant an attendance of 82,000 an hour. Assuming each person paid 3p on each visit that meant an expenditure of over £1,000 pounds an hour.

RELICS OF BUNTING. *The Irish News* understands that through the will of the late Mrs. Milligan Fox the Belfast University Library acquires the original MSS., and other relics of Edward Bunting, the famous Irish musician.

Shorthand for railway Porters. All the stationmasters and clerical staff on the D. and S. E. Railway have received notice, it is stated, to study shorthand and present themselves for examination in six months. The order has caused much uneasiness to the older officials, and to the station masters at small stations, almost all of whom received promotion from the rank of porter.

THE SUDDEN DEATH IN ENNISKILLEN. On going to call a lodger named Michael Feely, who belonged to the Garrison District, on Tuesday morning, Mrs. Leonard, Head Street, Enniskillen, found him dead in bed. It appears that the deceased who was an old-age pensioner was in the habit of rising at 12 or one o'clock each day. Mrs. Leonard kicked his door three times on Tuesday morning and on receiving no answer she decided to break the door open, and on entry found that the old man had expired during the night.

April 20th 1916. NOTES. The New Tax should have a good income from football matches, seeing that in Great Britain the number who witnessed them in one year has been as many as 40,000,000. At the Crystal Palace 120,000 people have been present at one cup tie match; and the charges for admission to those matches varying from 6d to 2s 6d.

Breakfast and dining cars are to be discontinued on the London and North Western railway system from the 1st of May next, but cold lunch tickets will be served to travellers.

A shell factory is to be established in the South of Ireland and perhaps other munitions factories also.

Fat cattle continue to fetch high prices. Mr. D. McCaffrey, Fivemiletown, paid £42 10 shillings to Mr. Robert Woods, Cullentra, on Friday for a bull.

The losses to the Germans during the 12th attack on Douaumont amounted to 30,000 men, it has been computed. And no gain for these heavy losses

The average increase in the cost of food in this country has been 49 per cent, while in Berlin food costs 85 per cent over the 1914 basis.

During the war and for six months after the Lord Lieutenant has ordered that the limits of age for candidates for Petty Sessions Clerkships shall be 41 to 50, except in the case of a present clerk, when it is 41 to 55, or in the case of a person discharged from the forces through injury or disease when the ages are to be from 21 to 50. I.R.

The seaplane raid carried out by British officers on villages near Constantinople containing munition depots etc. was the longest yet attempted of 300 miles.

For the week ending Thursday last 31 ships, of which 19 were British, were sunk by submarines, their total tonnage being at 85,045, of which Britain owned about 66,000 tons.

THE THIRD STAGE: A BRITISH SEAPLANE BEING LOWERED TO THE WATER FROM THE DECK OF THE PARENT SHIP.

April 20th 1916. SENSATIONAL REPORTS OF A CABINET CRISIS AND SINN FEIN TROUBLE.
Reports are current not only of the impending resignation of Mr. Lloyd George, but of important resignations also at the War Office unless the Cabinet decides in favour of compulsory service for all unattested married men. Mr. Lloyd George is concerned quite as much about the supply of labour for the making of munitions as he is about the supply of men for the army. The situation has been further complicated by the receipt of rather disturbing news from Ireland regarding the activities of the Sinn Feiners. In all the circumstances it is still a little doubtful whether Sir Edward Carson will proceed on Wednesday with his resolution in favour of compulsory service. I.R.

April 20th 1916. THE DUBLIN RATES AND THE CORPORATION'S EXTRAORDINARY ACTION.
An extraordinary situation has been created by the action of the Sinn Fein members of the Dublin Corporation who at the meeting held on Friday for the purpose of striking the municipal rates for the ensuing year, voted against the adoption of the poor rate which includes the police rate (£33,000.) Their attitude was inspired, so their spokesman declared, by the recent speech of Mr. Justice Kenny at the Dublin Commission with reference to the seditious campaign. Judge Kenny was referred to as 'this man' and his speech was described 'as most disgraceful. I.R.

April 20th 1916. KILLED BY THEIR OWN GUNS. GERMAN VICTIMS OF RUTHLESSNESS. It is sometimes asked, in view of their appalling losses, how the German infantry can be induced to charge again and again to certain death. A French staff officer gives the following explanation: - It would be a mistake to underrate the courage of the German infantry. They are not lacking in bravery; their officers are responsible for these butcheries. They still hold the old theory that men are only so much food for cannon, and success cannot be won without paying the price. Besides, many of the men are fatalists. If they were not it would make little difference for they have no choice. Behind them are their machine guns and they know that at the slightest sign of wavering their own gunners would not spare them. He therefore prefers to take the chance of being killed by the French. It frequently happens that the soldiers of the opposing armies get mixed up in a melee. At such moments of confused fighting the French artillery men cease firing. They must not kill their own men. Not so the German gunners. On the principle of making sure they fire into the mass, killing friends and foe alike. I.R.

April 20th 1916. THE DEATH OF LORD CLANRICKARDE – THE BEST HATED MAN OF HIS TIME IN IRELAND. The death has occurred at his London residence, 13 Hanover Square, in his 84th year, after a long illness, of the Marquis of Clanrickarde, who at one time was probably the most hated man in Ireland, and the most friendless even among his own class. A Non-resident landlord, he achieved the unenviable distinction of being the most ruthless of evictors, detested alike by his tenantry and the land owning classes, for the latter were exasperated that their general character should be besmirched by the acts of a man who was not the type but something apart by himself. His long and bitter fights with his tenantry form a black chapter in the Irish Land agitation, which was happily closed when, after lengthy litigation, his Galway estates were required by the Consolidated Districts Board for £238,000.

It was on the Clanrickarde estate that the Plan of Campaign was first suggested. Possibly the only time the Marquis was seen in Ireland was at the funeral of his father, and when his mother died he did not come over. Indeed not one of his tenants seem to have ever seen him, though such was his power that at one time it was said he could elect his grey mare to Parliament if he liked. His intervention in debate to denounce the Evicted Tenants Bill caused a sensation in the Gilded Chamber. His passionate, but thin and cracked voice railed against the offending measure. His pale face was convulsed with bitter feeling as the torrents of his wrath descended on the Bill and its authors. Two or three times producing from his waistcoat pocket a small vial containing a brown liquid he imbibed the stimulant and inveighed greater than ever against the Bill. His utterance, so dramatic, chilled rather than thrilled his hearers. No peer present give him the slightest suggestion of applause.

Nearly nine years ago a bill for the expulsion of Lord Clanrickarde, under the 10 minutes rule was made by Mr. Duffy. The measure passed its first reading by a very large majority, in which were three nephews of the Marquis, one said to be his favourite relative, but it never went any further.

A long, thin, pallid figure, shabbily dressed, with high cheekbones, a highly intellectual forehead and some 5 feet 7 inches in height describes him physically. The late Mr. Labouchere, who was with him at the British Embassy in Paris, described him as parsimonious and miserly unlike his spendthrift father and brother. When he came in to his estates they had a rent roll of £20,000 a year from poor land, and while his agents had to carry their lives in their hands, he remained in London immovable and impenetrable, while he drove his tenants to such exasperation as to make the estates the hotbed of the land revolution. Though he never recognized defeat even when Acts of Parliament were passed to deal with this case, Lord Clanrickarde had some good points as the landlord. In some ways Lord Clanrickarde really was not a bad landlord; indeed he was indulgent to appeals and allowed arrears to run up in many instances. He mentioned that when the Government valuers wanted part of the Clanrickarde estate some of the tenants who had not been evicted objected to the functions of these officials, contending that as they had not paid any rent for 12 or 14 years they were entitled by prescriptive right to occupy the land rent free. The agrarian records do not bear out the view that Lord Clanrickarde was a considerate landlord, but it was in the political aspect of the land war that he appeared to the worst advantage and cut an unenviable figure.

There was however another side to the Lord Clanrickarde character. Mean and eccentric in appearance and reported to be a miser, he was an ardent connoisseur and collector of art - rare pictures and china being the main objects of his activities in this direction. Lord Clanrickarde filled yet another role that of the moneylender. Furthermore until he was well past 80 he was an enthusiastic skater, and had the reputation of being an adept at skating on one leg. I.R.

April 20th 1916. COOLER AND LESS PERTURBED MEN NEVER MARCHED TO WHAT WAS CERTAIN DEATH FOR SO MANY. When the order came the men had just finished a spell in the trenches. They were cleaning their boots preparatory to a turn in billets. To have a well-earned rest taken from them so suddenly must have been annoying, but they showed no sign. In the 10 minutes left before the onward march began they went on with the boot cleaning as though they were getting ready for a day's holiday. In a quarter of an hour they were swinging along the road chanting one of the pretty songs of their country. In another half hour they were under fire from the German great guns that were dropping huge shells by the score, converting the smoothest of roads into a series of pits deep enough to bury half a dozen men at a time. Halfway down the road we came in sight of the detachment the Irish were to reinforce. They are awaiting a German attack, which is rapidly developing under cover of a heavy artillery fire design to harass the defenders of the position, and at the same time prevent reinforcements reaching them. Shells continue to drop amid the Irish and their losses are not slight. Still they press on with the cheerfulness of their race. Now the enemy attack on their comrades is being pressed home in real earnest. Clouds of enemy infantry settle down in front of the position and soon swarm over the parapet. It is only then that the wonderful Irish betray excitement. There is no holding them back, and their officers don't try to. A great cry, obviously a battle cry breaks from the lips that were chanting a baby's lullaby only a few minutes before and the tide of Irishmen sweeps onward irresistibly to overwhelm the Teuton foe. I am told that their cry was, Faugh-a-Ballagh. Nothing could be more sublime than that onward sweep against the increasing rain of German shells. The intrepid Irish seemed to cover the intervening yards at a single bound and range themselves by the side of their sorely pressed English comrades. The Germans were in overwhelming strength, but that didn't seem to trouble the Irishmen. Into the German hordes the Grenadiers flung scorers of hand grenades at 30 yards distance. Violent explosions followed and the effect on the closely packed enemy ranks was deadly. Before the enemy could recover the Irish were upon them with the spring suggestive of tigers defending their cubs against hostile attacks. In spite of their numbers, the Germans were helpless against that glorious dash. They were swept off their feet and scattered in great confusion. I.R.

Fermanagh Herald April 22nd 1916. PETTIGO HALF-HOLIDAY. We the merchants of Pettigo have agreed to close our business premises every Wednesday from the 1st of May at the hour of 1.00.

Fermanagh Herald April 22nd 1916. A GERMAN SHIP SUNK OF THE IRISH COAST. In an attempt to land arms in Ireland, Sir Roger Casement is arrested. The Secretary of the Admiralty announces: during the period between PM April 20 and PM April 21 an attempt to land arms and ammunition in Ireland was made by a vessel under the guise of a neutral merchant ship, but in reality a German auxiliary, in conjunction with a German submarine. The auxiliary sank, and a number of prisoners were made amongst whom was Sir Roger Casement. Sir Roger Casement was brought to London on Sunday morning. He was met at Euston by officers from Scotland Yard, and is now detained in military custody. It is understood that evidence as to his proceedings in Germany since the outbreak of war will be produced at his trial.

April 27th 1916. OPEN REBELLION! PROCLAMATION OF AN IRISH REPUBLIC. A RISING IN DUBLIN! THE CITY TAKEN POSSESSION OF BY SINN FEIN VOLUNTEERS. DUBLIN CASTLE TAKEN AND RECAPTURED. THE POST OFFICE SEIZED. SOLDIERS AND PEOPLE SHOT DOWN. THE CITY IN TERROR.
Liberty Hall in Dublin has been taken by the Navy and Army. The following Official statement of the position is issued by the Lord Lieutenant: - During the night of the 25th of April a Royal Naval reserve gunboat shelled and troops subsequently occupied Liberty Hall, the Headquarters of the Sinn Fein forces. Meanwhile large reinforcements have arrived in Dublin, including detachments of 10,000 troops from England, with Artillery, Engineering and Medical Corps. In other portions of the city the situation is well in hand, repairs to railway lines now are being rapidly affected. A Royal Proclamation was published yesterday (Wednesday) which substitutes trial by court martial for offences hitherto triable by Civil Court. I.R.

Ed:- Arthur Griffith 1871-1922 (See above) was an Irish journalist who founded the Sinn Fein movement in 1905 to emphasise the idea of national self-reliance. Because of his work as a writer and journalist the ideas of Sinn Fein had become well-known in Ireland. Politicians and newspapers knowing little or nothing about the IRB (Irish Republican Brotherhood) which was a secret organisation, incorrectly referred to the insurrection as "The Sinn Fein Rising" while in fact it was an IRB Rising.)

April 27th 1916. IT SEEMS LIKE A DREAM, YET IT IS ALL TRUE! THERE HAS BEEN AN INSURRECTION IN DUBLIN AND THE PROCLAMATION OF AN IRISH REPUBLIC BY SINN FEIN.
Rumours abound about an insurrection in the capital and the chief places being taken possession of by Sinn Fein Volunteers. The whole thing reads like the impossible. Owing to the cutting of the wires and breakdown of telegraphic communications, and the seizure of the General Post Office, Dublin, we have to depend for news upon travellers who have passed through the danger zone. The rebellion took place on Easter Monday morning, being a bank holiday and the day of Fairyhouse Races. It was a day when the military would be supposed to be on leave; and it was selected for the occasion by the Sinn Feiners, who had all arrangements made for an insurrection, move their battalions under arms, and prepared to seize the city.

1. The Post Office was taken possession of. 2. The outer portion of the Bank of Ireland was seized. 3. One of the minor barracks was taken by an armed party. 4. The bridges across the Liffey were seized and guards placed upon them and barricades raised along the quays. 5. Dublin Castle was for a time seized till it was recaptured. Tuesday morning saw a portion of the city in the hands of the rebels to the extent that they overawed the population. They disarmed police, they shot down soldiers returning on furlough, and numbers of innocent people were wounded. Points of vantage like the *Daily Express* office at Cork Hill, and the corner of Sackville Street and Lower Abbey Street were seized, the slates were ripped off the roofs and their machine guns placed in position to sweep the streets. One of the first places seized was the General Post Office, on which machine guns were placed; and machine guns were also placed on Messrs. Cleary's establishment opposite.

One informant saw a party of cavalry ride up Sackville Street, and the commanding officer, some men and several horses were shot down by men in upper windows. Telegraph and telephone communications were broken, wires cut, and railway bridges destroyed so as to delay help coming to the forces of the Government. Owing to the bridges being destroyed the trains could not bring troops from the Curragh and regiment after regiment had to march to Dublin. All motor cars were seized. Mr. Jack Lemmon and Mr. Harvey (Enniskillen)

were on their holidays and their car was seized. It was expected that all available cars around Enniskillen would have been seized for Government purposes also. The rush, the expedition of the whole plan, and the wonderful success which attended it at the outbreak, astounded the public who could scarcely believe it to be true.

There is no prospect at present of the military at Enniskillen being needed at Dublin. Mr. Birrell, who is largely responsible for the trouble, was in England, away from the country which he, by his policy, precipitated into such a state of rebellion. At Enniskillen a military guard was placed over the Sligo railway bridge at Killyhevlin and at the town bridges. In Dublin shops were looted in all directions and valuables taken, so that it was said gold rings could be bought cheaply in the streets; and big coats were cast out of the windows for a few shillings. Horses which were shot in the streets were permitted to lie there for barricades. Rolls of paper were seized in the *Irish Times* office to form barricades. Bicycle shops were raided by the rebels, and the bicycles were taken out by them to form entanglements. There has been some uneasiness in Blacklion, owing to the proximity to Glenfarne having a lot of Sinn Feiners but we do not think there is any cause for anxiety. There may be sympathisers but leaders and action and organisation are other things. I.R.

April 27th 1916. THE ROYAL INNISKILLING BAND CONCERT EVENING IN ENNISKILLEN TOWNHALL HAS BEEN CANCELLED OWING TO THE RISING IN DUBLIN AND THE STATE OF PUBLIC FEELING. Owing to the extraordinary state of things in Dublin and the country it is well to know that the chief authority in Enniskillen and district is vested in Colonel Sir John Leslie, Bart., under the Defence of the Realm Act; and if anything should arise to cause him to take over all public control, all the ordinary civil proceedings will be subordinate to military authority. Colonel Leslie has sent out cavalry patrols, placed guards on the bridges of Enniskillen and taken precautions. The soldiers are provided with ball cartridge and have strict orders to stop motor traffic. The police have taken charge of the petrol supply locally. I.R.

April 27th 1916. MOTOR CARS STOPPED. ARMS BROUGHT TO CAVAN AND TO SOUTH FERMANAGH AND THE BAWNBOY DISTRICT. About two weeks ago two motor cars conveyed a quantity of rifles and ammunition to County Cavan and South Fermanagh. They eluded the police and got distributing their arms. We have remarked for several Saturday nights that about 11.30 to 12 o'clock motor cars passing up Enniskillen Street, returning on Sunday night about the same time. Strange motor cars, conveying coffins, openly passed through our streets under the noses of the police; and the number of the coffins and drivers did not arouse any suspicion. These cars plied through the town by day and night till Colonel Sir John Leslie, Bart., took the matter in hand, when the civil power had failed; and now he has stopped all motor cars by guards on the two bridges. I.R.

April 27th 1916. LISNASKEA. DEFENDANT AND HIS PIG WERE BOTH ARRESTED AND LOCKED UP. Patrick Crudden, Slushill was arrested for being drunk and disorderly on the 19th of April. Constable Killduff said that defendant's language was not of the very best. The defendant said he was walking down the street with a pig on his back and the pig kicked him and he was not pleased with it and he may have said something wrong. The chairman of the magistrates asked was the pig alive and he was told indeed it was 'and could kick like a good one.' 'Was the pig in the barrack too?' The defendant said yes it was arrested. He was fined five shillings 6d and costs and Constable Reagan prosecuted the same defendant for kicking him on the shins on the 19th while in the barrack lock up after arrest for the charge proved above 'and only he was drunk he did not think that the defendant would have kicked him.' A fine of five shillings and costs was imposed. I.R.

MAY 1916

May 4th 1916. THE REBELLION CRUSHED. The Dublin Sinn Fein Rebellion of Monday, April 24, collapsed on the succeeding Saturday evening; and the foul blot on Ireland, destitute of excuse, and a disgrace before civilisation without one redeeming feature, was brought to an ignominious close. O, the infamy of it! That Irishmen who prate so much of their country as if it were more than any other, who rave so much of their breed as if endowed with superior virtues, should descend so low as to accept German gold to assassinate their own fellow countrymen; and with the hire of foreign corruption and murder in their pockets should hide to slay unarmed victims and shelter themselves in places of strength to shoot down children and women and priests and all those who trusted to the elements of brotherhood and the laws of civilisation. They assassinated, they fought behind shelter, they murdered unsuspecting victims, and then when hopelessly beaten cried 'Hands up, we give in.' The Hands Uppers' of Ireland are the scum…

Fancy Mr. Pearse, a dreamer, who some 10 or 12 years ago advocated in Enniskillen the formation of the Gaelic League, making it evident that what he was really driving at was a separation movement and other literary and professional men thinking they could become generals against trained men, and lead some thousands of enthusiastic dupes to success against the British army. The Gaelic League is as dead as the Rebellion and now some other Irish fools will try to devise some other fad with which to play on the simple souls who were led to believe in the purity of Irish Nationality – even when it was bought with German gold. I.R.

May 4th 1916. DUBLIN VICTIMS BURIED. Private Knox of the 12th (Reserve Battalion) Inniskillings, who met his death last week in Dublin, was buried in the New Cemetery, Enniskillen with full military honours on Sunday. Knox, it appears, was firing a bomb when it accidentally exploded and killed him.

During last week's Dublin Rebellion 2nd Lieutenant Crockett of the 12th Inniskillings, was accidentally killed by a bomb. Mr. Crockett's brother is in the Cadet Corps in Enniskillen. He belonged to Londonderry, and his remains were removed to that place for internment. I.R.

May 4th 1916. DUBLIN NEWS. THE ATTACK ON TCD. PROMPT AND DEADLY REPRISALS. On Tuesday the rebels took an ammunition shed at Bachelors Walk from which they had Trinity College under close and direct fire. On Wednesday at the suggestion of the provost Dr. Mahaffey a field gun was brought to the roof of the College and the ammunition shop was blown to pieces. 11 men who ran out of this were all killed by a machine gun. During those terrible days a term examination was held with exact ceremony within the walls of the ancient and dauntless University.

The Irish Times is officially informed that the damage done to structures and records in the Four Courts is not such that any great delay will take place in reopening. When the military authorities have handed over the custody of the buildings the work of clearing will occupy two or three days and it is anticipated that Monday 9th May at the latest shall see business resumed.

Uniform of 5th Camerons.

It was manifestly impossible to hold the General Synod in Dublin this week with any prospect of the attendance of the clergy and laity from the provinces owing to the outbreak of the rebellion in Dublin and elsewhere throughout Ireland, the Lord Primate intimated that the Synod would be postponed to some future date of which the members will all receive due notice. F.T.

May 4th 1916. REBELLION. The tales that are told of the crimes perpetuated under the aegis of the strangely established 'Republic' form amazing reading. It is almost inconceivable that such things could occur. The record of wholesale bloodshed, the deliberate sniping at innocent individuals whose sole crime was being on the public thoroughfares, the rabid, insane destruction of property, the wild incomprehensible notions of overcoming and crushing all authority – these things make one almost despair of the future of the country. Every blessing and privilege a people could enjoy has been granted to Ireland in fullest measure – shall we say in excess? The only gratitude manifested is revolution by a large section of the populace - horrors and barbarities almost incredible. Not for a score of years will it be possible for Dublin to recover from the devastation and ruin to which it has fallen victim. One of the pleasantest and handsome cities in Europe has been battered and bruised until it has become a picture of sadness and desolation. F.T.

May 4th 1916. THE REBELLION. INCIDENTS AND COMMENTS. The riots in Dublin are the subject of almost universal ridicule, mingled with severe reproaches addressed to Mr. Asquith because of his 'wait and see' policy wires the *Daily Mail*, New York correspondent. Of course the Sinn Feiners and the Clan-na-Gael separatists who form probably not more than five per cent of the Irish population of America are jubilant and are flooding the newspapers with all sorts of exorbitant statement alleged to have been cabled here in code regarding the extent of the trouble. Already they have issued a flamboyant call for a mass meeting to be held on behalf of the widows and orphans of the Dublin 'martyrs' and protest against the execution of Sir Rodger Casement.

The state of chaos in the city is such that one has to be in it to realise it. Few firms were able to pay wages on Friday or Saturday because no money could be obtained from the banks. There is electric light, but it will be a long time before the tramway service can be resumed because the Sinn Feiners have demolished the power station as well as wrecking many of the tramway cars.

Until Thursday the rebels were full of resolution and were adopting many ingenious devices for getting in ammunition. That day at Rathmines two coffins were opened by the guards; one contained a body and the other ammunition. A closed hearse was full of ammunition.

The G.P.O. Dublin

The Sinn Fein sharpshooters were mainly young men between 18 and 23 who had made themselves proficient at a range in the Wicklow Mountains. Military officers say that they were remarkably accurate marksman.

Connolly and his men gained possession of a wireless station at Steven's Green and by this agency sent out the proclamation of an Irish Republic to the world.

In the neighbourhood of the Custom House says Mr. Neville of Belfast I saw at least eight woman lying dead. Hundreds of others were wounded but these were carried away for treatment in the City Hospitals. In Mercer's Hospital alone over 600 cases were treated.

The remains of Constable Magee who was shot in Louth at the same time as Lieutenant R. L. Dunville of the Grenadier Guards was wounded were interred at Falcarragh, Co., Donegal. It appears that Constable Magee was carrying dispatches to his superior officer when he was held up on the roadside by a number of armed insurrectionists who took possession of the dispatches and after perusing the contents they placed him against the hedge and shot him. The constable received no fewer than four bullet wounds in the region of the heart and lived only 20 minutes. F.T.

May 4th 1916. COMPLETE SURRENDER IN DUBLIN. MANY PRISONERS SENT TO ENGLAND. The following communiques were issued by the Field Marshal Commanding-in-Chief of the Home Forces on Monday. All the rebels in Dublin have surrendered and the city is reported to be quite safe. The rebels in the country districts are surrendering to mobile columns. There were 1,000 prisoners in Dublin yesterday of whom 489 were sent to England last night. F.T.

May 4th 1916. MILITARY NOTES. PETTIGO MAN KILLED. Private S. T. Read, Canadian Infantry who has died at the Canadian General Hospital, Boulogne from a gunshot wound was the youngest son of Mr. Robert Read, Post Office, Pettigo. He enlisted at Saskatoon, Canada in July last where he was employed as

Dublin city centre, Easter 1916

clerk in the Bank of Commerce. Before getting his appointment at the Canadian Bank he was a pupil at the Belfast Royal Academical Institution. His brother Fred is serving in the Princess Patricia's and his eldest brother Alexander is a captain in the Black Watch. His sister Jennie who has been a military nurse since the commencement of the war was with him at his death. F.T.

May 4th 1916. CONCERT IN THE BARRACKS. In Enniskillen Barracks, on the night of the 26th an enjoyable concert was held in the gymnasium for the entertainment of the men who have been confined to barracks since the outbreak of the Dublin revolt. Each item was encored. When Captain Thomas, adjutant, announced that martial law had been proclaimed there was an outburst of enthusiasm. It required about 70 men to furnish all guards at the Enniskillen bridges for a day and at the changing of the guards the usual formalities were observed of the outgoing saluting the incoming guard etc. These guards inspired public confidence. I.R.

May 4th 1916. COLLAPSE OF THE SINN FEIN REBELLION IN DUBLIN. THE SINN FEIN REVOLT IS CRUSHED AND THE LEADERS MAKE AN UNCONDITIONAL SURRENDER. THE PHANTOM IRISH REPUBLIC WHICH EXISTED ONLY IN THE IMAGINATION OF SOME THOUSANDS OF

SINN FEINERS IN DUBLIN, BORN ON APRIL 24TH AND PERISHED FIVE DAYS LATER AMID UNIVERSAL RIDICULE AND CONDEMNATION. The bank of Ireland was saved because opposite is Trinity College, where the O.T.C. are stationed and the young officers had a warm reception in readiness. The rebels came along in great style anticipating no trouble in shooting down the half dozen soldiers who were always on guard at the bank and as they advanced there was a crack of rifle fire and some of the attacking party rolled over shot. The College had been transformed into a veritable fortress and in place of the usual windows there were sandbags loopholed, behind which armed officers were waiting to give battle to those who threatened the bank. The insurgents were stupefied for a moment and hesitated as to what they should do. Some of the group gave an inspiring lead to their fellows and with acclamation the crowd pressed on with their enterprise. Again came a volley and more victims fell. The rebels, realizing that so far as this adventure was concerned they were checkmated, turned and fled and that is how the Bank of Ireland was saved. I.R.

May 4th 1916. The footpaths of Sackville Street were one wild welter of disorder and debris. Troops of tatterdemalion boys and girls were having the time of their lives. The more youthful of them were smeared with butterscotch and toffee and chocolate from head to foot and carried parcels of similar confectionery and sweets galore. Young fellows by the dozen were in possession of packets and boxes of cigarettes, while the air was fragrant with the odour of choice cigars designed for other lips. Boxes of cigars were offered to passers-by for a shilling, while many old ladies were festooned with necklaces and trinkets looted from jeweller shops. In the midst of all the tragedy a touch of comedy was not wanting. It was provided by the spectacle of scorers of robust and elderly women squatting on the footpath endeavouring to compress their too ample feet into fashionable boots and shoes. I.R.

May 4th 1916. THE COUNTESS MARKIEVICZ. A STRANGE PERSONALITY. The capture of the Countess Markievicz at Dublin is an episode in the career of one of the strangest personalities in the 'Ireland for the Irish' movement. In England she was only known by repute in trade union circles but in Dublin she has been for years identified with extreme Socialism. During the regime of Jim Larkin at Liberty Hall, Countess Markievicz and Miss Larkin were in charge of the food distribution, and she was very active during the transport workers' strike in Dublin. When the exchequer failed, as it often did, the Countess unfailingly came to the rescue. The soup kitchen at Liberty Hall reached the highest point of efficiency, and indeed became eventually the only means of subsistence of many of the strikers. The Countess, apparently approaching middle age, was of undeniably attractive appearance. In the days of the strike she affected Irish dress and was usually a lively figure in the processions of strikers. It may be added that the lady before her marriage was Miss Constance Georgine Gore-Booth, the daughter of Sir Henry William Gore-Booth, fifth baronet of Lissadell, County Sligo. She is the organiser and trainer of the Scouts, who have supplied a large portion of the rebel forces. She is described as wearing a man's green uniform and carrying a rifle and bayonet. Countess Markievicz, who is an Irish woman of good family, is married to a Polish nobleman who is at present fighting against the Germans. I.R.

May 4th 1916. THE COUNTESS IN GREEN. HOW SHE SURRENDERED. LAST KISS TO HER REVOLVER. How Countess Markievicz surrendered with a force of 120 Sinn Feiners who had been in possession of the Royal College of Surgeons from the outbreak of the rebellion has been related. Countess Markievicz was in command of the party which had seized the College and when she found the position was hopeless she evidently decided that it was not worth taking any more risks. It was the last place in St., Stephen's

Green held by the rebels. At eight o'clock on Saturday morning the white flag was hoisted and a communication was sent to the officer commanding of the attacking forces to say that the Garrison would surrender at 11.00. At the appointed hour Countess Markievicz marched out of the College followed by her force walking two abreast. She was dressed entirely in green – green tunic, a green hat with a green feather in it, green putties and green boots. It was a rather impressive scene. She marched to where the opposing force was waiting and going up to the officer in command, saluted, put her revolver to her lips and kissed it before handing it to him, gave up her bandoleer and announce that she was ready. The men were disarmed and the squad was marched under an armed escort through Grafton Street and Dame Street to the castle. I.R.

May 4th 1916. SEVEN POLICEMEN WERE SHOT DEAD IN AN ATTACK IN COUNTY MEATH AND 18 WOUNDED. A Navan correspondent says – The indignation of the entire population of County Meath has been roused to the fullest extent by the perpetration in this peaceful county of the cold blooded and carefully planned attack on a force of local police seven of whom have been shot dead including one District Inspector and three civilian chauffeurs wounded, one of whom has since succumbed. These murders have been perpetrated by a body of Sinn Fein rebels numbering over 400 who have made their way from County Dublin. At midday on Friday the County Meath police authorities received information that the rebels had attacked Ashbourne police barracks. County Inspector Gray, District Inspector Henry Smyth, Navan and a force of some 50 constabulary left in motor cars for the district. The Sinn Feiners however had laid a carefully prepared attack, having secreted themselves in a small grove by the roadside at a place called Rathgate. In the field they had entrenched themselves and at each end of the road they had taken up a position for attack. Hardly had the police got out of the motors nearing the ascent to the hill when a fusillade of bullets were sent into their midst. Sergeant John Shanagher of Navan was shot through the heart almost as he was leaving his car. I.R.

May 4th 1916. REBELS IN JACOB'S FACTORY. SNIPING IN DUBLIN. Though the Republic is definitely at an end and its leaders in custody, fighting in Dublin has not quite ceased as yet. One or two points are still held by little groups of unyielding rebels, who make rather a solid resistance by shooting and sniping from behind barricaded positions and as an official expressed it 'there may be a series of Sidney Streets for a little time.' But all the main strongholds have surrendered. White flags were waved from window or roof or barricade. British soldiers at once accepted the signal, marched boldly into these strongholds and took prisoner the garrisons. Groups of these prisoners, some young and simple looking, others older and more sinister looking, but all dejected as they marched between strong guards of British soldiers were among the many queer sights to be seen in Dublin streets. One of the main strongholds that refused to surrender was Jacobs biscuit factory. A few days ago this place was a high centre of rebel activity. Rebel rifleman defended it over barricades made of flour and sugar in sacks. Girl nurses wearing red crosses on their arms and girls wearing green costumes cooked and attended to the needs of rebel fighters. Today the building is nothing but a husk of walls, jagged and blackened by shell and fire. The women had left, and the place was defended by a few remaining rebels who refused to surrender. The military by some means gave them intimation that if they did not yield the place would be blown to bits. They still refused. Preparations for the last act were quickly set in hand and field guns pounded the place with shells. I.R.

May 4th 1916. POSTAL OFFICIAL'S ARREST. THREE SINN FEINERS DROWNED. A further sensation has been added to the seizure of a boat with arms and ammunition in Tralee Bay by the arrest of a prominent member of the Tralee Irish Volunteers, Mr. Austin Stack

Austin Stack

and Cornelius Collins, one of the accountants of the G.P.O. Dublin who were charged with conspiracy and aiding and abetting the importation of arms from Germany. Both were remanded in custody. A man of unknown nationality who refused to disclose his identity was conveyed to Dublin under a strong escort. The bodies of two unknown men were recovered from the River Laune, near Killorglin. They are described as of the labouring class, and are believed to be natives of Limerick. Each had a revolver and some rounds of ammunition and the Sinn Fein badge. It appears that the previous night a motor car with three passengers and a chauffeur plunged over the quay wall at Ballykissane. The three passengers were drowned but the chauffeur escaped. The body of the third victim has not been recovered yet. I.R.

May 4th 1916. MEATH CAPITULATION. AN ENVOY TALKS WITH HIS GENERAL. An insurgent lieutenant with 10 men carrying a white flag entered Dublin from Meath on Saturday with a view to the surrender of the forces in that county. The lieutenant was allowed to have an interview with the prisoner Pearce to confirm the surrender and afterwards to return to Meath to make arrangements for the men to come in. Piles of rifles belonging to the rebels were on Saturday morning taken into the castle. I.R.

May 4th 1916. PRISONERS LANDED AT HOLYHEAD. At 3.00 on Monday morning over 400 Sinn Feiners arrived at Holyhead from Dublin being carefully guarded by troops who accompanied them with fixed bayonets. The majority of them wore ordinary civilian clothes which were dirt-stained. A few wore the uniform of the Irish volunteers. Many were hatless and without overcoats and shivered as they stood on the railway platform in the chilly hours at dawn. Several were mere youngsters, and there was a sprinkling of older men, but the party was mainly composed of young men. They appeared very dejected and bore not the slightest resemblance to a military force. They showed no inclination to enter into conversation. I.R.

May 4th 1916. IN EAST TYRONE A FLYING COLUMN AT WORK AND TROOPS SENT TO DUNGANNON. When the intimation of the rebellion became known in Dungannon there was evident uneasiness on the part of the local members of the Sinn Fein organisation and on that night a number of them were observed leaving their respective districts and returning next day and it is alleged that they had assembled during the night in the mountain district for the purpose of concealing arms. Prompt measures were at once taken and on Thursday morning a military flying column of 300 men under the command of Colonel Madden arrived in Dungannon in motor lorries. Without any halt the column proceeded to the Sinn Fein stronghold of Carrickmore where a box containing a very large quantity of ammunition in cases and filled bandoliers was discovered in the turf shed attached to a private residence. The box also contained a number of badges inscribed 'we will not have conscription.' The column returned to Dungannon, but on that night a party of military revisited Carrickmore district and arrested a man named Haskin, alleged to be a Sinn Fein organiser, who does not belong to the locality. He was handed over to the police authorities. Another man was apprehended in Portadown. I.R.

May 4th 1916. MR. REDMOND ON THE RISING. FINANCED BY GERMANY. DOUBLE-DYED TREASON. A BLOW TO HOME RULE. My first feeling, of course, on hearing of this insane movement was one of horror–almost despair. I ask myself whether Ireland, as so often before in her tragic history was to dash the cup of liberty from her lips? Was the insanity of a small section of our people once again to turn all other marvelous victories of the last few years into an irreparable defeat and to send her back, on the very eve of her final recognition as a free nation into another long night of slavery, incalculable suffering, weary and uncertain struggle?

Look at the Irish position today. In the short space of 40 years she has by a constitutional movement made an almost unbroken triumphal march from pauperism and slavery to prosperity and freedom. She has won back the possession of the Irish Land; she has stayed emigration; she at last began an era of national prosperity. Finally she succeeded in placing on the Statute book the greatest charter of freedom ever offered her since the days of Grattan. Is all this to be lost? I.R.

May 4th 1916. MARKIEVICZ AND OTHER LEADERS DISAPPEAR FROM DUBLIN. It will be gratifying news to most people to know that the Countess Markievicz was seen in the Castle yard on Tuesday morning and did not reappear in the streets, the fate which should have been hers years ago, before she lured many others to the same fate. She was seen to deliberately murder one policeman and to shoot at several others, and the bullets were expanding ones. Anyone postman, policeman, or soldier, in the King's uniform was shot at by her and other rebels. Kevin O'Duffy, Pearse, Donoghue have also disappeared and Connolly is in hospital with a broken leg and we assume that he will also disappear – perhaps the worst of the whole gang. There have been almost 300 rebels shot. Dray loads of them were removed from Steven's Green and there have been over 1,000 prisoners taken to England. Eoin O'Neill who had been the head, issued a manifesto on Easter Sunday forbidding the rising when he found that the German arms and ammunition which had been captured by a British cruiser had not arrived. For this reason rebel Cork did not rise. But the other leaders persisted. Pearce then became head as Commandant-General and Connolly second in command as General. I.R.

May 4th 1916. NO MORE U-BOAT TALKS. U.S. PRESIDENT FIRM. The German attempts to flatter American public opinion have elicited an authoritative statement reaffirming the President's determination to break off diplomatic relations should an unsatisfactory and evasive reply be returned to a specific demand that 'Germany shall immediately declare and effect the abandonment of the present submarine warfare'. The personal appeal from the Kaiser for a discussion of the issues will it is stated, have no effect on the Presidents attitude. I.R.

Fermanagh Herald May 6th 1916. THE RISING IN DUBLIN. The Irish War News is published today because a momentous scene has happened. The Irish Republic has been declared in Dublin, and a Provisional Government has been appointed to administer its affairs. The Irish Republic was proclaimed and a poster prominently displayed in Dublin at 9.30 a.m. today.

The following statement was made by Commander–General P. H. Pearce: - The Irish Republic was proclaimed in Dublin on Easter Monday April 24 at 12.00 p.m. Simultaneously with the issue of the proclamation the Dublin division of the Army of the Republic, including the Irish Volunteers, the Civilian Army, and Hibernian Rifles, occupied dominating positions in the city. The General Post Office was seized at 12.00 p.m. the Castle attacked at the same moment, and shortly afterwards the Four Courts were occupied. Irish troops hold the City Hall and dominate the Castle. Attacks were made next by the British forces and were everywhere repulsed.

It is stated that there was £7,000 in the Post Office for the payment of weekly pensions and other current disbursements when the insurgents entered into occupation on Monday and the employee's canteen yielded an abundant commissariat. But on the following morning the invaders made a breakfast hour descent on the Gresham Hotel across the way, and commandeered all the food supplies that they could lay hands on.

The Press Association is authorised to state that Mr. Redmond has placed himself absolutely at the disposal of the authorities and is in constant touch with them. He has instructed the Irish National Volunteers in all parts of Ireland to hold themselves at the disposal of the military authorities. In many places outside Dublin they have already on their own motion mobilised in support of the troops. On Friday the Tipperary Volunteers offered their services.

Fermanagh Herald May 6th 1916. NEWS IN BRIEF. RAILWAY TRAFFIC. In Ireland railway traffic has resumed. The first train from Dublin conveying passengers reached Belfast on Saturday evening. The Irish mails arrived at Euston station on Saturday evening, having come via Ardrossan and Glasgow.

THE CLERK OF DUNGANNON MARKETS reported at Monday's meeting of the Urban Council that the newspapers had recently stated that the city of Armagh had broken all previous records by sending off 30,000 dozen of eggs from the weekly market. As a matter of fact 42,000 dozen had been packed and sent off from

Dungannon market on the previous Thursday.

OMAGH MEN ARRIVE HOME. One Saturday afternoon some Omagh people who had been interned in Dublin for several days arrived back. When leaving they were escorted to the station by a force of military. Mr. A. E. Donnelly, solicitor, a member of Tyrone County Council, and other public Boards who had been spending Easter in Dublin, was amongst the arrivals and was able to give a vivid account of the conditions in the metropolis since Easter.

WAGES OF COLLIERY MECHANICS. At meetings with coal owners in Newcastle it was arranged that the wages of colliery mechanics in Northumberland should be advanced by seven pence per day, commencing today Monday, 1st May and that the wages of deputies be advanced also by seven pence per day, making the daily wage nine shillings and three pence.

Fermanagh Herald May 6th 1916. RAILWAYMEN AND IRELAND. Mr. J. H. Thomas, MP, addressing a large meeting of railwaymen at Northampton, said the rebellion in Ireland was treason of the worst kind, and it would be the greatest disservice to the country for any politicians to attempt to make political capital out of so tragic an incident. It was a suicidal policy to have introduced the recent Government Military Bill, and Labour was in no sense responsible for it. He was opposed to the introduction of any proposals merely to gratify the whim of any section of the people.

From a correspondent:- "The rebels are being gradually driven from house to house and the direction from which the firing comes is continually changing. The rebels, who know every inch of the city, get away from the soldiers and appear somewhere else. By means of knocking openings in the partition walls of houses, they have succeeded in some thoroughfares in establishing covered communications. They occupied a number of big houses which commanded important thoroughfares. They were burned out of one of these strongholds in Percy Place; and gas was employed by the military in dislodging them from part of the Post Office. The rebels had displayed a white flag in token of surrender, but on an officer of approaching to ascertain their meaning, he was shot dead. An R.A.M.C. man told me that there are few wounded rebels – many have been shot outright. The rebels had evidently got a great deal of ammunition. A number of over-curious civilians were hit. Out of 15 dead that I saw three were civilians. The population are making the most of the rebellion, and it is not the insurgents themselves who are guilty of most of the looting. On Thursday night I saw some women coming down Grafton Street carrying boxes of oranges taken from some shop, and passers-by were helping themselves.

There are numbers of women fighting with the rebels, and some have been shot and some captured, declared a gentlemen who arrived in London from Dublin to a representative of the Press Association. I saw a number of women marching into Dublin on Saturday last. Some of them had naval revolvers strapped around them. They were wearing a dark green uniform similar to that of the male insurgents and slouch hats. They consist largely of young women but there are a number of older ones among them. I believe they have had training with the men for they do not lack a certain discipline and organisation. There have been cases of military officers being shot from behind by a woman.

A SUMMARY OF THE REVOLT. The revolt began on Monday a little before noon. Information was received that the Castle had been attacked, and that St. Stephen's Green had been occupied and the Post Office seized. Telegraphic communication to the Curragh at once put into motion the reserve troops there, and they arrived in Dublin that night and the following morning. Meanwhile the situation at the Castle had been eased and strengthened. They did not take the Castle. All the rebels did was to shoot a policeman at the gate, and they were then held up. The Castle was never in danger but they obtained the Post Office.

Fermanagh Herald May 6th 1916. A special representative of the *Irish News* supplied a series of narrative incidents collected from returning passengers from Dublin. A well-known Belfast man says that he saw the armed Volunteers marched up to the Post Office, left wheel, quick march, and straight through the doorway. A typical Eastertide crowd gazed on the scene in a surprised way. He can only surmise what happened inside, but a few minutes later a scared-looking crowd of females of the staff hurried through the doorway. In a moment the crowd learned the sensational news that the G.P.O. was seized and in the hands of the Sinn Feiners. The incident created no panic and was regarded as somewhat amusing. Another body had executed a similar dramatic move at the Four Courts. Platoons of armed men marched here and there, clearing buildings and hurrying up ammunition and food. The Metropolitan Police, surprised, gaze for a minute on the scene and being without arms had to clear off the streets. Soon O'Connell Street became packed with people. The looting spirit broke out amongst the youthful section with the dread of the massive D.M.P. men removed. The youngsters had a sweet tooth and Noblett's toffee shop attracted – not a case of so near and yet so for now. The shop was taken possession of and Noblett's toffee became a universal favourite. In the side streets youths careered about on the latest three speed cycles taken from a depot nearby.

THE SURRENDER. The following community was issued – "All the rebels in Dublin have surrendered, and the city is reported to be quite safe. The rebels in the country districts are surrendering to mobile columns. There were 1000 prisoners in Dublin yesterday of whom 489 were sent to England last night. There are 188 dead soldiers and civilians in Dublin hospitals.

May 11th 1916. If the person who lost a small yellow and white cow in poor condition and then valued for about £11 which came to this address on the evening of the 28th of March last will communicate with me I will on his proving ownership to the satisfaction of the proper authorities and paying the cost of the animals maintenance and any other expenses in connection therewith including the insertion of this advertisement hand her over to him. The Constabulary have up to the present been unable to trace the owner J. O'R. Hoey, Greenhill, Brookeborough. F.T.

May 11th 1916. NO CONSCRIPTION FOR IRELAND. There was a debate in Parliament on Tuesday over a motion by Sir John Lonsdale to bring Ireland under the provisions of the new Military Service Bill. Mr. Asquith made it clear that owing to Nationalist opposition Ireland could not and would not be included. He admitted that Mr. Redmond's ipse dixit (Ipse Dixit. Latin, He himself said it. An unsupported statement that rests solely on the authority of the individual who makes it) was his authority for stating that Ireland objected to conscription. Despite earnest protest by Sir Edward Carson on behalf of Loyalist Ulster, Mr. Redmond's views prevailed and the motion was rejected. F.T.

May 11th 1916. PANIC AT GLASGOW CATTLE MARKET. UNPRECEDENTED PRICES. A veritable panic was witnessed during the proceedings in Glasgow cattle market yesterday when prices were obtained at figures unprecedented in the history of the establishment in the livestock section. Prices have been steadily rising on account of the great shortage but today all records went by the board when live cattle were obtained for the abnormal figure of 130 shillings the hundredweight. Normally prices were from about 72 shillings to 90 shillings. The day's price is the highest ever obtained and the outlook for retail traders is exceedingly serious. One gentleman closely associated with the trade declared that it will ruin many traders who have nothing less in front but to shut up their shops. The retail figure in consequence of this extraordinary rise in wholesale prices will be unthinkable for householders. F.T.

May 11th 1916. DERRYLIN MAN KILLED IN DUBLIN. A PATRIOTIC STUDENTS TRAGIC END. Among the many tragic incidents connected with the Dublin rebellion was one which will appall the people throughout this district. Private John A. Thompson, nephew of Mr. William Swan, Drumany, was a student at Trinity College, Dublin. Some months ago joined the 10th (Pals) Battalion of the Royal Dublin Fusiliers. When the rebellion broke out in the metropolis he was sent on duty with his comrades to the Castle on Easter Monday and during the fighting was shot through the heart and killed immediately. He was only 19 years of age and was a lad of much promise. On Monday his remains were sent by train to Enniskillen and on Tuesday the funeral took place to Callowhill, Derrylin and was very largely attended by the people of the district. F.T.

May 11th 1916. INNISKILLING CASUALTIES. SECOND LIEUTENANT TRIMBLE KILLED. ENNISKILLEN BOYS KILLED AND WOUNDED. During the past week the tragic consequences of war have been brought home to Enniskillen people more forcibly and more sadly than ever by the news, official and otherwise, of the death and wounding in action of several brave young fellows who were either natives of, or were well known in the town. The first official intimation which reached Enniskillen on Friday bore the sad tidings of the death through being gassed of Second Lieutenant Noel Desmond Trimble, Royal Inniskilling Fusiliers, son of Mr. W Copeland Trimble, J.P. Enniskillen. He was only 20 years of age and had only been a few weeks at the front. He won many prizes at Portora School and was a very clever pianist and won 1st prizes at Dublin, Derry and Sligo. Two of his brothers are on active service, Reginald, being a lieutenant at Salonika and Alwyn being a second lieutenant also with the 16th Irish Division. A pathetic incident is that Alwyn was at the burial of his brother which took place in the little cemetery set apart for local boys just behind the lines. Very general and sincere sympathy has been felt for Mr. Trimble and family in their bereavement. (Ed. Considering the bitter and very personal antipathy expressed by Mr. Trimble towards the *Fermanagh Times* and its editor this is a generous response to this sad news.) F.T.

SEC.-LIEUT. N. D. TRIMBLE,

Royal Inniskilling Fusiliers, son of Mr. W. C. Trimble, J.P., Enniskillen, died in action as a result of being gassed. He was an old Portora boy, where his attainments won him considerable notice. Prior to the war he

May 11th 1916. PUTTING DOWN THE RISING. SEVERE CASUALTY LIST. In the House of Commons on Tuesday Mr. Asquith gave the casualties suffered by the Crown forces in Dublin – officers, 17 killed and 46 wounded; other ranks, 86 killed, 311 wounded, nine missing; R.I.C., 12 killed and 23 wounded. D.M.P., (Dublin Metropolitan Police) Three killed and three wounded; Navy, one killed two wounded; Loyal Volunteers five killed three wounded. Total killed 124, wounded 388, missing nine. F.T.

May 11th 1916. THE PRICE OF TREASON. FOUR MORE REBELS DOOMED. 83 SENTENCED TO DATE. These include, shot, 12; life sentence, 4, 10 years, 21, 8 years, 2; five years, 3, three years 36, 2 years 2, one year 3. F.T.

May 11th 1916. DISLOYAL OFFICIALS. The Government we are told is now conducting a vigorous examination of their offices in Dublin to purge them off disloyal officials. It is a case of late again. For years it has been openly known that Dublin's officialdom was honeycombed with sedition and neither the Old Woman, Lord Aberdeen, nor the champion bungler, Birrell, would at all interfere. Lord Wimborne came upon the scene too late to do anything in this direction. The men dreamers, who wear long hair, and the lady faddists who wear short hair had crazes that were pretty well known. The Department of Agriculture was believed to be a favourite rebel nest, and in some counties their inspectors and instructors were believed to be organizers, while the Technical and Art Department furnished others. Briefly, Government positions and money were used to organize the country for the overthrow of the Government. The General Post Office in Dublin was known to contain a number of rebel officials. I.R.

May 11th 1916. BIG CATTLE PRICES. Record prices were paid for cattle in Enniskillen fair on yesterday (Wednesday). The prices are the highest yet reached. Twelve to 15 months old calves reached as high as £14 and £20 was a low price for springing heifers, in some cases as much as £30 being paid. Young sucking pigs were £2 10 shillings each and beef was over 50 shillings per hundredweight. I.R.

May 11th 1916. FULL COMPULSORY SERVICE. Sir Edward and his committee have triumphed. The government has been compelled to introduce a Compulsory Service Bill for all males in Great Britain of military age. Mr. Asquith had stated to the Labour Members on one occasion that if such a Bill would be introduced that would be brought in by another Prime Minister; but he has been compelled to abandon the fad as to voluntary service as well as that of pseudo Free Trade by the necessities of the situation. One drawback of this bill is that it is unjust to Irish soldiers. Time expired men are not to be allowed to leave the army. The principal works with fairness now in England where compulsion will be in force, but in Ireland the loyal and willing hearts are to be kept in the army at the front when the slackers, the rebels, and the wastrels of society are to be allowed to remain. This is a United Kingdom and the law that is put in force for the necessary defence of the Kingdom should have been applied to Ireland as well as to England and Scotland. I.R.

May 11th 1916. THE DUBLIN REBELLION. THE FATE OF SOME CONSPIRATORS. A ROMANCE – MARRIED AT NIGHT. MANY REBELS TRIED AND SHOT. REDMOND'S PLEA FOR LENIENCY. PENAL SERVITUDE FOR OTHERS. Of the seven leaders of the rebellion, those who signed the Republican Proclamation, four were court-martialed and found guilty and shot on Thursday morning – namely –Joseph Plunkett, Edward Daly, Michael O'Hanrahan, and William Pearce. Sentenced to death but commuted to penal servitude for life by the General Officer commanding-in-chief Constance Georgina Markievicz and Henry O'Hanrahan. Major McBride who was executed on Friday was a man of about 50 years of age and was an employee of Dublin Corporation. During the Boer war he fought with the Irish contingent on the side of the Boers. At Mount Jerome Cemetery internments had to be carried out under crossfire from the military at Portobello Barracks and the Volunteers from Rialto Bridge. At Glasnevin Cemetery 50 internment had been arranged for, and the gravediggers were having their busiest day. In one corner is a large closed in grave in which at least a dozen rebels were recently interred. The body of The O'Rahilly has found its last resting place at Glasnevin. I.R.

May 11th 1916. AT LONG LAST MR. BIRRELL RESIGNS. The House of Commons on the 3rd witnessed one of the most moving personal scenes that have taken place in the long succession of the ups and downs, the rise and the fall of great men. Mr. Birrell sat in a corner seat greatly perturbed. Five days of Dublin under its trial of blood and fire had searched him, as he afterwards hinted to the depths. Mr. Birrell was almost overcome with emotion, and it seemed he would be unable to carry on. But there was no noticeable halt in the fairly long speech. I.R.

May 11th 1916. REBELS MARCH ON GALWAY. STOPPED BY SHELLS FROM A DESTROYER. The Sinn Feiners numbering 400 captured Oranmore and made prisoners of the police. The sergeant defended himself with a rifle and revolver and was eventually rescued. Later the rebels marched on Galway where they were checked by shells discharged from a destroyer which had just arrived in the bay. Some prominent persons were arrested. At the house of one of them the police discovered 600 sovereigns and on others incriminating documents were found. I.R.

May 11th 1916. THE LOSSES OF DUBLIN. A special meeting of the Dublin Corporation has been summoned at the request of the Local Government Board for Ireland to deal with applications from the Guardians of the North and South Dublin Union for to have the Act of 1898 put into force to enable the widespread destitution resulting from the rebellion to be dealt with. Until these applications have been considered the Guardians have no power to obtain overdrafts for relief purposes or give outdoor relief to able-bodied persons. The Council of the Dublin Chamber of Commerce has expressed its views very strongly on what they describe as the gross and unjustifiable laxity long continued of the Irish Administration. It therefore considers that the Government should atone for its misdeeds by providing from the Treasury without delay the funds necessary to restore the buildings and property destroyed during the rising. I.R.

May 11th 1916. SINN FEINERS IN THE G.P.O. AN EXTRAORDINARY REVELATION. A young woman who was a clerk in the General Post Office when it was taken by the Sinn Feiners said: - 'Suddenly we were aware that something extraordinary was happening. A certain number of our officials were visibly nervous and the reason for this quickly developed. Many men whose faces I had never seen came into the building. All of them were armed. They were given complete possession by the officials, who aided them in stacking up numerous boxes containing arms and ammunition and money – the latter 'legal tender of the Irish Republic.' More men thronged into the building and everyone who was not openly identified with the revolt were searched and turned into the street. Before I was ordered to leave I discovered that a good sized army of rebels had been in the building since day break, probably having arrived during the night. They swarmed over the place from the basement to the roof and rapidly made preparations for defence. Tables were piled against the windows all over the building. As I walked out into the street a rebel sentry stood guard at the door. I suppose that the munitions and money which I saw had been stored in the basement and vaults for weeks'. This young woman is from a respectable Irish family of comfortable means. I.R.

May 11th 1916. 7TH AND 8TH INNISKILLINGS GASSED BY THE GERMANS. HOW OUR BOYS SUFFERED YET DROVE THE ENEMY BACK. THREE DAYS FIGHTING. ENNISKILLEN IN MOURNING. SORROW IN SEVERAL HOMES. THERE WERE OVER 500 CASUALTIES. Enniskillen is in mourning. In both the main street and side streets there are sorrow stricken homes. In the dawn of Thursday 27th of April the German attacked the British lines under a heavy hail of shrapnel. The 7th Inniskillings held the first line of trenches, the 8th were in reserve in front billets not in trenches. The first bombardment did not inflict much injury on the front lines and it passed to the reserve to form a barrage or curtain of fire. This warned the troops for an attack in force. The Germans then discharged the most dreaded of all deadly things, a heavy cloud of poisonous gas about 5.00 a.m. The gas came slowly over the 100 yards from the front enemy line and for a time hung over the enemy trenches so that their own men were seen running away from it. The gas came diagonally to the 7th who manned the trench and opened rapid fire on the enemy but there raiding parties got up on B Companies flanks, where the first two lines were close together, and in some cases got actually into the trenches trying to take some prisoners. Some of them were shot down on the way back, while our artillery bombarded them the whole time. About an hour later a further discharge was effected from the enemy lines of the dreaded gas, thicker than before. But no enemy attack followed that. The enemy had suffered severely from his former experience. Next day the 8th

Inniskillings went to the front line while the 7th were in reserve and again at daylight the gas appeared again, denser than ever but the 8th did not flinch. They did not flee before the dreaded thing. They held their ground despite the terrible nature of the gas cloud and they suffered severely from it, perhaps more than the 7th and drove back the advancing enemy. We are not informed whether the gas helmets in use by the 8th were deficient or whether some of them had gas helmets at all but the gas laid several of our boys low, among whom were Lt. F. P. M. Leonard, Sec. Lieut. Noel D. Trimble, Second-Lieutenant Milligan, Second-Lieutenant P. H. Hall, Sergeant Major Finnegan, late of Enniskillen, Sergeant James Fox, Woaghternerry, Sergeant Curran, Lance Corporal F. Smith, Ashwoods, Lance Corporal Peter Drum, Cross Street - also in hospital badly gassed: - Captain J Ritty, Captain J. E. Knott, Sergeant McGlade, (an old 27th man), Corporal Frank Roche, Mary Street, Corp. Jim Leonard, late of Market Street, Lance Corporal Freddie Grome, Queen Street, Pte. W. Hynes, Gas Lane, Thomas Donnelly, Market Street, Ptk. Carney, Nugent's Entry, wounded, Gerald Martin (grandson of Mr. Patrick Crumley M.P., Pte. J. Jones, Fartagh, Monea. We fear that there is a long list of sufferers not yet issued to add to these. The 7th Battalion has 263 casualties, and the 8th must have had the same or more - over 500 casualties. I.R.

May 11th 1916. THE REBELLION CONDEMNED AT THE LISNASKEA BOARD OF GUARDIANS ON SATURDAY. Mr. J. Maguire said he had a resolution to propose regarding the disgraceful 'rising' in Dublin. They all knew it had been promoted by the Germans and financed by German gold. The resolution he proposed was that the Board view with abhorrence the recent disgraceful conduct of a small section of irreconcilables in Dublin and other parts, placing on record a disapproval of such conduct, the object of which was to embarrass the Government in the present grave crisis and to aid and assist the Germans.
Mr. William Irvine, seconding the resolution said there was not a member of the Board – with the probable exception of one who was not present – who would not support the resolution. There was a small section of the Irish people who would always be found to act against the English Government at all costs. He hoped the Government would take strong measures to put the rebellion down but that they would not go to extremes in dealing with the unfortunate dupes who had been led into it. The Chairman, Mr. Burns, having given the resolution his whole hearted support, it was passed unanimously. I.R.

May 11th 1916. GALLANT AIRMAN'S FATE. Flight Sub-Lieutenant T. R. Liddle, aged 20 has been killed in England. An officer referring to the deceased said 'I have never met such a keen youth about aviation and they could not keep him out of the air.' Deceased was a grandson of Mr. Hugh Liddle, Ballymakenny, Lisnaskea. At the time of the accident with his machine he was 1,000 feet up on the air. It dived downwards striking the earth between two railway tracks. Strange to say though the unfortunate lad's body was dreadfully smashed up; his face was untouched and had a smile upon at. Death was instantaneous. I.R.

May 11th 1916. A SOLDIER CONGRATULATED. Colonel Sir John Leslie, 12th Battalion Royal Inniskilling Fusiliers (Reserve), Ulster Division, addressing the troops of the Battalion who were through the fighting in Dublin since Monday week, said he had been directed by the General to sincerely thank them for their bravery during the trying time. Company Sergeant Major McGahey, a justice of the peace for Derry City and a member of the Derry Corporation was called out to the front, and when Colonel Sir John Leslie shook hands with him he said he and the 12th Inniskillings were proud of him for the magnificent example he had shown to the men, rallying them time and again when subjected to heavy firing by the rebels. Company Sergeant McGahey, in reply, said he had only done his duty. It is understood company Sergeant Major McGahey's name is being sent to the General for his bravery. I.R.

May 11th 1916. BELCOO. The Rev. Mr. Caulfield, Catholic Curate of the parish of Cleenish, asked the prayers of the congregation at Holywell for the Sinn Feiners who had fallen in Dublin, from the altar; and we are told that the request was not cordially received. I.R.

May 11th 1916. SIR ROGER CASEMENT AND HIS TRIAL IN ENGLAND. There is much speculation as to the coming trial of Sir Rodger Casement, and some comment has been heard as to the discrimination between the arch-traitor and the other rebels. It is pointed out, however, that as he was arrested before martial law was proclaimed he has the right to a civil trial, and as the crime of which he is accused is presumably that of assisting the King's enemies in Germany the proper tribunal is the English High Court. In this connection a London newspaper gives currency to the remarkable statement that Sir Rodger has expressed the wish that his defence should be in the hands of Sir Edward Carson. While this might be regarded as a tribute to Sir Edward's professional ability, and certainly gives no confirmation to the suggestion that the prisoner's mental condition has been affected there is little likelihood the wish will be gratified. There is nothing extraordinary of course in council taking on the defence of a client of totally different political views, but the circumstances are so exceptional in the present case that Sir Edward's acceptance of the brief would be out of the question. Sir F. E. Smith, as Attorney- General will naturally conduct the prosecution. I.R.

May 11th 1916. GASSED AT THE FRONT. THE LAST OF POOR FINNEGAN. HOW IT OCCURRED. The following is a copy of a letter from Lieutenant E. Gallacher, 7th Inniskillings. Poor Finnegan referred to in it, was a well-known newspaper man in Enniskillen and a prominent National Volunteer.

30-4-16 Dear Harry, - Just on my way somewhere; we are in a hospital train, and it's like our own officers mess, so many of the old hands are here, gassed. As for the Irish, they easily carry the day, men and officers. I was gassed in the second attack (gas) after having a good half hour bowling over Bosches and looking forward to another good time. My platoon sergeant, poor Finnegan – was with me and he did buck us up; he kept shouting on the Bosches 'Come on Fritz; we have some lovely presents for you,' and they got them. Then when the Bosche saw he had failed he sent us more gas and it was terrible seeing poor fellows dropping on all sides. Then I felt my own time coming; words could not describe it. I had my helmet on, but it must have had some defect. However, I began to feel the gas: first it made me gasp; and then it turned me blue; my chest weighed a ton and my head was ready to crack and I coughed until I thought I would cough my insides up. I thought I would try and find the dressing station. On my way I came across poor Finnegan and he was as bad; we got on about 100 yards when we both collapsed. We just clung to one another and Finnegan said 'Sir, we have no chance.' I agreed as I was exhausted. Finnegan shouted out: 'By God, Sir isn't it terrible to die like this! If we had only got a sporting chance; but no one could beat this. After half lying, half standing, clinging to one another for about 10 minutes and going through terrible agony, I said to Finnegan, come on let us make one last effort, and we did. I helped poor Finnegan along. At last he said, 'Go on sir, I am done.' However we plodded along, creeping and walking in a trench with two feet of mud. I found myself at the dressing station about done up. I sent out a party for Finnegan, but he could not be found. He was found that night dead. A plucky soldier – he had no fear. Our boys did well. Harry, if you could have seen them it would have delighted you. There was no pause, every man went at it, and after the first attack they actually fought as to which company had the best 'bag' outside their parapet and to hear them bragging 'that fellows helmet beside your big shell hole is on our side of the wire. It was glorious and I was just thinking how pleased the people at home will be when this will be told in full. Then in a day's time I got a paper and what do I see? This terrible rebel rising in Ireland. Poor old Ireland! Betrayed again! I am getting along as well as can be expected. It takes time to get the gas out of one's system. However a few weeks will make me fairly up to the knocker. Best love to all in Dunwiley. Harry. May be home sooner than I expected. I.R.

Fermanagh Herald May 13th 1916. THE RISING IN DUBLIN. TWELVE EXECUTIONS. OTHER SENTENCES COMMUTED. MR. REDMOND MAKES AN APPEAL FOR LENIENCY. The following was officially communicated from the Command Headquarters, Parkgate, Dublin, on Wednesday morning: - three signatories of the notice proclaiming the Irish Republic – P. H. Pearce, T. MacDonagh, and P. J. Clark – have been tried by a Field –General Courts-martial and sentenced to death. This sentence having been duly confirmed, the three above mentioned men were shot this morning. The trial of further prisoners is proceeding.

T. McDonagh

Fermanagh Herald May 13th 1916. THE FERMANAGH HERALD EDITORIAL –THE SINN FEIN RISING. The aftermath of the Sinn Fein rising has been so dreadful that the average mind tries to avoid the contemplation of it. Shooting and penal servitude for varying terms have been the fate of several of the more prominent leaders, and many hundreds of the rank and file were also suffering the results of the folly that has thrown a funeral pall over Dublin and other parts of the country. It is a bitter lesson, and we trust that it will never be forgotten or misapplied. The Fenians with numerous examples of the most loathsome political corruption and the complete absence of a proper constitutional alternative, conspired, struck and were sacrificed; the revolt of 1916 was not only unnational, judging by the restricted and unrepresentative sources from which its strength was gathered, but without a shred of justification. Certainly, while the Home Rule Act remains inoperative the country has a technical grievance.

Fermanagh Herald May 13th 1916. JOTTINGS. MR. MURPHY, COUNTY COURT JUDGE WAS SHOT DEAD in Stephens Green on Easter Tuesday. He was passing the Unionist Club, and raised his hand to salute a friend in a window, when he was sniped.

JAMES CONNOLLY STILL LIES IN DUBLIN CASTLE HOSPITAL, slowly recovering from his wounds. One of his legs is fractured below the knee joint. His ward is guarded by six soldiers with fixed bayonets.

THE REMAINS OF THE LATE MR. SHEEHY–SKEFFINGTON, who was shot in Portobello Barracks on the 26th of April, were removed from the barracks on Monday morning by permission of the military authorities for internment in Glasnevin Cemetery. The funeral took place at one o'clock.

AN ENNISKILLEN FOOTBALLER FALLS IN ACTION. Word has been received in Enniskillen that Lance Corporal James Leonard, of the Royal Dublin Fusiliers has fallen in action from the effects of gas poisoning. It will be remembered that Lance Corporal Leonard's parents resided in Market Street, Enniskillen. Some five years ago he left Enniskillen and joined the London Police Force where he was deservedly popular with all his brother officers. The deceased soldier was well known in local football circles and he played on many occasions for the Celtic Football Club.

Fermanagh Herald May 13th 1916. ENNISKILLEN MEN KILLED IN ACTION. Word has also been received by his relatives that Sergeant J Smith, of the Inniskillings has fallen in action. Captain J. E. Knott, has written the following letter to Mrs. Smith, Waternerry, Enniskillen giving an account of the manner in which her son died. "Your son was on a wiring party in charge of an officer, and most unfortunately the party was discovered by the enemy and fired on and your son was badly hit. The officer came in and reported that your son was unconscious. A Sergeant McNiff of this company volunteered to go out with the officer and try and bring him in. They went out very gallantly under heavy fire, and lifted up your son, who unfortunately at that moment was hit again by a bullet which caused his death. Sergeant McNiff at the same time was slightly wounded, and they had to return, your son being quite dead. It was impossible without losing more lives to bring him in that night, but two officers and two men brought him in under fire last night, and he was buried this afternoon in the burial ground here, the position of which you will be notified later."

Fermanagh Herald May 13th 1916. ENNISKILLEN GAELIC LEAGUE. The following paragraph appeared in last week's *Impartial Reporter*: - This Mr. Pearse had been an ardent Sinn Feiner and organiser of the Irish Language movement, and years ago he succeeded in forming a branch in Enniskillen, with the Rev. Jas. Tierney, then Roman Catholic Curate of Enniskillen, as president. This statement is untrue. The Lough Erne Branch of the Gaelic League was established many years before Mr. Pearse visited Enniskillen. He came to the town to deliver a lecture under its auspices, and the chair was occupied by the President, Rev. John Tierney. It was at that time and still is a vigorous branch, and Father Tierney was the third president who had held office since its formation.

Fermanagh Herald May 13th 1916. OBITER DICTA. A PRESBYTERIAN ORATION. Ireland deeply deplores the unfortunate rebellion. It has been condemned in every quarter, while Mr. John Redmond and the "Leader" of the people of Ulster have stated that it would be highly injudicious for anyone to endeavour to make party or other capital out of the deplorable affair. The Ulster loyalists are following Sir Edward Carson's instructions to the letter, and the individual making the really best effort is an Enniskillen Presbyterian minister, the Rev. Mr. A. J. Jenkins – who, judging by a recent harangue delivered by him, evidently forms his opinion on local affairs by reading the Unionist press. His services were required on a recent Sunday to officiate at Divine service for the Presbyterian soldiers in the Enniskillen Barracks. Let us consider what is the Rev. Mr. Jenkin's idea of what constitutes Divine Service. As reported in the Impartial Reporter this Rev. Gentleman in the course of his remarks, abused – not criticised – "perverted history in the day schools of this country," cast a slur on local Nationalists, the magistrate, juries, and officials. Now he says in effect that the recent trouble is the outcome of a conflict between a true and a false religion.

Needless to say, in the Rev. Mr. Jenkins' opinion the Protestant religion is not the false religion. This terrible discrepancy in belief is, we are told by this learned Churchman, due to the teaching of perverted history in the day schools of this country. In what manner and since when, have our religions been founded on historical facts? Was Mr. Jenkins living on the Moon before he came to Enniskillen? Did he never hear the slogan cry, "Ulster will fight etc.? Did he ever hear that preparations were made in Ulster for civil war? Has he not been told that members of his own congregation drilled others and were drilled themselves? Did he never see pictures of the gun-running episodes, the nurses who had been trained to bandage the wounded etc.? Perhaps he didn't. As a Belfast contemporary says: - in every legal essential the gun-running exploit at Larne was an act of Rebellion as contemptuous of the Crown authority as the deeds of the men who raised the flag of insurrection on the Dublin Post Office.

Fermanagh Herald May 13th 1916. A TRAGIC PARALLEL. Amongst the multitude of heart–saddening episodes connected with the revolt in Dublin one tragic romance will probably live in the public memory for many generations to come – the marriage of Joseph Plunkett, a young and gifted member of the revolutionary party, to Miss Grace Gifford, the sister of Thomas MacDonagh's widow. The names of MacDonagh and Plunkett were affixed to the Provisional Government's declaration. Both were young men of ability and writers of verse. McDonagh was one of the first three victims of Marshall Law in practical application. Plunkett was shot on Thursday morning, May 4. He was to have been married that morning; and the announcement

Grace Gifford and Joseph Plunket

has been made that the marriage was performed and that the young lady became the bride of the doomed lover a few hours before his death at the hands of the law. Thus two sisters were widowed within the week. Their story is one of the most pathetic in Ireland's annals; but it had a remarkable, though not quite exact, parallel in the story of Dublin County many centuries ago. Dalton's History of Drogheda has the following passage – of the monuments most worthy of note in the chapel of Malahide is an altar tomb ornamented with an effigy, in bold relief, of a female habited in the costume of the 14th century, and representing the Honourable Maud Plunkett, wife of Sir Richard Talbot. She had been previously married to Mr. Hussey, son of the Baron of Galtrim, who was slain on the day of her nuptials, leaving her the singular celebrity of having been a maid, wife, and widow all on the same day. Gerald Griffin tells the story in a familiar ballad: -

The joy bells are ringing in gay Malahide
The fresh wind is singing along the seaside;
The maids are assembling with garlands of flowers,
And the harp strings are trembling in all the glad bowers.

Hark! 'mid the gay clamour that compassed their ear,
Loud accents in anger come mingling afar!
The foe's on the border; his weapons resound
Where the lines in disorder, unguarded are found.

The lords of the Pale and their followers where at Malahide; the O'Tooles made a foray into South Dublin from their Wicklow fastness; and the call to arms reaches the wedding party, who mounted "in hot haste" and rode to meet the Gaelic invaders. Of course the O'Tooles retreated – suffering losses they went back to their Wicklow fastness.

Fermanagh Herald May 13th 1916. NEWS IN BRIEF. DERRY LABOURERS STRIKE SETTLED. The strike of the Derry dockers engaged in the discharge of coal boats has been settled, the men who demanded an increase of 2d per ton, having accepted a temporary advance of 1½ d per ton.

SCARCITY OF POTATOES. There was a great scarcity of potatoes at the Sheffield market. This was due to the stoppage of the Irish supply and the almost entire depletion of English-grown stocks.

LIGHTING REGULATIONS. Fines inflicted under the lighting regulations at Newcastle-on-Tyne were over 40 including one on a schoolboy for using a flashlight in the street.

BORROWED WAR BADGES. At Birmingham two men from Wolverhampton were each fined £5 for wearing borrowed war-work badges. A recruiting clerk said that if the matter had not been detected the men would have undoubtedly escaped military service.

STREET BETTING. A fine of £20 plus advocates fee, was imposed on Henry Simpson, 167, Tulketh Brow, Ashton-on-Ribble, by the Preston magistrates for street betting. Simpson, who had several times previously been fined for similar offences, described himself has retired spinner, but the police described him as a bookmaker.

Fermanagh Herald May 13th 1916. HIS DISAGREEABLE EXPERIENCE DURING THE DUBLIN TROUBLES. The experience of County Court Judge Johnston and his family was very disagreeable. On Easter Monday men were observed to be working on the railway line at Lansdowne Road, which is close to Judge Johnston's house. The rails were torn up, and trenches were dug. At 1.00 on Easter Monday night the family was awakened by a loud knocking at the door. The judge himself went down to ascertain the cause, and on opening the door armed men pushed their way in, stating they had orders to occupy the house in order to prevent troops coming along the railway from Kingstown or along Lansdowne Road and Shelburne Road into Beggars Bush Barracks. The family was first ordered to leave the upstairs bedrooms and stay in the dining room flat. The rebels then broke the walls between the bedrooms and opened other spaces, through which the various approaches could be commanded. Next day passed quietly until eight o'clock in the evening when the rebel leader informed the judge that he had received information to the effect that military reinforcements were coming in by Kingstown, and that he had been instructed to put the house in a position of defence. The family was then ordered to take up their quarters in the basement and to remain there. The rebels tore up the beds and bedding, and placed all movable pieces of furniture at the windows and doors making barricades.

Shooting was going on from and at this house all that night. At 10.00 on Wednesday morning the rebels evacuated the house, leaving behind them four rifles, one complete suit of uniform, a considerable quantity of ammunition and military equipment. During the time the rebels had possession of the place they were as considerate as possible to the judge and his family.

Fermanagh Herald May 13th 1916. 30,000 BRITISH PRISONERS. Mr. Tenant informs Mr. G. Lambert in a written answer that there are 26,800 British and Colonial prisoners in the hands of the Germans, two with the Austrians, 449 with the Bulgarians, and 9,796 in the hands of the Turks. This is the latest information in possession of the War Office.

Fermanagh Herald May 13th 1916. OBITUARY. MR. JOHN MOOHAN, GLASGOW. The interment took place on Tuesday 2nd of May from the residence of Mr. Terence Brennan, 23 Martyr Street, Glasgow of the remains of Mr. John Moohan, son of Mrs. Moohan, wine merchant, Belleek, Co., Fermanagh, Ireland, a much esteemed and highly respected family in that district. Deceased was resident in Glasgow during the past 20 years and during that period he was a highly esteemed member of Saint Aloysius congregation, Garnethill. An exemplary Catholic, a true Irishmen, he was always ready and willing to assist in any organisation of Irish or Catholic origin.

May 18th 1916. THE SHOOTING OF JAMES CONNOLLY AND JOHN MCDERMOTT in Dublin on Friday completes the number of those who were sentenced to the death penalty for participation in the recent rebellion. Bulmer Hobson, one of the Sinn Fein leaders opposed the outbreak. We hope that this phase of the death chapter of Irish mourning is over and forever but we confess with sadness that we much fear the mercurial temperament of our Nationalist peasantry will always leave them a prey to the political mountebank and scheming conspirator. Let us hope that our fears will prove illusory. I.R.

Seán Mac Diarmada (English: John MacDermott; 28 February 1883 – 12 May 1916),

May 18th 1916. WINSTON CHURCHILL SHOULD STAY IN THE TRENCHES. Discussing the rumour that Mr. Churchill aspires to be Mr. Burrell's successor, *The New York Sun* says he should not be appointed, as he is temperamentally unfit for the post. Moreover why should he not return to the trenches and stay there. In no small measure he was responsible for the ill-starred Gallipoli campaign in which so many lives were needlessly sacrificed. There are enough politicians muddling things in England without the ex-Admiralty Lord taking a hand again. Having put on the uniform of a soldier and been promoted to colonel for no particular reason, Mr. Churchill should do his bit at the front till the end of the war – Morning Post. F.T.

May 18th 1916. NELSON DEFIES THE SINN FEINERS. It is confirmed beyond doubt that no less than four futile attempts were made by the rebels to destroy the Nelson Monument. The explosions took place one morning at intervals of 10 minutes but the Pillar stood firm as a rock and defied the reckless dynamiters. They had not however done with the monument to the hero of many battles. Snipers were placed on the roof of the Post Office and extensive pot shots took place at the statue. F.T.

May 18th 1916. SCHOOL AND SEDITION. A correspondent of the Belfast Newsletter writes – A Roman Catholic head-constable of the R.I.C observed to me yesterday that a good deal of the seditious spirit abroad in Ireland may be firmly attributed to the history teaching imparted by the Christian Brothers. The teaching was exposed before the Royal Commission presided over by Lord Powis. The past is brooded over.

Nicholas Breakspear became Pope Adrian IV in 1154.

Exaggerated accounts of the misrule of former times were given. Such well attested facts as the Sale of Ireland by Nicholas Brakespeare (Adrian 1V) are suppressed. Pure fictions are substituted for true history. It is no wonder that such schools breed traitors. The history teaching in most of the Roman Catholics National schools is little better. Some of the history textbooks sanctioned for use in these State supported schools are a disgrace. Barbarities perpetrated by Irish rebels are denied. False assertions about England are made and the state of affairs will go from bad to worse until a system of public non-sectarian schools is established. Clericalized education is the enemy that has generated the sedition that prevails. Pseudo history is the instrument that he employs. F.T.

May 18th 1916. THE LISNASKEA GUARDIANS. THE CHAIRMAN SAYS THE EXECUTION OF REBELS WAS COLD BLOODED MURDERS. If there had been a larger attendance of members of the Lisnaskea Board of Guardians on Saturday last a very stormy scene might have resulted from some remarks made by the Chairman Mister J. McElgun about the rising in Dublin and the punishment of the leaders of the rebellion. There were only four Guardians present however and so Mr. McElgunn's protests that the rebels after they had laid down their arms were murdered in cold blood did not receive the attention that might have been expected. Had there been anyone present to take the chairman's remarks seriously no doubt an angry discussion would have taken place. F.T.

May 18th 1916. BALLYSHANNON GUARDIANS. At the meeting of the Guardians on Saturday the following resolution was passed on the motion of Mister P. McNulty:- That we protest in the strongest possible manner against the continuance of martial law in Ireland and demand a return to constitutional law. We consider that the wholesale executions and sentences to long terms of imprisonment are barbarious and reminiscent of the horrors through which Ireland has so often passed under English military law. We also demand the cessation of wholesale arrests throughout the country. F.T.

May 18th 1916. PROMPT ACTION AND HOW THE REBELS WERE FOILED. The reason why the military and R.I.C throughout the country were appraised of the outbreak of the rebellion in time to prevent the country being practically in the hands of the insurgents: as soon as the news reached Kingsbridge that the G.P.O. was taken all outgoing trains were stopped by Mr. Neale and the private wires of the company used to warn the police and military of the situation in Dublin. The trains were sent on to Newbridge to convey troops from the Curragh. In a few hours Kingsbridge terminus was held by several thousand troops. As a result of Mr. Neale's prompt action the R.I.C. in many parts of the South were enabled to be mobilised at headquarters this being notably the case at Tullamore. I.R.

May 18th 1916. SINN FEIN PRISONERS. PEARCE'S EXECUTION. WANTED TO SEE HIS MOTHER. Mr. Tennant informs Mr. Ginnell that P. H. Pearse, the Irish rebel, surrendered unconditionally. His desire to see his mother before his execution was not refused, but endeavour was made to meet it, the Rev Father Aloysius being sent in a car to bring her. Owing to the firing which was going on however the car could not get through. Mr. Ginnell asked why W. Pearce, his young brother, a minor and not a signatory to the proclamation was shot. Mr. Tennant – he was convicted by a court martial. Mr. Ginnell asked by whose order during the fighting in Dublin little boys and girls running about in terror were caught by soldiers and shot out of hand on the pretext that they were carrying messages. Mr. Tennant – no such order was given, and there was no evidence to lead one to believe in the truth of the allegations in question. (Cheers) Mr. Ginnell 'will any inquiry be made?' Mr. Tenant – 'No.' Answering a further question by Mr. Ginnell, Mr. Tennant said it was found impracticable in the first instance to allow mourners to attend the

Margaret Pearce

funerals of those who fell in the riots in Dublin, but as soon as possible one mourner was allowed to attend. In many cases it was necessary for the purpose of identification to open the coffin. Mr. Tennant in reply to Mr. Byrne, Dublin, said the government hoped soon to make their decision as to the method of dealing with the prisoners deported from Ireland. There was every desire to be as leniently with these prisoners as the circumstances permitted. I.R.

May 18th 1916. AN ENGLISH VIEW OF THE RISING. SLUM INFLUENCE ON THE RISING. The *Daily Mail* publishes the following from its Special Correspondent in Dublin. 'This is a supreme occasion in Irish history. The rebellion has given the British Government an opportunity to end long years of misunderstanding, bitter faction struggles, and bad rule, and to lay the foundation for peace and prosperity of Ireland that may be enduring. In short all the terrible struggles that have centred around the cries of 'Home Rule' and 'Ireland a Nation' may be ended by a wise policy at this hour. Such a unique opportunity may never arise again. If it is neglected, if wrong decisions are given, Ireland will be plunged into controversies more racking than any that have gone before, and the separation between Ireland and England will become a sword for both. This is indeed, the parting of the ways. To avert a tragedy and to gain a splendid future for Ireland, English people with whom the decision really lies must make a supreme effort to understand the state of affairs.

Calmly reviewed what were the causes of the rebellion? Quite frankly, the leaders sought separation from England and the creation of an independent Ireland. To attain what seemed to them ideal they were even prepared to accept the help of England's enemies. They shut their eyes to difficulties, when every shadow of hope became to them a certainty. At the last hour half of them headed by John McNeill shrank from self-delusion and drew back. Orders for the insurrection throughout Ireland were hurriedly cancelled. The other half headed by Connolly succumbing to their delusions were prepared to risk all and determined to raise the Republican flag in Dublin. In the end these men met the inevitable failure of death. The first cannon shell fired at Liberty Hall sounded their knell. They had never thought of artillery. But to the last Conolly believed that if John McNeill had not broken away and countermanded the orders for a general rising they might have won. I have before me an order of his days only the day before the surrender in which he expresses that view.

The leaders, therefore, were absolutely blood-guilty traitors to Britain but in some ways their sentiments were worthy of respect. Theirs was an intense local patriotism. They believed in Ireland. They believed that she would never prosper or be happy under British rule. They knew that there were 16,000 families in Dublin living on less than £1 a week. They saw the infinite misery of the Dublin slums, the foulest spot in Europe, where a quarter of the total population are forced to live in the indescribable squalor of one room tenements – I quote from official records – and they believed that this was due to England's neglect as, indeed, it was; and that the Irish Republic would end these things.

Therefore they struck, and as far as they could exercise direct control over the rebel army they tried to fight a clean fight. The begged their followers not to disgrace the Republican flag. They posted guards to prevent looting. He treated prisoners fairly. They fought with magnificent courage. Nevertheless, their control was not far reaching and they were disgraced by the anarchy of some of their fellows. But it is necessary to point out their virtues, because it is those and their ideals that non-rebel Irishmen are remembering day.

Of their followers a different story has to be told. They were roughly of three classes. First there were the anarchists and their near kinsmen, the looting rabble. They were the men who sacked houses and shot women and children when cornered and desperate. They are the inevitable produce of rebellion. Secondly there were more or less innocent dupes who all obeyed the mobilisation order without any knowledge of what they were being led into but who once involved could not dropout. These were the great majority. Thirdly there were the dreamers like their leaders of a new and regenerated Irish nation. Such men are slow of thought but fixed ideas. What are to us the visions of a night are to them the dreams of a lifetime. Irish history was taught to them all wrong. They had learned of the injustices of England and never of the good results of our rule and they had lived in the slums. These men supplied the motive power of the rebel lines.

A consideration of their sentiment is of the utmost importance because stripped of the deliberate disloyalty it is that of the vast majority of Nationalists and establishes a bond of sympathy between them and the rebels. Unless this bond is recognized by a policy such as I have outlined it will become closer and men now loyal will champion the rebels and be driven into more active distrust of English rule. I.R.

Fermanagh Herald May 20th 1916. JOTTINGS. Two Irishmen, charged at Altrincham, Cheshire, with being absentees were very defiant, and said that they were determined not to join the Army. They declared they would rather be shot than do so. They also pleaded that they were not liable as their homes were in Ireland, but they had lived here for some time. They were handed over to the military authorities.

Ex–Quartermaster Sergeant James Hall, Gortmore Terrace, Omagh, has received intimation that his son, Lance-Corporal Frank Hall has been killed in action. Lance-Corporal Hall had 10 years' service with the Royal Inniskillings Fusiliers, and had seen service in China, India, Crete, and Malta. He took part in the landing at Gallipoli where he was wounded, but was subsequently able to re-join his battalion, and remained with it until the evacuation of the Peninsula. Shell fire in the trenches is stated to have been the cause of death.

Mr. James McManus, J.P., of Rathkeeland, Brookeborough, received £100 for three head of cattle in Enniskillen fair on the 10th Inst., – a fat bull, fat cow, and a springer.

Fermanagh Herald May 20th 1916. THE BELLEEK POTTERY. Belleek Pottery works has had to be closed at times owing to an insufficient supply of water. At the last meeting of the Lough Erne Drainage Board a letter was read from Mr. Michael Maguire, solicitor, Ballyshannon referring to previous correspondence and pointing out that from the 27th of December, 1915, for a period of almost three months, the Belleek pottery works were rendered idle at times, and partially idle, the remainder of the time. He added: - the Lough Erne Drainage Board does not appear to appreciate their obligation to give an uninterrupted and sufficient supply of water to the works. The manipulation of the gates at Belleek appears to be exercised in a most arbitrary manner. On the 26th of April the works were again rendered idle owing to an insufficient supply of water at the wheel, and the same state of affairs continues. Mr. Maguire said it was the intention of the pottery company to take action against the Drainage Board and to recover damages already suffered by the pottery. One of the members of the Board is reported to have said that was a pity some of the shells in Dublin did not reach Belleek and blow it out of it. The letter was marked "read." Mr. Clegg and Mr. Porter agreed that the lake was too high at present and instructions were ordered to be sent to the gatekeeper to let more water off than he had been doing.

Fermanagh Herald May 20th 1916. MORE SENTENCES. FOURTEEN MEN ARE DEALT WITH. The following results of the trials by Field General Courtmartial are announced: -sentenced to death, and sentenced commuted to penal servitude, Edward de Valera, penal servitude for life.

The trial for the murder of Head Constable Rowe took place at Cork on May 4th with the following results: - William Kent – acquitted. Thomas Kent – found guilty and sentenced to death, and the execution took place on the 9th Inst. The trials by courtmartial of those who took an active part in the rising in Dublin are practically finished. Those arrested in the provinces have been dealt with. Lists of the rebels sent to be detained in England are being published in the Press as soon as they have been verified.

In view of the gravity of the rebellion and its connection with German intrigue and propaganda, and in view of the great loss of life and destruction of property resulting therefrom, the General Officer Commander-in-chief has found it imperative to inflict the most severe sentences on those who organized this detestable rising and on those commanders who took an active part in the actual fighting which occurred. It is hoped that these examples will be sufficient to act as a deterrent to intrigue, and to bring home to them that the murder of his Majesty's liege subjects or other acts calculated to imperil the safety of the nation will not be tolerated.

Fermanagh Herald May 20th 1916. THE DEATH OF MR. SHEEHY SKEFFINGTON. HIS WIDOW'S STATEMENT. I last saw my husband on Tuesday evening, April 25th, at Westmoreland Chambers. He had called a meeting there to stop looting and was waiting to see if any people would attend same. In the neighbourhood of Portobello Bridge he was arrested unarmed and unresisting. He never carried or possessed any arm of any description, being as is well known, a pacifist and opposed to the use of physical force. He was conducted in military custody to Portobello Barracks where he was shot without trial on that night or early on the following morning. No priest was summoned to attend him, no notification has ever since been given his wife or to his family of his death and no message written before his death has been allowed to reach me. On Friday night in April 28th a large military force surrounded my husband's house in 20 Grosvenor Place, fired without warning on the windows in front, and burst through without waiting for the door to be opened. They put myself, my son, aged seven, to whom they shouted "hands up," and my maid under arrest, and remained in the house over 3 hours. The found no ammunition of any kind, but burst locks etc and took away with them by a large amount of documents, newspapers, letters, and books, as well as personal property such as linen tablecloths, trunks, photographs of Keir Hardie and M. Davitt, a picture of Kilmainham prisoners of 1882 etc.

Mr. Sheehy Skeffington

Fermanagh Herald May 20th 1916. THE EDERNEY BRANCH OF THE UNITED IRISH LEAGUE IS REORGANISED. REFERENCES TO THE "RISING." A large influential and enthusiastic meeting of the Nationalists of the parish of Blackbog was held at Ederney on Sunday evening for the purposes of reorganising the local branch of the National Organisation. Mr. J. P. Convery delivered an instructive address on the good work accomplished by the Irish Party on behalf of the people of Ireland. His reception was not less enthusiastic than the many rounds of loud and vociferous applause with which the oration was punctuated, and that he made a deep impression on his audience was proved by the fact that large numbers came forward and were enrolled. It was from every viewpoint a most successful evening's work. Mr. William Maguire J.P. was moved to the chair and said that he had never seen such a large and influential gathering in that district before.

May 25th 1916. GERMAN DESPERATION. TERRIFIC FIGHTING ON ALL FRONTS. APPALLING CASUALTIES AROUND BY VERDUN. BRITISH REVERSE IN FRANCE. A communique on aviation issued on Saturday with reference to an air raid on Dunkirk states that Sub Lieutenant Nivarre brought down his 11th German aeroplane which fell on our lines.

The Germans succeeded according to the official report from British Headquarters in penetrating our position at the north end of the Vimy ridge and entering our frontline trenches on a front of about 1,500 yards and depth varying from 100 to 300 yards. The preceding bombardment was exceedingly heavy and lasted all day. The British artillery is reported in return, to be heavily bombarding the German position. There was great mining activity on the rest of the front. F.T.

May 25th 1916. SELF-CONDEMNED. DUBLIN CASTLE HAS BEEN DAMNED by its own set. Never has a more thorough exposure been given of its failure and Do-nothing policy than by Mr. Matthew Nahan and Mr. Augustine Birrell in their evidence before the Royal Commission. They had the whole evidence before them of a most dangerous conspiracy among the Sinn Fein party in Ireland and they DID NOTHING. Was there ever a more incompetent set of bunglers? They admitted that they had received the official reports speaking of the danger of the conspiracy; that they knew of its growth in power and extension; that they knew of the rehearsal of the attack on Dublin Castle and other points of vantage, and yet the Chief Secretary and the Under Secretary did nothing! Surely, Mr. Birrell, who was mainly responsible, should be impeached! They knew of the fiery speeches by Father Flanagan in the South near Cork and did nothing. They knew of the anti-recruiting circular of Dr. O'Dwyer, Bishop of Limerick yet did not place him under arrest, and they would undoubtedly have arrested a humble man who had written the same letter. I.R.

Mr. Augustine Birrell

May 25th 1916. DAYLIGHT SAVING. The clocks had their time indicators moved forward on last Saturday night; and in Enniskillen and other towns the new hours were observed as if nothing had taken place except at morning Mass in the Roman Catholic Chapels. In some of the villages the clocks were not disturbed – even in progressive Lisbellaw and matters moved as before but as everything proceeded on the new timetable on Monday morning the people soon awoke to the necessity of 'putting on the clock.' The change is welcomed everywhere as a distinct advance for the better. I.R.

IMPARTIAL REPORTER OWN GOAL. An Irishman's Diary - JOHN HORGAN – Irish Times. The 1916 Rising was a journalist's nightmare. Censorship was in force and many papers at first published little more than the official communiqués. But some of the nightmares were of journalists' own making and, as the anniversary approaches, one episode provides a telling example of the dangers of rushing into print without checking the facts. The central figure of this episode was William Egbert Trimble, whose family owned the Impartial Reporter of Enniskillen, edited in 1916 by his father, William Copeland Trimble. The Impartial Reporter and Farmers' Journal, to give it its full masthead title, was a unionist paper that was usually, and understandably, known in its area of circulation as the "'Partial". The 'Partial prided itself in being the first Irish newspaper to report the Rising, and was almost certainly the first of the non-Dublin papers to send its own reporter to the capital. By May 11th, W.E.T was in full voice, and his column on "Some Incidents of the Rising", was redolent not only of his journalistic fervour but of his politics. One item in his column, headed "An Enniskillen Traitor", cut straight to the chase. "One of the rebel leaders was an Enniskillener, and an old Portora boy. George Irvine, a bookworm and student, an exhibitioner and Gaelic scholar, whose father kept a religious repository in Bridge-street . . . was one of the leading revolutionary spirits in Dublin. He donned the Irish kilt, and for his pernicious teaching of anti-British ideas, he was got rid of both by the Rathmines School and St Andrews School Boards. Then he went to the Church of Ireland Diocesan School in Molesworth-street, and his presence there and teaching had been tolerated for years till it was cut short last week by his being sentenced to death, commuted to ten years' penal servitude. He took every opportunity of instilling into the minds of his students pernicious teaching.

So far, so sensational. However, two weeks later, a letter from Mr Irvine's sister, then living in Dublin, appeared in the Impartial acknowledging that George had taken part in the Rising, and had been sentenced to 10 years, she set out to demonstrate that everything else that had been published about him was a "pure fabrication". It was not the kind of letter any editor likes to receive, let alone publish. George had never taught in Rathmines and had been popular and well respected. He had gone out on Easter Monday expecting only to participate in a "long march". Noting that he had been
employed in Molesworth Street for 11 years, his loyal sister observed that if he had taken "every opportunity of instilling into the minds of his pupils pernicious teachings", he "would not have lasted there a minute, let alone eleven years." She added: "Let his own opinions be what they will, right or
wrong, George Irvine was at least honest and did the work he was paid to do, and to the satisfaction of both the Board and the headmaster.

Challenging Trimble's view of her brother as a gloomy student bookworm, she then delivered the coup de grâce. "He is by the way the exact opposite. You are evidently mixing his identity with that of his elder brother,

Mr. W. Irvine, B.A., ex-Sch. TCD, though, of course, neither of them is known to you at all. The latter man taught for some years in St. Andrews College, Rathmines, and other places and he certainly was not 'got rid of' in any of them." The older brother, she noted, was not only one of the finest classical scholars in Dublin, but had actually given up a position in a good Dublin "grinding" college to join the army on the outbreak of war (with the consent and approbation of his "rebel" brother), and was currently serving with a trench mortar battery in France. He was also a fine Gaelic scholar. "I have yet to learn", she added caustically, "that the latter fact has in any way
impaired his usefulness, either as a teacher or a soldier." You can almost hear the grinding of teeth as Trimble snr composed his brief, sourpuss reply to this salvo: "This letter is a natural one for a sister to write. We have always heard good things of Mr. Wm. Irvine, who, like his unhappy brother, were good sons to their mother. — Ed. I.R." See more at www.irishtimes.com

Fermanagh Herald May 27th 1916. Fully 200 Sinn Fein prisoners arrived in Glasgow on Saturday at Stobcross Quay. There they disembarked from the overnight boat from Ireland. The prisoners were mostly young fellows, their ages ranging from 20 to 30. None of them wore the uniform of the Irish Volunteers, being attired for the most part in everyday clothes. They had been brought over under military escort. One section, comprising about half of them was conveyed by an escort with fixed bayonets to Barlinnie Prison, Glasgow. The remainder were dispatched by a special train from Buchanan Street station to the penitentiary at Perth. The men were marched to the station, but were taken by quiet thoroughfares.

Fermanagh Herald May 27th 1916. In an article on the Sinn Fein revolt written from Dublin to the Nation by H.W.M. it is recorded that Connolly when, on being carried to his execution, was asked to pray for the shooting party. He replied, "I will say a prayer for all brave men who do their duty."

Fermanagh Herald May 27th 1916. THE TOTAL NUMBER OF SENTENCES AND EXECUTIONS. The following was published on Monday: Executions, 15; Life Sentences, 6; 20 Years, 1; 10 Years, 28; 8 Years, 2; 5 Years, 14; 3 Years, 53, 2 Years 2; 1 Year, 15; 6 Months, 3; Deportations, 1958. Total 2097.

A Sinn Fein prisoner 1916.

June 1916

June 1st 1916. THE DUBLIN REBELLION. MORE SENSATIONAL EVIDENCE BEFORE THE ROYAL COMMISSION. COMPLICITY OF SOME PRIESTS AND WARNINGS THAT WHERE UNHEEDED.
The Royal Committee appointed to inquire into the recent Irish rebellion resumed its sittings on Thursday at the Shelburne Hotel, Dublin. Sir Neville Chamberlain, Inspector General of the Royal Irish Constabulary stated that the recent rebellion necessarily drew attention to the facilities offered during recent years for the acquisition of arms without the restrictions imposed by the Peace Preservation Act and there should have been an extension to Ireland of measures intended to prevent the sending of arms. The Sinn Fein movement came into existence in 1905 and was at first in moderate movement but it got into the hands of extreme men. It became allied to revolutionaries and spread to various parts of the country. During 1908 the bond between the Sinn Fein movement and Irish Republican Brotherhood became closer and the Gaelic Athletic Association endorsed its doctrines. In 1909 a poster appeared in Gaelic declaring the men who joined the British Army and Navy were enemies of their country and one appeal was in the words, 'let us rout the foreigner out of Ireland.' The Irish Boy Scout movement started by Countess Markievicz in 1910 was really a training school for young rebels. The formation of the National Volunteers was suggested by and was the result of the Ulster Volunteer movement. I.R.

June 1st 1916. BIG ROMAN CATHOLIC SCHEME FOR DUBLIN. ARCHBISHOP WALSH AND THE CATHEDRAL 'GAP'. A GRANDIOSE BUILDING IN SACKVILLE STREET. The Roman Catholic Church is ever on the watch for opportunities of self-aggrandisement. Were that the special object of the Christian Ministry no other religious body could at all approach the Irish Hierarchy. Out of the terrors and horrors of the Sinn Fein insurrection it is now sought to make capital – to provide for a great and grand Cathedral in the most conspicuous part of Dublin. Sackville Street is the most central thoroughfare in the city. It is likewise and naturally the city's most important business rendezvous. The patriots transformed the greater part of its fine trading establishments and offices into heaps of bricks and rubbish. The result is pitiful, a deplorable picture of desolation.

St Mary's Church, known also as St Mary's Pro-Cathedral, Dublin.

The British Government is about to make amends for the criminal neglect of Mr. Birrell which led up to the devastation and allot some three millions of money for the clearance of the ground, the rebuilding of premises, and the reestablishment of the merchants and others whose property was so cruelly destroyed. Now enters upon the scene the very worthy and vigilant Roman Catholic Archbishop of Dublin. Referring to the new planning scheme which has been engaging attention for some time his Grace says: - my interest in the project lay chiefly in its connection with the opportunity it seemed to afford for making at all events a beginning of the work of providing us with a Catholic Cathedral in Dublin and of thus filling the gap created centuries ago in the provision for public worship in of the city by the transfer of our old Cathedrals of Saint Patrick's and Christ Church to the use of our Protestant fellow citizens.

June 1st 1916. CORRUPTION OF MAGISTRATES. Sir Morgan O'Connell, Killarney, in his evidence said that scores of men had been put on the Bench in Kerry who are not fit for the position of J. P. and they only attended sittings of Petty Sessions to carry out the most open and flagrant jobbery. The Roman Catholic Bishop of Kerry has issued a pastoral protest against the unabashed corruption of these men as magistrates. Witness put in a copy of the pastoral. He entered a protest against certain statements which Mr. Birrell made in his evidence before the Commission. He regarded Mr. Birrell and his government as entirely responsible for the present position of affairs. I.R.

June 1st 1916. CAUSES OF POOR RECRUITING. The reasons for the poor recruiting amongst the farming and shop keeping classes are; 1.Ancient history and prejudice and the attitude of the official Nationalist party up to the outbreak of the war; 2. The Roman Catholic clergy as a body who were on the whole lukewarm on the subject of recruiting; 3.The farmers and shopkeepers had always looked down upon the Army as a profession for their sons; 4. The persistent campaign against recruiting carried out since before the Boer War by the Sinn Fein anti-British party; 5. The spread of the Sinn Fein Irish Volunteer movement; 6. A proportion estimated at over 4,500 of Irish Nationalist Volunteers (Redmondite) who would go over to the Sinn Feiners in the event of conscription. I.R.

June 1st 1916. WHY AUSTRIANS FIGHT HARD. Several Austrian prisoners state that the tenacity of the Austrian soldiers is due to three reasons; first, the enormous difficulties of surrendering without been killed; secondly the risk of being shot by the Austrian machine guns which are kept in the rear of the marching columns; and lastly the prospect of dying of hunger if the war is lost. I.R.

June 1st 1916. £30,000 FOR COUNTY FERMANAGH. PLENTY OF WORK IN TIMBER FOR WAR MUNITIONS. For so far Fermanagh has received little benefit from the huge sums spent on the making of war munitions. The starting of a war munitions factory was talked of but nothing practical was done. Fermanagh is unsuitable for the manufacture of munitions in the ordinary sense of the term but the large amount of timber that grow in different parts of the county are at present a valuable asset and these are now being purchased by the government. Mr. F. R. Brown, F.A.S.I who is an expert in forestry has been appointed by the government for the purchase of timber in the northern quarter of Ireland. Already tracks of forest have been bought and others are in progress of purchase. All the timber bought will have to be sawn locally and this will mean a large circulation of money. The estimated total cost of trees in Fermanagh to be bought is £30,000. The trees from Glenfarne and Glenade and Mr. Faussett's will be brought to Florencecourt station where a powerful engine and saw mill supplied by the government will be erected by Mr. John Humphries of Enniskillen. Mr. Humphreys has been guaranteed five years' work and upwards of 3,000 tons of timber will be forthcoming for this mill for a start. At Inishmore Hall a similar mill will be worked by Mr. Robert Daly; while the existing sawmills will be utilised for the smaller quantities of timber. For instance if a farmer sells 50 or 100 trees in the Maguiresbridge district such trees would be cut by Mr. James Morrison, of Maguiresbridge and the like quantity in the neighbourhood of Enniskillen would come to the local sawmill. The carting and labour in connection with this work will give much local employment. The timber is to be cut into props for mines, sleepers for the railways, and other purposes for the carrying on of the war. I.R.

June 1st 1916. NOTES. Mr. James Quigley, County Surveyor of Meath and a brother of Father Quigley of the orphanage, Bundoran, is to be tried before a court martial in Dublin for taking part in the recent rebellion.

Second-Lieutenant Edwin White, Royal Irish Rifles, of Lisbellaw, is at present in hospital suffering from shell shock, this being his second wound within a month. Second Lieutenant McMeekin, 12th Inniskillings, who left for the front a few weeks ago, is also suffering from shell shock.

Russian Military Cross. Mrs. Carney, Abbey Street, Enniskillen has received from the government the Cross of the order of Saint George which had been awarded to her son Sergeant James Carney, 27th Inniskillings, who unfortunately did not live to receive the decoration which was awarded for rescuing a wounded comrade in October, 1914. Sergeant Carney was killed in January last.

In loving remembrance of my dear brother 26658 Thomas Cassidy 7th Royal Inniskilling Fusiliers a native of a Irvinestown who was killed in action on April 27. R.I.P

Died of wounds on the 29th of April Private Francis Donnelly 8th Royal Inniskillings in action in France aged 19 years. He had lived in Market Street

Russian Military Cross

Enniskillen and had four brothers in the army. His death is deeply deplored by his comrades and by all who knew him. I.R.

Fermanagh Herald June 3rd 1916. THE PORTOBELLO BARRACKS CASE. Replying to Mr. Dillon and Mr. Devlin, Mr. Asquith said – As far as I am aware Sheehy-Skeffington, Dixon, and McIntyre were the only prisoners shot in Portobello Barrack. The officer who is alleged to be responsible is about to be tried by court martial and the proceedings will be public. The matter is, therefore, sub judice and until the trial is over I cannot determine the precise scope or our method of the inquiry which I promised.

Fermanagh Herald June 3rd 1916. ON THE EVE OF HIS EXECUTION P. H. PEARCE, PRESIDENT OF THE IRISH REPUBLIC WROTE HIS LAST LETTER. This letter was written from Kilmainham Prison to his mother: - My Dearest Mother – I have been hoping up to now that it would be possible to see you, but that does not seem possible. Goodbye, dear, dear mother. Through you goodbye to Wow-Wow, M.B., Willie, Miss Byrne, Michael, cousin Maggie, and everyone at St. Enda's. I hope and believe that Willie and St. Enda's boys will be safe. I have written two papers about financial affairs, and one about my books, which I want you to get. With them are poems which I want added to the poems and manuscripts in the big bookcase. You asked me to write a little poem which would seem to be said by you about me. I have written it, and one copy is in Arbour Hill Barracks with the other papers, and Fr. Aloysius has taken charge of another copy of it. I have just received Holy Communion. I am happy except for the great grief of parting from you. This is the death I should have asked for, if God had given me the choice, of all other deaths – to die a soldier's death for Ireland and for freedom. We have done right. People will say hard things about us now, but later on they will praise us. Do not grieve for all this, but think of it as a sacrifice which God asked of me and off you. Goodbye, again, dear mother. May God bless you for your great love for me and for your great faith, and may He remember all you have so bravely suffered. I hope soon to see papa, and in a little while we shall all be together again. Willie, Mary Bridget, and mother, goodbye. I have no words to tell you of my love of you and how my heart yearns to you all. I will call to you in my heart at the last moment. Your son, Pat. (Wow-Wow was a pet name for a sister. Willie, above referred to, a brother, was afterwards executed.)

June 8th 1916. LORD KITCHENER DROWNED AT SEA OFF THE ORKNEYS WITH ALL HIS STAFF ON HIS WAY TO RUSSIA. We deeply regret to announce that H.M.S. 'Hampshire' with Lord Kitchener and his staff of seven on board was sunk on Monday night about 8.00 to the west of the Orkneys either by a mine or a torpedo. Four boats were seen by observers on shore to leave the ship. Patrol vessels and destroyers at once proceeded to the spot and a party was sent along the coast to search. Only some bodies, that of Lord Kitchener's Secretary and a capsized boat have been found up to the present. At the time of his death Lord Kitchener was on his way to Russia, whither he was going at the special invitation of the Russian Emperor on an important mission, and also to confer with the military authorities. He was, it is understood going to Archangel, and thence to Petrograd. He was expected back in London for the reassembling of Parliament. I.R.

Lord Kitchener

June 8th 1916. GREAT NAVAL FIGHT BETWEEN THE BRITISH AND GERMAN FLEETS WITH HEAVY LOSSES ON BOTH SIDES. OUR BATTLESHIPS SWEEP THE SEAS AND THE GERMANS WITHDRAW TO THEIR BASE WITH TREMENDOUS LOSS OF LIFE. On the afternoon of Wednesday 31st of May a naval engagement took place off the coast of Jutland. The British ships on which the brunt of the fighting fell were the Battle Cruiser Fleet and some cruisers and light cruisers supported by four fast battleships. Among those losses were heavy. The German Battle Fleet aided by low visibility avoided a prolonged action with our main forces and soon after these appeared on the scene the enemy returned to port though not before receiving severe damage from our battleships. The battle cruisers *Queen Mary*, *Indefatigable*, *Invincible* and the cruisers *Defence* and *Black Prince* were sunk. The *Warrior* was disabled and soon after being towed for some time had to be abandoned by her crew. It is also known that the destroyers *Tipperary*, *Turbulent*, *Fortune*, *Sparrowhawk*, and *Ardent* were lost and six others are not yet accounted for. F.T.

June 8th 1916. A NATION IN MOURNING. THE BRITISH EMPIRE IS IN THE MOURNING. Our most illustrious a soldier, our greatest military organiser and administrator Earl Kitchener of Khartoum has been tragically removed from amongst us by the ruthless hand of death. Not only throughout our own nation but amongst all our Allies in the field this deplorable news has created a deep and most painful impression. Public opinion everywhere has been inexpressibly shocked and oppressed by the lamentable intelligence. His strong, yet silent, personality, his iron determination, his calm imperturbability in the face of danger imparted strength, confidence and a sense of security to his colleagues in the War Office and to the great masses of our people amongst whom he was held not only in the most profound respect but in positive affection. F.T.

June 8th 1916. EXTRAORDINARY WAGES. GLASGOW PLUMBERS DEMANDS THE HIGHEST EVER KNOWN. At a mass meeting of Glasgow plumbers it was unanimously resolved to make a demand for an advance of twopence per hour which would bring the wages up to 1 shilling I penny per hour – the highest ever known in the trade. This would also be the highest rate of wages in the building trade. F.T.

June 8th 1916. CURIOUS FIND AT CLOGHER. MAN'S BODY DISCOVERED IN BOG. An extraordinary find was made by Mr. David Robinson, farmer during turf cutting operations in Annagarvey bog near Clogher last week. About 5 feet from the surface Mr. Robinson's spade struck some hard substance. He and his men then discovered that it was the remains of a horse's head. Searching further they were somewhat horrified to find alongside, the intact skeleton of a man lying face upwards and with two stones half a hundredweight each placed on the legs. The teeth were perfectly sound. The men raised the remains and were quite satisfied as to them being those of a fully developed man before they reinterred them. The affair has caused a good deal of curious surprise locally as no light can be thrown on the affair. F.T.

June 8th 1916. MILITARY NOTES. PORTORA'S SPLENDID RECORD. We learn from the current issue of 'Portora' the ably edited and interesting little magazine published in connection with the Portora Royal School that 189 'old boys' are serving with the colours. It is felt that the list is far from complete and it is earnestly requested that those who know of any 'old boys' who have joined will send particulars to the Editor. Of the 189 with the colours 17 have been killed in action, three have died from wounds, 12 have been wounded, and two have been wounded and are prisoners of war. Amongst the honours won by Portora boys are the following: - one Distinguished Conduct Medal, two Military Crosses, while six 'old boys' have been mentioned in dispatches. This is truly a splendid record and should make Enniskillen more proud than ever of their local Royal School. F.T.

June 8th 1916. WHAT ARE OUR 5,041,000 SOLDIERS DOING? Much attention has been paid to Mr. Winston Churchill's remarkable speech in the Commons last week in which he asked, 'Where are our five million men?' Mr. Churchill's speech was almost the first practical contribution we have yet had to the question of the supply and use of the men for the army, says the *Manchester Guardian*. Here is what Mr. Churchill said: - 'The thing that struck a visitor to our armies in France or Flanders and no doubt our Armies in the east were in a similar condition, was the very large number of officers and men in the prime of their military manhood, who never went or only very rarely went under the fire of the enemy. In fact they perceived one of the clearest and one of the grimmest class distinctions ever drawn in this world – the distinction between the trench population and the non-trench population. All our soldiers, officers and men are brave and honest and were doing their duty but the fact remains that the trench population lived almost continually under the fire of the enemy; it returned again and again after being wounded twice sometimes three times and was continually subjected to the hardest of tests men had ever been called upon to bear while all the time the non-trench population, many of them enjoying better food and getting higher wages than were drawn by the men under fire every day, had also a share of the decorations so disproportionate that it had passed into a byword. F.T.

June 8th 1916. THE GREATEST SEA FIGHT OF ALL TIME OCCURRED on the afternoon and night of Wednesday, May 31 in the North Sea within from 80 to 100 miles off the coast of Jutland (Denmark.) For 22 months the British navy has been longing for the opportunity to get to grips with the German Navy and at last the decoy of Admiral Jellicoe, under the command of Sir David Beatty lured the German High Seas Fleet into the open. The decoy British Fleet consisted of some five battle and light cruisers and some destroyers followed by four battle ships; and when the Germans saw how small in comparison was the force before him to his own mighty fleet he offered battle and firing at a distance of from 5 to 6 miles began. Sir David knew that he was hopelessly outnumbered but he looked to the help of the main British Fleet before he should be discomfited. The German enemy had all the enormous weight of Dreadnought battleships against our cruisers, in addition to great superiority in numbers, the proportion being estimated at 3 to 1 but the British never flinched and the battle proceeded until the German Commander-in-Chief Herr Scheere learned of the approach of the main British Fleet and turned tail at once. Sir David Beattie was 'too many' for him and with the squadron intercepted the flying Germans trying to hold them until his leader would join them; but the Germans forced their way through the line at enormous loss to themselves and with great loss to us and sought shelter behind their minefield and under the guns of their fortresses.

Admiral Jellicoe

When the first news arrived of this great sea fight in which 100 ships were engaged some gloom was occasioned at home by the loss of so many ships and between 5,000 and 6,000 men. The Kaiser was elevated; he ordered Berlin to be beflagged and Germans went wild over their 'victory.' But when the new facts became known that a squadron of ours had given battle to the German Fleet and the squadron had inflicted such losses on the enemy and that the vaunted German Fleet had fled to the security of their harbours leaving our main fleet untouched, the country was able to see in clearer prospective that Sir David had scored a success and proved to the world that the supremacy of the sea still rested with England. I.R.

June 8th 1916. NINETEEN TRAIN LOADS OF DEAD. According to reports from the frontier the Landsturm soldiers in Belgium have had their rifles taken from them and have been armed with old models. The modern weapons obtained are all being sent to the Verdun region, where there is a great need for them. Nineteen trains loaded with dead bodies have arrived at Seraing from the district around Hill 304. The corpses are now being incinerated in the blast furnaces. I.R.

June 8th 1916. SAFE ARRIVAL IN ENNISKILLEN ALTHOUGH HIS SHIP WAS DESTROYED. Seaman Gunner Reid arrived home in Enniskillen on Monday last having escaped a watery grave during the battle in the North Sea last week. He has had an adventurous career during the present war. He has taken part in four big naval battles since the outbreak of the war and has not even a scratch or a flesh tear although he went through the big battle last week off Jutland and saw his ship battered to pieces and left a drifting wreck. He served on the *Glasgow* not only in the fight of Coronal but also in the battle of the Falkland Islands in December 1914. On arrival at home waters the *Glasgow* crew were paid off and Reid was transferred to a destroyer attached to the Home Fleet. Getting nearer to the Germans he was laying the aft gun when two 13 inch shells struck the destroyer amidships smashing up her boilers and turbines and also exploded a torpedo that was about to be discharged. The survivors were picked up by a Norwegian sailing ship and transferred to the destroyer which had succeeded in torpedoing the *Frauenlob*. He tells how each time when in a tight corner and was laying his gun he prayed to God. On occasions he got down on his knees and asked for strength and power to do his best and his prayers were answered. 'I will never laugh about religion again,' he said 'what he had seen, what he had experienced and his near death so often, and the miraculous deliverance he has had, has changed his outlook and made him realise that there is a Power that controls the destinies of men.' (Seamen Gunner Reid is a son of Mr. Reid, Barrack Warden, Main Barracks, Enniskillen.) I.R.

June 8th 1916. ALSO IN THE NORTH SEA FIGHT. Fermanagh was represented in the great naval battle also by Gunner John J. Cullen, A. B., of H.M.S. *Warrior* which played such an important prominent part in the battle. There were nearly 300 Irishmen on the *Warrior* so on sea as well as on land our brave lads faced the enemy in the real Nelson spirit. The Admiralty wired to his father, Constable J. Cullen, Maguiresbridge on Sunday that his son's name was not in the list of casualties and therefore assumed he must be alive and safe. The *Warrior* accounted for two German cruisers and one destroyer and was at one time attacked by six large German ships of Dreadnought class it was nothing short of a miracle how she escaped being sunk at that moment. But she went down when being towed to port. Gunner Cullen succeeded in sinking a German submarine in the North Sea when on a trawler some time ago. I.R.

H.M.S. Warrior

June 8th 1916. AMONG THE KILLED. Midshipman Desmond F. C. L. Tottenham, H.M.S. *Invincible*, killed in action was the second son of Captain C.G.L. Tottenham of Tudenham Park, Westmeath, whose family owned Glenfarne Hall, County Leitrim before it was occupied by the late Sir Edward Harland, of Belfast. Captain Gore is a cousin of Mr. P. M. Tottenham who was married in 1909 to Miss Angel Archdale, D.L. of Riversdale, County Fermanagh. His son who has now had died for his country was 19 ½ years of age.

Sub lieutenant P. J. Vance, son of Mr. J. G. S. Vance, manager of the Belfast Central branch of the Belfast Bank and formerly of Enniskillen was killed in the battle off the coast of Jutland. He was on the destroyer *Shark* which took a prominent part in the battle. I.R.

June 15th 1916. REBELS OF CORK. When the news of the sea fight got to Cork the Sinn Feiners paraded the streets and nothing was done to stop them. They were rejoicing prematurely over the defeat of the British Navy and also – is it prematurely? - over the German Emperor's gift of Home Rule in Ireland. For let there be no mistake about it, if Home Rule is given to Ireland now it will be a real victory for the Germans. I.R.

June 15th 1916. A GARRISON TRADER COMMITTED TO JAIL AND HIS WIFE WARNED. In the Bankruptcy Court Dublin on Friday before Mr. Justice Pim, the case of Daniel Magee, Garrison County Fermanagh was listed for the examination of witnesses. The bankrupt had carried on a small general store and had been in business six years and had returned his liabilities as about £930, his assets consisting of debts amounting to £80, stock-in-trade £60 and cash in hand of 18s and 6d. It was inconceivable he said where the stock and cash had gone to not to speak of the profits that had been made upon the goods. The bankrupt and his wife were examined and the former stated he had been married 12 months. He admitted that portion of his goods were stored away in the house of a man named Carson. Several bags had been left in his house. Several chests of tea had also been left with his brother James Magee. An anonymous letter signed 'Observer' called attention to other houses in which goods were concealed but the witness said to his knowledge there was no stock in the places indicated. He lent about £50 to a man O'Connor who he said spent it backing horses and then went away. He attributed his failure to his own mismanagement of his affairs. When he was failing he sought to join the army but he would not be taken. It was not true to say that he had plenty of money. He could not explain now where his goods had gone to. Mr. Justice Pim made an order for the committal of the bankrupt and with regard to his wife he said he did not believe a word of what she had sworn. She would have to come before him again and would have to tell the truth or go to jail. As to some of the other witnesses he also cautioned them that if they did not make full and true disclosure of what they knew about the bankrupt's stock they would be similarly dealt with. F.T.

June 15th 1916. PROTESTING CONVENTION IN OMAGH. STRONG DISSIDENTING VIEWS OF THE ROMAN CATHOLIC BISHOPS. Rev Monsignor O'Doherty, P.P. presided at the Nationalist Convention held in Omagh last week. The Roman Catholic Bishop of Derry wrote: - I heartily join my voice with you in protesting against any proposal that would be inconsistent with the ideal of an Ireland one and undivided which Nationalist Ulster has ever kept before her in the strenuous part she had of necessity to play in the struggle for Home Rule during the past quarter of a century. One could hardly believe any responsible statesman would make the suggestions you dread unless he wanted to alienate the goodwill of Nationalist Ireland. I would like to know on what principle the destinies of three such Nationalist proportions as Tyrone, Fermanagh and Derry City are to be sacrificed to the treasonable threats of Sir Edward Carson and his followers. F.T.

June 15th 1916. STATE PURCHASE OF PUBLIC HOUSES. A £250,000 EXPERIMENT. The Carlisle and District Licensing Vintners Association have received a communication from the Liquor Control Board intimating that they had decided it is necessary to control liquor traffic in the Western Border area. They intend to acquire compulsorily or by agreement premises in the area in respect of licenced premises and breweries in Carlisle and neighbourhood. Drunkenness has been greatly on the increase in Carlisle recently and the chief constable said some days ago that for the last month there had been 100 convictions, which was a record for the city.

Ed. Huge munitions facilities were near Carlisle and greatly increased wages led to more drinking. H.M. Factory, Gretna (or officially, His Majesty's Factory, Gretna) was the UK's largest Cordite factory during World War I. The government-owned facility was adjacent to the Solway Firth, near Gretna, Dumfries and Galloway. It was built by the Ministry of Munitions in direct response to the Shell Crisis of 1915. H.M. Factory, Gretna stretched 12 miles (19 km) from Mossband near Longtown in the east, to Dornock / Eastriggs in the west straddling the Scottish / English border. The facility consisted of four large production sites and two purpose-built townships. The facility had its own independent transport network, power source, and water supply system. To prevent problems with the influx of navvies and munition workers, authorities implemented the introduction of the State Management Scheme which curtailed alcohol sales through the nationalisation of pubs and breweries in the vicinity. Munitions production started in April 1916. By 1917 the largest proportion of the workforce was women: 11,576 women to 5,066 men. At its peak, the factories produced 800 tons (812 tonne) of Cordite RDB per week, more than all the other munitions plants in Britain combined. Cordite was colloquially known as the "Devil's Porridge"; the name comes from Sir Arthur Conan Doyle who wrote in 1917: "The nitro-glycerine on the one side and the gun-cotton on the other are kneaded into a sort of a devil's porridge".) I.R.

June 15th 1916. QUEEN MARY'S SINKING. A gunlayer of the battle cruiser *Tiger* which participated in the recent North Sea battle says – at 4.00 in the afternoon of the engagement every man in the British battle cruiser squadron, each vessel of which had been singling out by an opposing vessel, realised that the Germans had not only a preponderance of guns but more than double the number of vessels. They commenced a concentrated fire and every gun of the German Squadron was first turned on the *Lion* but hardly a shell hit her although two asphyxiating projectiles fell on her upper deck. Later the German guns were concentrated on the *Queen Mary*. They had been poking about for some minutes without effect. Then every shell that the Germans threw seemed suddenly to strike at the battle cruisers at once. It was as if a whirlwind were smashing a forest and reminded one very much of the rending that is heard where a big vessel is launched and the stays are being smashed. A minute and a half and all that could be seen of the *Queen Mary* was her keel and then that disappeared. We were engaged at 15,000 yards by two battleships in addition to some half dozen submarines which were popping up everywhere. The loss of one submarine is given out but I know two were sunk - one had been rammed by a British battleship while the *New Zealander* blew another to pieces with her quick-firers. I.R.

June 15th 1916. PAINFUL DISCLOSURES ABOUT THE BELLEEK LACE CLASS. A remarkable discussion took place at the meeting of the Fermanagh Technical Committee on Friday last as to the present situation of the Committee's class in Belleek, occasioned by the illness of the teacher there a Mrs. Gallacher. The complaints against her were twofold. That she got herself into such a condition in which she became ill; and that her cash was £50 short. Mrs. Gallacher is now a Mrs. McBrien. Father McMahon said she had since been married morally and licitly to McBrien who was a Protestant and now a Roman Catholic. That was the cause of the whole matter today and it was most unjust he said. I.R.

June 22nd 1916. DEATHS. Second Lieutenant W. O. E. Morris. We learn as we go to press, of Second Lieutenant Morris, the King's Liverpool Regiment (8th), second son of Captain and Quartermaster W. A. Morris, 1st Inniskillings was killed in action on the 17th Inst. in France. Second Lieutenant Corscadden, Royal Irish Rifles whose death is announced as a result of wounds was the youngest son of Mr. P Corscadden, Hollymount, near Manorhamilton, County Leitrim, and was 27 years old. I.R.

June 22nd 1916. SPHAGNUM MOSS DRESSINGS. The manufacture of Sphagnum Moss Dressings in Ulster for the use of our wounded soldiers has grown since the outbreak of the war until it is now an enterprise of the greatest importance, the dressings having been found to be of the highest value in the treatment of wounds. The matter of the regulation of the supply of moss and the coordination of the various working parties has been before the Director General of Voluntary Organisation and he has authorised the setting up of a Provincial Association for this purpose. Meanwhile the Fermanagh War Guild under the presidency of Mrs. Archdale of Riversdale has been gathering quantities of it in this country; and we learn from the letters of Mr. G. A. Millihan of the Sphagnum Moss Depot that their fortnightly supplies to the War Hospitals Supply Committee is particularly good and well picked. There is a good moss and inferior moss and the Fermanagh Guild have been particular to send only the best quality well picked. I.R.

June 22nd 1916. WHAT WILL THE CLERGY DO? A great deal will depend in the National Conference in Belfast tomorrow on the action of the clergy. Of these about 150 will be present and the complaint is already made that more than one priest will not be admitted from one parish, when all the Nationalist District Councilors are being admitted. If the clergy and the officials of the Hibernians and the Foresters were of one mind they could carry the meeting. The Ulster Roman Catholic Bishops have according to Dr. McHugh of Derry decided against the proposals; and if this be so, we may expect that all the clergy will be hostile. The fear with them is that education may pass out of the hands of the clergy into lay hands in the six counties under the new condition of things which is a purely imaginary grievance as there will not be a separate Ulster Government; and it is much more likely to come into operation at an early date under an Irish Parliament in Dublin, for no secret has been made of the intention of Irish laymen to take the control of education out of the hands of clerical managers and place it on a new basis. I.R.

July 1916

Fermanagh Herald July 1st 1916. TYRONE, FERMANAGH, AND DERRY CITY. 265 of the delegates who attended the Conference in Belfast on Friday last registered their votes against the ill-conceived and preposterous proposal to exclude six Ulster counties from the operation of the Home Rule Act, and thus proved to the world that the spirit of Irish Nationality is indestructible. By a majority of 210 the delegates consented to the proposal to cut up Ireland into fragments, but the vast majority of the men of Tyrone, Fermanagh and Derry City stood out resolutely against the Lloyd-Georgian scheme and showed that no influence, no matter how strong, or no argument no matter how eloquent, could lessen the intensity of their devotion to the National ideal – the right of the Irish people to full self-government. In another column we published an analysis of the voting, from which it will be seen that 52 Tyrone delegates voted for exclusion and 102 against, that 28 Fermanagh delegates voted for and 51 against, and that only seven of the delegates of Derry City voted for the proposal, when 30 declared against it. By a majority of 96 the delegates of the land of the O'Neill's and the Maguires and of the brave and historic City of Derry have emphatically condemned the attempt which is being made to deprive them of their National rights.

July 6th 1916. MILITARY NOTES. The *Winnipeg Telegram* announces that Brigadier General L. J. Lipsett of Winnipeg who belongs to an old Ballyshannon family has been promoted to be commander of the Third Canadian Division to succeed Major General Mercer who was killed a few weeks ago. General Lipsett at the present is in command of a brigade at the front. Formerly a captain in the British Regular Army, General Lipsett was lent to the Canadian Militia Department for the purpose of assisting in military organization. After war broke out he was appointed to command the Nineteenth Regiment afterwards the 8th Battalion which unit under his leadership won undying fame in the great fight at Ypres.

Brigadier General L. J. Lipsett.

Mr. Matthew McManus, Gubrawooly, Swanlinbar has had the misfortune to lose three sons in the war. Private James McManus, Royal Munster Fusiliers; Private Thomas McManus, Royal Munster Fusiliers and Private Patrick McManus, Royal Inniskilling Fusiliers have all died of wounds. A fourth son is serving in the Irish Guards and a fifth has just volunteered for service.

Captain Sir Basil S Brooke, Bart 10th Royal Hussars of Colebrooke, County Fermanagh has had the honour of being received at Buckingham Palace and decorated with the Military Cross awarded to him on the occasion of the King's birthday, in recognition of his gallantry and devotion to duty in the field. F.T.

July 6th 1916. DEATH OF THE RIGHT HON EDWARD ARCHDALE. Amongst all sections of the community throughout Fermanagh the announcement of the death of the Right Hon Edward Archdale, P.C., Castle Archdale will be read with unfeigned regret. He had been ailing for a short time and in the doctor's hands but no person suspected that the end was near so that the news when it became known on Tuesday created somewhat of a shock among his many friends. Being the head of the Archdale family in Fermanagh he was held in universal respect by people of all religions and political persuasion. In 1908 he married Mrs. Elizabeth Clark, daughter of the late Nicholas Harwood, H.M. Dockyard, Pembroke and widow of Captain Wingfield Clark, Leicestershire Regiment. Prior to 1880 he had been engaged as a civil engineer laying submarine cables in various parts of the world. When the Wyndham Land Act came into operation in 1903 he was the first landlord in Ireland to give his tenants the advantages of that measure and sold to them on very reasonable terms which were afterwards quoted and taken as a standard for all the rest of the country. In religious matters the late Mr. Archdale was an earnest and enthusiastic member of the Church of Ireland and some years ago build and presented to the Parish of Castle Archdale at his own expense one of the most beautiful little churches in Ireland. F.T.

July 6th 1916. SOME STRIKING GAINS. EIGHT VILLAGES ARE TAKEN. On a front of 25 miles the Allies on the western front commenced the expected great offensive on the extreme right of the British line and left of the French and on both sides of the Somme early on Saturday morning. The artillery preparation by the British for the subsequent infantry assault is described as altogether unparalleled. 7 miles of trenches have been captured by the British on a front of about 20 miles north of the Somme. I.R.

July 6th 1916. A PRUSSIAN BATTALION SURRENDERS. On Monday an entire battalion of the 186th Regiment of the Prussian Infantry surrendered to the British near Fricourt. The Battalion had been rushed up to replace very heavy casualties. On detraining it was at once moved into the trenches. After a short show of resistance 20 officers and 600 men of the Prussian Battalion left the trenches and came towards the British taking signs of surrender. The battalion was chiefly drawn from the Upper Rhine. I.R.

July 6th 1916. TRIBUTE TO ULSTER DIVISION. MAGNIFICENT IN ATTACK. General Sir George Richardson, K.C.B. commanding the UVF has received a letter dated 30th of June from Major General Nugent commanding the Ulster Division in which the following passage occurs. 'Before you get this we shall have put the banner of the Ulster Division to the supreme test. I have no fear of the result. I am certain no general in the army out here has a finer Division, fitter and cleaner. I am certain they will be magnificent in attack and we could hardly have had a better date calculated to inspire our men of the north. It makes me very sad to think what the price may be, but I am certain the officers and men reckon nothing of that. (General Nugent's reference is to the 1st of July the original date of the Battle of the Boyne in 1690.)

(Ed. It is currently celebrated on the 12th of July because in 1582 Pope Gregory XIII reformed the Julian calendar because it introduced an error of 1 day every 128 years. The introduction of the Gregorian calendar allowed for the realignment with astronomical events like equinoxes and solstices, however a number of days had to be dropped when the change was made. The Gregorian calendar was not adopted until much later in Great Britain and America. It wasn't until September 1752 that 11 days were dropped to switch to the Gregorian calendar. Although the Gregorian calendar is named after Pope Gregory XIII, it is an adaptation of a calendar designed by Italian doctor, astronomer and philosopher Luigi Lilio.) I.R.

July 6th 1916. 250 German dead. A British soldier wounded in the course of one of our raids into the enemy's territory says that when he and his comrades invaded the German trenches they counted 250 dead. The reconnoitering party pushed ahead to the second line without meeting any resistance. There they found a few of the enemy who had survived the bombardment and gas attacks. They surrendered without hesitation. The party took back to the British lines 60 prisoners, two machine guns, and one bomb thrower. The methodical destruction of the enemy's defence works is proceeding according to schedule, the bombardment intended to level the German trenches being particularly active on that section of the front line between Ypres and Albert, (where our 11th Battalion have been.) In one of their more daring raids on the 1st the men repulsed a counterattack in the open and got as far as the last line of enemy trenches. The corpses there all gave evidence of the efficacy of the gas sent forward from the British lines. Saturday was an excellent day for Sir Douglas Haig's forces and the Duke of Wurttemberg and the Crown Prince of Bavarian are not likely to forget the losses inflicted on them by our heavy cannon, field guns and trench mortars. The French military experts assert that the 'Tommies' are marvelous. They feel confident knowing that there is no scarcity of munitions. I.R.

July 6th 1916. WHY IT SHOULD NOT BE SO? A VERSE WITH MORAL.
By 2629 Sargent C. Maguire force RI. Inniskilling Fusiliers.

Brave Father Pat and Parson Sloane
Went out to France together,
And in the muddy trenches there,
Faced wild and stormy weather
The men received them with a smile,
For both despite their station,
Would always help a needy one
No matter his 'Persuasion.'

For instance parson Sloane would rush
Without regard to danger,
Across some bullet strewn ground
To help a Connaught Ranger,
And Father Pat himself was known
To stretch a helping hand
When the battle-roar was loudest
Just to save an Ulster man.

And thus we get the moral
As it rushes o'er the foam,
If Irishmen unite in France
Why not the same at home. I.R.

July 13th 1916. ULSTER MEN'S GALLANTRY A GLOWING TRIBUTE THAT WILL BE REMEMBERED AS LONG AS HISTORY IS READ. *The Times* special correspondent at the British Headquarters in a dispatch on the great offensive says – back on the high ground behind, the enemy had massed an immense amount of artillery – guns ranging from 77 mm to 250 mm in size. At one point there was a mass of machine gun positions dug into the ground behind. Above this point were other machine guns. Against this front our men charged under a fire that cannot be described or imagined without one man faltering or turning back. It was as splendid as any action of human bravery could be. Above this point the Ulster troops behaved in a way that will be remembered as long as history is read or written. It is said that the Royal Irish Fusiliers were first out of the trenches. The Royal Irish Rifles went through what was an absolute hell, went over the German parapets and killed the men in the machine gun emplacements with their bayonets. The Inniskillings rushed and cleared out certain positions in the enemy's lines which had been named respectively as 'Enniskillen' 'Omagh' and 'Strabane' and it is said that they all went forward shouting 'no surrender' and 'remember the Boyne.' They were subject to a murderous crossfire. I.R.

July 13th 1916. ENNISKILLEN MAN'S ACCOUNT OF THE ULSTER DIVISION TO ATTACK. Lance Corporal J. Quinn, Royal Irish Rifles (Ulster Division) writing to his father, Mr. Thomas Quinn, The Diamond, Enniskillen describing the great advance says: - I expect you had word from Willie. He was wounded in the arm during the attack. I got out all right but it was a proper hell. The machine guns mowed our fellows down like sheep. Poor George Geddes was killed beside us. Our Colonel was also killed and all our company officers either killed or wounded. We went in with over 200 men in the company and came back with 57 but we took four lines of the "Allemandes" trenches. The --- Battalion (Fermanagh and Donegal Regiment) got it pretty bad too. I saw a lot of them lying killed over the top. I did not come across Tommy Johnson (Drummee) and nobody can tell me anything about him. I saw William Nelson, son of Mrs. Nelson, East Bridge Street, Enniskillen. He was wounded in the foot and leg. You could not have but pity for the poor devils the Germans. They ran out to us with their hands up and begged for mercy. Some of them got the bayonet. One poor fellow had the two eyes blown out of his head and he was a frightful looking case. We took about 1,000 prisoners altogether. They never even showed fight when we tackled them but they laid down their arms and begged for mercy. Our poor Colonel refused to stay behind. He led us into the charges and about halfway across got the head carried off him by a shell. Our fellows fairly went mad over it and showed the 'Allemande' no mercy. We carried out all we were asked to do with honour. Our division has made a name for itself. Our troops are progressing splendidly now and have taken four or five villages. You need not worry about Willie as I saw him when he was getting his arm dressed. He got hit about the muscle of the arm by a machine gun bullet. I had some miraculous escapes myself. I was hit six times with pieces of shrapnel but none did me any harm. Thank God we are both safe. F.T.

July 13th 1916. OBITUARY. The death of Admiral Sir St. George Caulfield D'Arcy-Irvine K.C.B. has taken place at Aixles-Bains. He was the third son of the Rev George Marcus Irvine and grandson of Major George Marcus Irvine of Castle Irvine. Born in 1833 he entered the Navy in 1845 and served in the River San Juan Expedition in Nicaragua and in the Black Sea and Baltic during the Crimean war; went up the Dardanelles during the Turco-Russian War of 1878 and commanded the *Penelope* at the bombardment of Alexandria. As Senior Lieutenant on the *Doris* he escorted King Edward as Prince of Wales during his tour in the East in 1862. He was second in command of the Channel Squadron in 1888/9. He married in 1868 the only daughter of Admiral Sir Horatio Austin. F.T.

July 13th 1916. LINE THINNED BUT UNWAVERING. BY AN EYEWITNESS. I am not an Ulsterman but on Saturday, the 1st of July as I followed their amazing attack I felt that I would rather be an Ulsterman than anything else in the world. My position enabled me to watch the commencement of their attack from the wood in which they had formed up but which long prior to the hour of the assault was being overwhelmed with shell fire so that the trees were stripped and the top half of the wood ceased to be anything but a slope of bare stumps with numerous shell holes peppered in the chalk. It looked as if nothing could live in the wood and indeed the losses were heavy, before they started two companies of one battalion being sadly reduced in the assembly trenches.

When I saw that the men emerge through the smoke and form up as if on parade I could hardly believe my eyes. Then I saw them attack beginning at a slow walk over No Man's Land and then suddenly let loose as they charged over the two front lines of the enemy trenches shouting 'no surrender boys!' The enemy gunfire raked them from the left and machine guns in the village enfiladed them on the right but battalion after battalion came out of the awful wood as steadily as I have seen them at Ballykinlar, Clandeboys or Shane's Castle. The enemy's third line was soon taken and still the waves went on getting thinner and thinner but without hesitation. The enemy's fourth line fell before these men who would not be stopped. There remained the fifth line.

Representatives of the neighbouring corps and division who could not withhold their praise that what they had seen said no human beings could get to it until the flanks of the Ulster division were cleared. This was recognized and the attack on the last German line was countermanded. The order arrived too late or perhaps the Ulstermen mindful that was the anniversary of the Boyne would not be denied but pressed on between three fires. I could only see a small portion of this advance but could watch our men work forward seemingly to escape the shell fire by a miracle and I saw parties of them now much reduced indeed enter the fifth line of the enemy trenches our final objective. It could not be held so that the Ulstermen were the target of the concentrated hostile guns and machine guns behind and on both flanks though the enemy in front were vanquished and retreating. The order was given to retire but some preferred to die in the ground they had won so hardly. As I write they still hold the German first two lines and occasionally batches of German prisoners are passed back over the deadly zone; over 500 have arrived but the Ulster men took many more who did not survive the fire of their own German guns. My pen cannot describe adequately the hundreds of heroic acts that I witnessed. I.R.

July 13th 1916. A SOLEMN TIME. IN BELFAST on yesterday afternoon for 5 minutes the whole city ceased to move. All the tramcars, pedestrians, and machinery stopped for 5 minutes to permit relatives of soldiers and others to think of what all our brave boys at the war were doing for us at home. Blinds were drawn; policemen stood to attention, and many thousands uttered a prayer, till the hand of the clock relieved the mournful strain. I.R.

"The Battle of the Somme". HistoryLearningSite.co.uk. 2014. Web.
The Battle of the Somme started in July 1st 1916. It lasted until November 1916. For many people, the Battle of the Somme was the battle that symbolised the horrors of warfare in World War One; this one battle had a marked effect on overall casualty figures and seemed to epitomise the futility of trench warfare. For many years those who led the British campaign have received a lot of criticism for the way the Battle of the Somme was fought – especially Douglas Haig. This criticism was based on the appalling casualty figures suffered by the British and the French. By the end of the battle, the British Army had suffered 420,000 casualties including nearly 60,000 on the first day alone. The French lost 200,000 men and the Germans nearly 500,000. Ironically, going over the top at the Somme was the first taste of battle many of these men had, as many were part of "Kitchener's Volunteer Army" persuaded to volunteer by posters showing Lord Kitchener himself summoning these men to arms to show their patriotism.

Why was the battle fought? For a number of months the French had been taking severe losses at Verdun – to the east of Paris. To relieve the French, the Allied High Command decided to attack the Germans to the north of Verdun therefore requiring the Germans to move some of their men away from the Verdun battlefield thus relieving the French. After the war, Sir William Robertson, Chief of the Imperial General Staff, explained what this strategy was: Remembering the dissatisfaction of ministers at the end of 1915, because the operations had not come up to their expectations, the General Staff took the precaution to make quite clear beforehand the nature of success which the Somme campaign might yield. The necessity of relieving pressure on the French Army at Verdun remains, and is more urgent than ever. This is, therefore, the first objective to be obtained by the combined British and French offensive. The second objective is to inflict as heavy losses as possible upon the German armies.

Ironically, the head of the French Army, General Foch, believed that the attack in the Somme would achieve little - this view was shared by some leading British commanders such as General Henry Rawlinson. However, orders from the army's political masters in London and Paris ensured that the battle would take place.

Just how backward military thinking was then is shown by the fact that the British put a regiment of cavalry on standby when the attack started to exploit the hole that would be created by a devastating infantry attack. British military faith was still being placed on cavalry attacks in 1916 when the nature of war in the previous two years would have clearly indicated that cavalry was no longer viable. This shows how conservative military thinking was during this war. The battle at the Somme started with a weeklong artillery bombardment of the German lines. 1,738,000 shells were fired at the Germans. The logic behind this was so that the artillery guns would destroy the German trenches and barbed wire placed in front of the trenches. The use of artillery was heavily supported by Field Marshall Haig: The enemy's position to be attacked was of a very considerable character, situated on a high, undulating tract of ground. (They had) deep trenches....bomb proof shelters......wire entanglements forty yards broad often as thick as a man's finger. Defences of this nature could only be attacked with the prospect of success after careful artillery preparation. In fact, the Germans had deep dugouts for their men and all they had to do when the bombardment started was to move these men into the relative safety of the deep dugouts. When the bombardment stopped, the Germans would have known that this would have been the signal for an infantry advance. They moved from the safety of their dugouts and manned their machine guns to face the British and French.

18th King George's Own Lancers near Mametz, on the Somme, 15 July 1916.

The British soldiers advanced across a 25-mile front. By the end of the battle, in November 1916, the Allied forces had advanced along a thirty-mile strip that was seven miles deep at its maximum. Lord Kitchener was a supporter of the theory of attrition - that eventually you would grind down your enemy and they would have to yield. He saw the military success of the battle as all-important. However, it did have dire political and social consequences in Britain. Many spoke of the "lost generation". Many people found it difficult to justify the near 88,000 Allied men lost for every one mile gained in the advance. However, during the battle, media information on the battle was less than accurate. This was written by John Irvine of the "Daily Express" on July 3rd 1916 - though his report would have been scrutinised by the British military and government and he could only have used what information the military gave him.

"A perceptible slackening of our fire soon after seven was the first indication given to us that our gallant soldiers were about to leap from their trenches and advance against the enemy. Non-combatants, of course, were not permitted to witness this spectacle, but I am informed that the vigour and eagerness of the first assault were worthy of the best traditions of the British Army. We had not to wait long for news, and it was wholly satisfactory and encouraging. The message received at ten o'clock ran something like this: "On a front of twenty miles north and south of the Somme, we and our French allies have advanced and taken the German first line of trenches. We are attacking vigorously Fricourt, la Boiselle and Mametz. German prisoners are surrendering freely, and a good many already fallen into our hands."

"The Daily Chronicle" published a similar report on the battle on July 3rd: At about 7.30 o'clock this morning a vigorous attack was launched by the British Army. The front extends over some 20 miles north of the Somme. The assault was preceded by a terrific bombardment, lasting about an hour and a half. It is too early to as yet give

anything but the barest particulars, as the fighting is developing in intensity, but the British troops have already occupied the German front line. Many prisoners have already fallen into our hands, and as far as can be ascertained our casualties have not been heavy.

However, those who fought there knew what really happened - if they survived: 'The next morning (July 2nd) we gunners surveyed the dreadful scene in front of us......it became clear that the Germans always had a commanding view of No Man's Land. (The British) attack had been brutally repulsed. Hundreds of dead were strung out like wreckage washed up to a high water-mark. Quite as many died on the enemy wire as on the ground, like fish caught in the net. They hung there in grotesque postures. Some looked as if they were praying; they had died on their knees and the wire had prevented their fall. Machine gun fire had done its terrible work.' George Coppard, machine gunner at the Battle of the Somme.

In the course of the battle, 51 Victoria Crosses were won by British soldiers. 31 were won by NCO's and 20 by officers. Of these 51 medals, 17 were awarded posthumously - 10 to NCO's and 7 to officers.

July 13th 1916. THE FUNERAL OF MR. ARCHDALE. A BRIEF ACCOUNT OF THE FAMILY. The funeral of the Right Hon. Edward Archdale, P. C., H. M. Lieutenant for County Tyrone, took place on Friday last, amid every demonstration of public respect. The country gentry, the clergy, the farmers of the Archdale Estate and the general public were largely represented. A brief service was held in the church of Castle Archdale in which the Right Rev. Morris Day, D. D., Bishop of Clogher, the Rev. R. Watson, rector of the parish, Rev Canon Ruddell, Clones and Rev. C Robinson, D.D. rector of Magheraculmoney took part. The choir sang hymns suitable to the occasion.

The Bishop in the course of a brief address said they had all lost a very dear friend in Edward Archdale. His acquaintance with the deceased began about eight years ago at the consecration of that church which deceased had built for the Glory of God and for the worshippers of the parish. He had never met a more conscientious gentleman and the deceased was an earnest faithful simple-minded Christian and may God grant that his good work commenced an earth would be continued he added. The Dead March from Saul was played as the coffin was borne out of the church and the interment took place in the Archdale burying ground at Templemaghery.

St. Patrick's, Castle Archdale

The Archdall family is one of the most influential and distinguished in the north west of Ireland. It is just over three centuries since John Archdale; the founder came to Fermanagh from Norfolk, having received a grant of several hundred acres from Elizabeth. The patent granting these lands was dated 13th of July, 1612. The said John Archdale married the daughter of Sir William Temple, Knight, who was provost of Trinity College Dublin and four years after his arrival in the county was its High Sheriff in 1616. The estate before its sale under the Irish Land Purchase Act in 1904 grew greatly in dimensions and extended well into County Tyrone.

Castle Archdale

The history of the family since its arrival from Norfolk is in many respects the history of Fermanagh. Since the Act of Union a member of the family down to 1885 when new forces came into operation sat continuously as one of its parliamentary representatives. The chain was only once broken in 1802 for a short period of three years. Mr. Mervyn Archdall, a general in the army and Lieutenant Governor of the Isle of Wight, who was born in 1763, sat in 11 Parliaments for the county and on his death in 1839 representation passed to a nephew. Mr. W. Archdale was elected at the general election of 1874 and held it until 1885 when he was displaced by Mr. William Redmond M. P. Mr. W. Archdale died in 1899 and was succeeded by Edward Archdale who broke the tradition of the family by never being elected to the House of Commons. He sold the entire estates in 1904 and devoted himself to farming upon his own account. He also broke the family tradition in politics becoming an ardent Liberal and Home Ruler. He was appointed Lord Lieutenant of Tyrone in 1913 on the death of the Earl of Belmore. I.R.

July 13th 1916. NOTES. A big cattle drive by about 500 men and women in County Roscommon, last week shows a revival of the revolutionary spirit.

Glasgow Corporation having passed a demand for total prohibition of excisable liquor, the Central Control Board do not think, with the danger of shebeening, that the demand can be completed at the present moment. Our Royal Flying Corps has rendered admirable services in the fight of the Somme. Nine German 'sausages' were destroyed inside two weeks and our airships have harassed the enemy night and day in some cases coming down to within 900 feet of the ground and shelling regiments in hiding places.

A gold stripe is to be permitted to be sown on the uniform of every officer or man wounded during the present war.

Aerial torpedoes, a British invention, are working destruction on German trenches and dugouts. Examination of wounded Italian soldiers has proved conclusively that the Austrian enemy use expanding bullets, as did the Sinn Feiners in the rising. I.R.

July 13th 1916. MAGUIRESBRIDGE. The committee of the Maguiresbridge U.L.L. unanimously condemned the action of the Irish Party in dealing with the Ulster question and called upon the member for Fermanagh to safeguard the interests of the county. They also condemned 'the corner boy tactics of the Belfast oligarchy' and add 'whereas there were only 84 delegates entitled to vote for Fermanagh and as all possible voters did not attend and whereas 94 votes were recorded, we are at a loss to know how the extra votes were obtained or if the oligarchy have adopted plural voting for Ireland.' A meeting to further the interest of the forthcoming gathering in Derry was held in the Lisnaskea Chapel grounds, the Rev Thomas Duffy, P.P. in the chair. Only six parishioners went for exclusion. I.R.

July 13th 1916. SUSPENSION OF THE 12TH. A MESSAGE TO ORANGEMEN. Sir James H. Strong, Bart., Tynan Abbey, Armagh, in a message to the Orangemen of Ireland, of whom he is Grand Master, states: as I have reason to know that very considerable irritation is being felt at the suspension for this year of the July celebrations, I think it right to state that the unanimous resolution of the Grand Lodge of Ireland was passed after the matter had been considered by all the County Grand Masters and by the Central Committee of the Grand Lodge. The reasons in favour of the decision (which the Lodge most reluctantly came to) appear to be overwhelming. We must avoid anything which might give an excuse for any relaxation of the proclamation in respect of disloyal and doubtful gatherings affecting the peace and security of our friends in the South of Ireland. No one can now hold us responsible for any mistakes that may be made in this respect. I would add that at a time when munition workers in England and Scotland are giving up their holidays any disregard of the wishes of the military authorities would have been looked upon as treason by people with whom we must have a very good character. In conclusion, I would claim for the officers of the Orange Institution a reasonable amount of confidence and consideration in the very difficult duties which we have to discharge at the present time. I.R.

July 13th 1916. THE SACRIFICE. CASUALTIES IN RECENT FIGHTING. HEAVY LOCAL LIST. The recent severe fighting has resulted in heavy casualties in the Ulster Division. Official intimation has not yet come through from the War Office, except in some cases, but the friends of those wounded have received letters or field postcards from those wounded and they also tell of others killed. The list below is far from complete and is not official.

Some of the officers: Captain H. H.G. Butler who is suffering from shell shock is a son of the late Hon. Henry Cavendish Butler, half-brother of the fifth Earl of Lanesborough. Captain Butler's home is at Innis Rath, Lisnaskea and he has been in command of the A. Company 11th Batt., Inniskillings in succession to Major Falls.

Captain J. S. Myles who has been wounded is the second son of the late Mr. John Myles, merchant, Ballyshannon, and has played a prominent part in recent years in the progress of that town in which has as well as in Bundoran, he installed electric light. He was a stalwart rugby forward and member of the Ulster team that some years ago played a series of matches in Canada where he had the misfortune to have an ankle severely injured.

Captain W. T. Sewell missing believed killed was serving in the 11th Inniskillings.

Captain B St. G French killed came to the Royal Inniskilling Fusiliers early in the present year.

Captain W.S.H. Pelly 9th Inniskillings reported missing is the son of Rev. C.H. Pelly M.A. (now in Canada and former rector of Killybegs County Donegal.

Captain H. Bryan Brooke, Gordon Highlanders seriously wounded while leading his company on Saturday last is a son of Captain H.V. Brooke, Bairley, Aberdeen and a grandson of the second Brooke baronet of Colebrook, County Fermanagh. Captain H.V. Brooke and Mrs. Brooke left for France last week. Captain Brooke has already lost his eldest son Captain J.A.O. Brooke and also a son in law while two other sons have been wounded. The Victoria Cross was awarded to his son who was killed. Local rank and file. Private Simpson, killed Castlecoole Enniskillen; George McRae, killed Enniskillen, was a shunter on the SL&ANC railway and one of the most popular men in the company. William Emerson, wounded Mill Street Enniskillen. His father Private James Emerson is in the 12th Inniskillings and his other brother and two brothers-in-law are also serving. William Weir severely wounded is the son of Mr. Weir, Inishmore, Lisbellaw. John Edwards, wounded is a son of Mr. John R. Edwards, Coa, Ballinamallard. He had been gassed early in the campaign. William Patten, gassed, son of Mr. John Patten, Ballinamallard. Sergeant Frank Armstrong missing believed killed, Makeny. Sergeant R. Law wounded from Carn, Irvinestown; Robert McClintock, killed, Kesh, Robert Graham wounded son of Mr. George Graham, Drumpeen, Lisnarick, John Little, reported killed, Manoo, Kesh. John Ellis, wounded, Ederney. Harry Ellis, wounded, Ederney, etc., etc. etc. I.R.

July 13th 1916. HOW IRVINESTOWN FARED - A LETTER FROM THE FIGHTING LINE. Mrs. Little, Irvinestown has received a letter from her son George who tells of the fate of several of the Irvinestown lads at the front. He says they have had a hard time a few days ago and it was a big row with the Germans. We lost a lot of men and we took their trenches from them. It was terrible but thank God, I have come out of it all right. I am sorry to say that all the boys from Irvinestown except T. Moore, Thomas Johnston, Robert McGahey, and myself have not come out of it safe. Poor Archie Heaney is missing, so is Billy McAleer and the rest of our wounded. I think Alex Carruthers is killed. We are very sorry for all our chums and we are very lonely since we lost them. Poor Tommy Creighton is wounded and Bertie Stewart is missing. Poor George Lowry from below Pettigo is wounded too. I saw Freddie Mitchell on Thursday last and he is looking well; he came over to see me in the trenches. He asked for the *Impartial Reporter* to be sent on to him as usual. I.R.

Fermanagh Herald July 15th 1916. PARTITIONISTS AT WORK. It must be borne in mind that when the Liberal Government brought forth its humiliating Councils Bill as a substitute for Home Rule and Mr. Redmond, in a speech in the House of Common, accepted it there was no Sinn Fein difficulty, neither was there when power over the Irish Post Office, Customs and Excise was withheld from Ireland under the Better Government Act, nor when Mr. Lloyd-George aimed what he considered a deadly blow against the Irish Liquor Trade. The Irish Parliamentary Party on the latter occasion confessed that there was no possibility of defeating the Lloyd George scheme, but when those engaged in the Liquor Trade in Ireland raised a storm the surrender flag was hauled down, and the "Wizard of Wales" reproached the government with having quailed before a mob of enraged Irish publicans – not with having quailed before the Irish Parliamentary Party, whose weakness he had well learned to appreciate.

Mr. Lloyd-George.

Fermanagh Herald July 15th 1916. FERMANAGH NATIONALISTS AND THE UNCLEAN CUT. STRONG PROTEST AGAINST EXCLUSION. THE IRISH PARTY'S ACTIVITIES CONDEMNED. Boho A.O.H. on last Sunday held a meeting of the local Division. The attendance was large and the following resolution was passed. Proposed by Bro. Tracy, D. C., and seconded by Bro Maguire: - that we again most emphatically protest against the exclusion of the Ulster counties. We claim that if we are to have an Irish Parliament we must have Home Rule, and a Parliament for all Ireland. We also protest against the action of the officers of the Fermanagh County Board A. O. H. who voted for exclusion at the Ulster conference, and also those who refused to attend and question their authority for so doing, and beg to dissociate ourselves with the conduct of those so called Irishmen. (Ed. Similar protest meetings are noted in the paper for Monea, Tempo, Brookeborough, Maguiresbridge, Lisnaskea, and the Parish of Devenish etc.)

July 20th 1916. THE ERRATIC MR. GINNELL. HYSTERICAL EXCITEMENT AND DRESS. Mr. Ginnell who has been arrested for an alleged offence under the Defence of the Realm Act is one of the strangest characters in the House of Commons. Even on the Irish Nationalist benches it would be difficult to find anyone quite so explosive as the member for North Westmeath. Every day he addresses a string of supplementary questions to Ministers on the Treasury bench, and his quaint comments on the answers are a source of constant amusement to the House. There are times, however, when Mr. Ginnell positively frightens the House of Commons. These are on the rare occasions when he makes a set speech and works himself into such a state of hysterical excitement the members are literally afraid that he will suffer a physical collapse. It was Mr. Ginnell who the other day excited protests from Unionist members because he came down to the House wearing the Sinn Fein colours in his buttonhole. The Speaker refused to interfere on the ground that it was no part of his business to take notice of what members wore. I.R.

Laurence Ginnell

July 20th 1916. THE IRISH HAY AND STRAW. THE WAR DEPARTMENT REGULATIONS. The Government require the entire 1916 crop of hay and oats and wheat straw grown in Ireland. Any balances of the crops of 1915 are not however affected by the order. Accordingly whilst farmers and stock owners are at liberty to use the normal quantities of forage for consumption by animals in their possession or control, none of these crops can be disposed of, except to the Military Authorities in the absence of a licence from the District Purchasing Officer of the District in which the crop stands. The maximum price payable for first quality seed hay is £5 7s 6d; for oat straw £3 5s; for wheat straw £3 per ton; other quantities of each being bought at their respective values. A bailer will be supplied by the army authorities. I.R.

July 20th 1916. SINN FEIN DISORDER. After midnight on Thursday a party of 1,000 Sinn Feiners chagrined at the non-arrival of released rebellion prisoners paraded the streets of Cork shouting rebel cries and booing and hissing soldiers. They smashed the windows of the recruiting office, and things looked dangerous for a time, but the disorderly crowd dispersed on the arrival of police reinforcements. Shots were fired around Carrigodrohid House the residence of Captain Phillips, chief recruiting officer. The gate pillars were smeared with tar and the inscription 'Up with the Republic' was painted. A skull and crossbones device accompanied this inscription. I.R.

July 20th 1916. NOTES. Petrol will become a scarcer commodity than ever next month. Pleasure riding will be impossible and trade car supply will be cut down by 40 per cent.

The war is now costing over six million a day.

Gas shells captured from the Germans are now fired back by our men to those who invented them.

It takes £1 now to buy would cost 12 shillings and five pence before the war in England. Seven of our men were found dead from the heat in India when being transported by train and of 32 others sent to hospital five died. An order has now been made not to move drafts in hot weather.

Derry has commenced to consider the reduction of lamps in street lighting. When will Enniskillen commence? Half of the light is absolutely wasted in Enniskillen from 10.30 to an hour before sunrise.

Dublin rebels assemble at the North Wall, Dublin in the evening to hiss and hoot departing soldiers. Expressions such as 'to hell with soldiers etc.' are heard and insulting language is heard. Such cowardly ruffians should be flung into the Liffey. Meantime they are helping to ruin their city. I.R.

July 20th 1916. AN INNISKILLING APPOINTED INSPECTOR GENERAL OF THE R.I.C. The new Inspector General of the Royal Irish Constabulary, in succession to Sir Neville Chamberlain, retired, is Brigadier General John Aloysius Byrne, who came to Dublin with Sir John Maxwell in the rebellion week as his Deputy Adjutant General. General Byrne who is 42 and is Roman Catholic in religion joined the Royal Inniskillings in 1893 and was promoted Brigadier General last April. He served in the South African War and afterwards as assistant Adjutant General in the War Office. It is probable that the new Inspector General will make important changes in the organisation of the Royal Irish Constabulary. I.R.

Brigadier General Byrne.

July 20th 1916. THE NATIONALIST REVOLT AGAINST ULSTER EXCLUSION AND THE IRISH PARTY. Enniskillen Nationalists, at a meeting on Sunday evening at which the Rev D. Gormley, C.C. presided, protested in the strongest manner against the partition of Ireland and more especially against the exclusion of Fermanagh with its preponderating Nationalist majority. Fr. Gormley said that, after all their trials they were asked to give away part of their country. Partition would create a continual state of turmoil for all time. When it was mooted at Buckingham Palace, Fermanagh protested and since has been always hostile to division. Young men were encouraged to volunteer at the outbreak of the war on the understanding that they were fighting Ireland's battle and that as a reward they were to be given Home Rule. Notwithstanding all that, owing to the way the Irish Party were moving they were now going to get nothing. The men from Fermanagh who voted for exclusion at the Belfast Conference had neither the intelligence of a monkey nor the courage of a mouse. (Hear hear). I.R.

July 27th 1916. THE 1ST OF JULY BATTLE BY A SOLDIER WHO TOOK PART IN IT. Mr. Robert Johnston, Scollan, Irvinestown has received a letter from his son Tom, in the 11th Inniskillings which makes special reference to the 1st of July. In the course of it he says – the old Division is gone in strength but that the old spirit is there. I don't mind telling you that I shared many a tear for the chums that are gone. It was awful: it was not for nothing we advanced on the 1st of July. The General Officer commanding said that we did far more than was expected of us, and much was expected at that. Our Brigade did the best: we took the front lines of German trenches in 25 minutes under a murderous fire of shrapnel and machine guns, and had to fall back again on account of the Divisions being held upon right and left, as we were not expected to go so far. Our losses were heavy, about 500 in all. Our company returned with 62 men out of 212 and only 11 left of my old platoon that took part in it. Our Brigade alone took 400 prisoners. I never saw our brave chaps so far beat before and everyone was proud of what the Division had done, all telling how the Germans had behaved crying 'Kamerade, Kamerade,' the whole time and put up their hands by the score. I.R.

July 27th 1916. THE NATIONALIST REVOLT AGAINST THE IRISH PARTY. A BIG MEETING IN DERRY WILL NOT HAVE EXCLUSION. MEMBERS RESIGNATIONS DEMANDED. Alderman C. O'Neill, D.L. presided at a meeting of over 2,000 people representative of Nationalist opinion in Derry City and counties Derry, Tyrone and Fermanagh on Thursday in Saint Column's Hall, Derry to protest against the Lloyd George exclusion proposals. Contingents from Enniskillen, Omagh, Strabane, Dungannon, Coleraine and Magherafelt attended. Mention of the names of Irish party leaders particularly Messers Redmond and Devlin were vigorously groaned. I.R.

Fermanagh Herald July 29th 1916. LLOYD GEORGE'S SCHEME DROPPED. THE PERMANENCY OF THE PROPOSED EXCLUSION. A DEBATE IN THE HOUSE OF COMMONS. SUCCESS OF THE ANTI-EXCLUSION PROTEST. RECRIMINATIONS AMONGST THE PLOTTERS.

Fermanagh Herald July 29th 1916. ENNISKILLEN OFFICER KILLED IN ACTION. We deeply regret to announce the death of Second Lieutenant Cormick Wray, a son of Mr. John F. Wray, LL.B., Enniskillen, who was killed in action in France on the 16th of June. He went to the front in April last on entering his 21st year. Much sympathy is felt for his bereaved parents.

SEC.-LT. CORMACK WRAY, Royal Inniskilling Fusiliers, son of Mr. J. F. Wray, LL.B., solicitor, Enniskillen, was killed in action after most gallantly leading a raiding party.

Tuesday 18-7-16. My dear Sir, - you will have before this received the grievous news of the death of your son, Second Lieutenant C. P. J. Wray as the result of wounds received on the night of the 15th Inst. He was in command of a raiding party that entered the enemy trench on that night in conjunction with the firing of two mines and the occupation of two craters. He carried out the raid very successfully securing a prisoner and much valuable information, and got back to our trench. He then learned that some of his men were still out and that fighting was going on in the direction he had come from on the nearest crater. He at once went out again and took a leading part in the defence of that crater, where he was eventually hit by a bomb or a rifle grenade. He was at once got back into the front trench, and died there almost immediately. He acted very gallantly as everyone expected he would, and with the determination to do his duty which had always been evident. We greatly deplore the loss of the gallant and efficient officer, and sympathise very keenly with you and your family. Believe me, my dear Sir, yours sincerely, H. W. Dalzell Walton, Lt. Col., C. O. 8th Inniskillings.

AUGUST 1916

Fermanagh Herald August 5th 1916. LISNASKEA WORKHOUSE. A SWORN INQUIRY HELD. WOMAN'S TRYING EXPERIENCE. Mr. Robinson, Local Government Board Inspector opened a sworn an inquiry in the Lisnaskea Workhouse into a charge against Mr. P. Lunny, Workhouse master, of having refused admission to the workhouse of a woman named Miss Annie Brown, with the result that she was confined on the public roadway near the workhouse gate. Mr. M. E. Knight, solicitor, Clones, appeared on behalf of Annie Brown. Miss Brown said that she was hired for the last 14 months at Tully, Maguiresbridge. On the 12th of May she was about to be delivered of a child, and she left Mr.

Lisnaskea Workhouse

Morrison's house for the purpose of coming to the Lisnaskea workhouse. She walked to Lisnaskea and called at Dr. Knox's house and saw Mrs. Knox, the Doctor not being in at that time. Mrs. Knox told her to go to Mr. Lunny, the workhouse master, and tell him the doctor was not at home and that perhaps that the ticket of admission would be sent when the doctor came home. The workhouse Porter sent her up to master Lunny in his room and she told him she wanted in to the hospital at once and explained her condition. The master said he would not admit her without a ticket and that she might not be coming to him to create mischief. He told her to go down to the Porter's lodge if she wished. Witness said that the lodge was the place where tramps were put. She again went back to Mrs. Knox who brought her into the kitchen fire and she remained there till the doctor came. Dr. Knox then gave her a ticket, and she left to return to the workhouse. It was about 9.30 when she went across to the workhouse gate where she wasn't able to get in because the gate was locked and she had her child on the roadside.

In his evidence the master said that he had offered to admit her to the probationary ward which was well kept and if the woman Brown had accepted his proposal to go there she would have been seen by the matron before entering it. He said in a great many cases women tried to get into the hospital long before the birth of their child, but it was not the practice to allow them in too near the birth.

August 10th 1916. A TRAGEDY NEAR CLONES. TWO GIRLS DROWNED. A shocking accident occurred in Studdert's bog, Clonkeelan, Clones, with two young women, sisters, being drowned in a bog hole on the brink of which they had been working at turf during the day. Their names were Maggie Ellen Smith, aged 19 and Kate Smith page 17, daughters of Mr. Patrick Smith, farmer, Tullyalt, Scotshouse. It appears that the girls left home in the morning to work in the bog and about 3.00 p.m. they went to a neighbouring house where they prepared tea and then returned to their work. This was the last time they were seen alive, and as they had not returned home at a late hour the father proceeded to the bog and was horrified to find their bodies in a bog hole. It is believed that one of the girls fell into the water and that the other had lost her life in an attempt to save her sister. I.R.

August 10th 1916. Tied to a wagon for 2 hours a day. It has been enquired from Mr. Lloyd George whether a driver was convicted of very slightly exceeding the speed limit and that the field court martial awarded 30 days field punishment entailing been strapped to a wagon in full view of the troops for 2 hours a day and the loss of 90 days' pay and the loss to the man's wife of his allotment. Mr. Foster in written answer said that the court martial was quite within its rights in awarding the punishment named. Very strict regulations have been laid down to prevent reckless driving in France – the authorities there are having had their attention called to a number of cases were children had been injured owing to that cause. I.R.

August 10th 1916. CASEMENT HANGED. CHANGED HIS RELIGION BEFORE HIS EXECUTION. LAST WORDS ON THE SCAFFOLD. CROWD CHEERED DEATH BELL. Rodger David Casement was executed at Pentonville Prison on Thursday morning. There was a dramatic scene in the condemned cell shortly before the execution. Casement expressed a desire to be received into the Roman Catholic Church and a messenger was immediately dispatched to the Catholic Chaplin, Rev. Dean Ring, of Commercial Road who with Rev. Fr McCarroll arrived quickly to visit the condemned man and for about a quarter of an hour the two priests remained with him preparing him for the final scene. His confession was heard and he was given Holy Communion. A few minutes before 9.00 Ellis, the executioner, entered the condemned cell. Thereupon Casement stood erect and made a slight gesture towards him.

Pentonville Prison

On the stroke of nine the little procession headed by the two priests, with Casement following between the two warders who have looked after him since his incarceration left the cell and walked towards the execution shed only some four or 5 yards away. The Litany of the dying was recited by the priests, Casement responding in low tones 'Lord have mercy on my soul.' As the reached the execution shed Ellis approached the condemned man and he was quickly pinioned. The chaplains, the Governor of the prison, the Under Sheriff of London and the Under Sheriff of Middlesex then took up their position in front of the scaffold and Casement took his place on the drop board. A touching scene was witnessed at the back of the prison where a group of some 30 Irishmen, among them an MP and women had assembled. Just as the tolling of the bell intimated that the execution had duly taken place they fell on their knees and with bowed heads remained a few moments silently praying for the repose of the criminal's soul. The priest said a prayer and Casement replied 'Into thy hands O Lord I commend my spirit.' Later the condemned man said 'Lord Jesu receive my soul.' Casement's last words were – 'I die for my country.' Ellis the hangman a Rochdale hairdresser arrived at Pentonville prison on Wednesday night and at once made his preparations. He examined the trapdoor in the execution shed and tested it thoroughly with a bag the equivalent of Casement's weight to see that all was in working order. Ellis remained in the prison throughout the night. Casement himself was never under any delusion as to what his fate would be and he acknowledges the extreme fairness of the Crown in the way in which the evidence was presented. If the Crown had so desired evidence of a much more startling nature than that given at the trial could have been produced. I.R.

Roger Casement's grave in Glasnevin Cemetery.

August 10th 1916. LINCOLN FARMERS REFUSE TO EMPLOY IRISH HARVESTERS. In the Lincolnshire Fens where it has been customary to employ Irish harvestmen in considerable numbers a difficulty has arisen which threatens serious trouble. At Deeping St. Nicholas near Spalding the local labourers determinedly refuse to work with the Irishmen and farmers are refusing to employ them. The grievance of the English labourers is that whilst Englishmen in Ireland receiving one shilling per day as government pay the Irish labourers – excluded from the Military Service Act – take their places in England at five and six and seven shillings per day. The difficulty is accentuated by the attitude of the local shopkeepers and innkeepers, who decline to accommodate the Irishmen, or have anything to do with them. In addition to the grievances as to the Irish escaping military service while the English labourers are being called up, the farmers attribute the position to some extent to the Irish rebellion. Last year no such difficulty was experienced. I.R.

August 17th 1916. RECRUITING IN FERMANAGH. A recruiting party of the Inniskillings has visited some of the country villages but no recruits. There were plenty of young men in Enniskillen of serviceable at the age on Tuesday and there are plenty elsewhere and we share the general opinion of all who wish the country well when we say that the government is merely tinkering with this matter of recruiting. There are at least 150,000 sound men able to bear arms in Ireland. Youths in England aged 18 years and eight months are now about to be called up for military service, but they are not to go abroad until 19. Irish harvesters have returned to the West owing to their being refused employment in England. 12,000 acres of his Scotch estate have been given by the Duke of Sutherland for the settlement of ex-soldiers and ex-sailors on the land. This magnificent gift will help to make amends for the notorious Sutherland land clearance of hundreds of crofters from their Highland holdings which aroused a storm of indignation at the time and has never been forgotten. I.R.

August 17th 1916. CASUALTIES. After 12 months in suspense Mrs. D'Arcy, Toneyloman, Enniskillen has received information that her husband Lance Corporal John D'Arcy, 5th Inniskillings was killed in action on 15th August, 1915 at the Dardanelles. Deceased was missing and through the Red Cross Mrs. D'Arcy got at last definite information. There are five little children in the family now left without a father.
Privates James, Robert and Joseph Simpson, have all been killed. They served with the 11th Royal Inniskillings and were the sons of Mr. T and Mrs. Simpson Castlecoole, Enniskillen.
When applications were made to the War Office during the present war for Commissions in the army and the query sheet showed that the applicant had been educated at Enniskillen Royal School and a certificate sent from the headmaster at Portora to that effect there was no delay in granting the application. I.R.

August 24th 1916. THE CASE OF MR. MCHUGH, PETTIGO, IN PARLIAMENT. Mr. Duke in answer to a question of Mr. McHugh's removal from the Magistry, Mr. Duke said he had been appointed as a justice of the peace in the year 1911 and was also a magistrate by virtue of his office as chairman of Fermanagh County Council. In November 1915 he wrote a letter in which he suggested that he might use, for the promotion of his own interests, his position as chairman of a pension committee. Upon his admission that he had written this letter the Lord Chancellor removed him from the magistracy. The Lord Chancellor has no intention of restoring Mr. McHugh to the commission of the peace. F.T.

Main Street, Pettigo

Fermanagh Herald August 25th 1916. THE CLOSING OF CLOGHER WORKHOUSE. Clogher Guardians are the first to put into operation the amalgamation scheme devised by the Poor Law Boards in County Tyrone for the closing of the workhouses. On Saturday the body of Clogher workhouse and casual wards were closed and the inmates removed by rail to Enniskillen Union where there will be chargeable at the rate of seven shillings per head per week to the Clogher Union. The net saving to the ratepayers by the change is estimated at £251 a year. The infirmary and hospital are retained and meetings of the Guardians and Rural Council will go on as usual. The Master and Matron are discharged and compensated.

August 31st 1916. THE GREAT SCANDAL. The Labourers' Act was like some others in this country – intended for a good object and badly abused. We know in some local Unions of many others beside agricultural labourers who occupied cottages, such as tailors and carpenters. Glenties supplied the case of a military captain occupying a labourer's cottage and Delvin County Westmeath affords an instance of cottage tenants owning farms of land. One tenant had 8 acres of land and 20 cattle at grass; he never worked for others, except when he cut meadows with his cutting machine and two horses. Other tenants there, as reported on by Mr. Peck Beresford, Local Government Inspector, held 15, 16, 18, and 25 acres! In some cases the Inspector reported the tenants had never lived in their cottages earning money in England at munitions work. Yet with all these cases of scandalous maladministration a deserving woman and her family could not obtain a cottage so that she had for shelter to make a sort of tent out of a few blankets fixed on bent sticks.

The Inspector also says – 'this woman has also living with her and under the same conditions her married daughter, the mother of two infants and the wife of a soldier at present in France. Mrs. Connolly's own husband was killed in France. Seeing the appalling circumstances in which the family existed, I thought there must be some excellent reason which weighed with the Council in their resolve not to give her a house; and I, therefore decided to make enquiries regarding her. From the police had learned that she bore an untarnished character and from other sources I obtained the same information. That the council could have acted as they have done in regard to this particular case passes my comprehension. These scandals of course are invariably with the Nationalist Boards and in the Delvin case the Board refused to do anything. I.R.

August 31st 1916. BUNDORAN. Both the parish churches were crowded in Bundoran on last Sunday. In the Protestant church the Rev Godfrey Day son of the Bishop of Clogher was the preacher and there was not room enough for all who sought admission. Several had to leave the building for want of accommodation. The most Rev Dr. Mulhern, Bishop of Dromore, and recently parish priest of Bundoran was the preacher in the Roman Catholic Church which likewise was crowded, with numbers standing.

Bundoran

Bundoran itself never before had such a crowd of visitors and these were increased by 5 excursions so that the streets during the day were anything but pleasant for Protestant folk who like a quiet Sunday.

One excursion party from Letterkenny of the Hibernians to Ballyshannon by the Donegal railway kept cars busy between Ballyshannon and Bundoran so that the traffic was abnormal. Not one perch of the road but had jaunting cars and motor cars and bicycles; and dense and dangerous as was the traffic entirely imperilling human life, not a solitary policeman was on the 3 miles of road which was congested with traffic. Nor was this all. Cars were overcrowded. Some of them had eight and nine passengers, so that the poor horses had a severe time; and the law which allows 1 foot 4 inches to each passenger was successfully ignored when there were no police to take steps to enforce the law. Drivers can drive furiously through the street and no notice is taken of it though the streets be crowded. The police take things very easily as seen in Bundoran.

It is noticeable that just as the nobility and country gentry who used to visit Bundoran half a century ago forsook it so the professional and better commercial classes are leaving it now. Rossnowlagh, this year was to some extent Enniskillen by the sea; and Portrush had six or seven Enniskillen families at one time while others favoured Castlerock. Protestant people greatly dislike a noisy Sunday and a Bundoran Sunday to them is very disconcerting. The body of a drowned woman was washed ashore at Bundoran on Monday last. Her name is stated to be Mrs. Glancy and she was a native of the place. I.R.

August 31st 1916. BALLYCONNELL a special court was held in in the R.I.C barracks before Mr. J. A. Bennison, J.P. when the police had in custody a servant boy named James McKiernan on a charge of being an absentee under the Military Service Act. It appears the boy had been working in Glasgow and had signed the registration papers and had failed to return. After formal evidence he was conveyed to Armagh jail pending the arrival of a military escort from Scotland.

In the Ballyconnell fair on Monday, Mr. F. J. Clancy, Ballyconnell, sold to Mr. Charlie Moan, Lisnaskea, a six year old springing cow for the fabulous price of £40. This is the highest price ever known to be paid in Ballyconnell for a beast of its class. Other classes of cattle sold from £33 to £35, young calves from £4 to £6 10 and young pigs from five to £6 two and sixpence per pair. I.R.

August 31st 1916. IRISH HARVESTERS WARNED OFF. A good many Irish labourers have, according to the *Glasgow Herald* offered themselves to Lothian farmers but without exception their services have been declined. The farm servants decline to work alongside men who are attempting to fill the places of farm hands now serving in the army. I.R.

SEPTEMBER 1916

Fermanagh Herald September 2nd 1916. OBITER DICTA. Some days ago I happened to be in Dublin on my way to England. I remained in Dublin for some days with the special purpose of getting the views of several persons with regard to the action of the Irish Party in consenting to exclusion. Dublin repudiates Mr. John Redmond. The people of her capital –with the exception of a few who cannot see further than their noses – have done with the Irish Party under its present leadership. What has lessened the popularity of Mr. Redmond? Simply and solely, the very idea of consenting to partition. In my opinion, and mind you it is the opinion of practically all of Dublin, John Redmond has been the greatest failure we have ever had the misfortune to send to Westminster to guard the destinies of our sorely tried country.

La Mitrailleuse, 1915, Christopher Richard Wynne Nevinson 1889-1946, presented by Contemporary Art Society

September 7th 1916. NOTES. Second Lieutenant J. J. Flower, B. A., T.C.D., Lancashire Fusiliers, seriously wounded again on August 26th and now in hospital is a son of Rev. Ed Flowers, Ballagh Rectory, Belleek.

Corporal Bernard McManus of the 1st Royal Inniskillings was killed by gas poisoning on the 8th of August. He was a good son to his mother, Mrs. McManus Strand Street Enniskillen. Miss McManus was a daughter of Mrs. McGurn who kept a stall at the angle of the old Townhall 50 years ago.

The increase of two shillings and six pence a week to old age pensioners if extended to all of them would amount to between six and seven million pounds; and this huge sum could be made up by stopping the expenditure on strong drink for one fortnight only or handing over that sum usually spent during that time in drink to the Treasury. I.R.

September 7th 1916. LOUGH DERG. There were 11,000 pilgrims to Lough Derg, County Donegal this year. This meant an average of 44,000 shillings to the Railway Company; 11,000 shillings to the car drivers, 11,000 shillings to the owner of the ferry who pays £50 a year to Colonel Sir John Leslie for the privilege; and how many thousands to the Prior of Lough Derg for board and keep only the Prior knows. I.R.

September 7th 1916. ENNISKILLEN ROYAL SCHOOLS. Enniskillen Royal School will open on the 22nd Inst., with an increased number of pupils and full teaching staff. The number of boys has kept steadily increasing. The Royal School for Girls will open on the 21st Inst., in Darling Street with more pupils than had been originally contemplated so eager are parents to take advantage of a higher class education. The teaching staff is of a high order and the premises have been placed in the best of order for both boarding and day pupils. I.R.

September 7th 1916. NEW BIG PUSH ON THE SOMME. OVER 6,500 PRISONERS CAPTURED IN TWO DAYS. The number of prisoners taken is a convincing indication of the completeness of our success. Up to Sunday the great Allied movement begun on July 1 had resulted in over 35,000 Germans being captured so that up till Tuesday at least 42,000 of the enemy have been accounted for in this way alone. Their losses in killed and wounded have of course been proportionately great.

Fermanagh Herald September 9th 1916. BIG ZEPPELIN RAID. THIRTEEN AIRSHIPS OVER ENGLAND. On Saturday night the Eastern coast was attacked by thirteen airships. Three only were able to approach the outskirts of London. One was heavily engaged by anti-aircraft guns and aeroplanes, and she burst into flames and fell rapidly towards earth. The ship was destroyed and wreckage, engines and half-burnt bodies of the crew were found at Cuffley near Enfield. The other two ships which approached London were driven off. One man and one woman were killed and 11 men and women and three children were injured.

The War Office announces that it was Lieutenant W. L. Robinson, Worcester Regiment, R.F.C., who brought down the Zeppelin on Sunday morning, and that the King has been greatly pleased to award him the V.C. He attacked an enemy airship, the announcement says, under circumstances of great difficulty and danger and sent it crashing to the ground as a flaming wreck. He had been in the air for more than 2 hours, and had previously attacked another airship during his flight.

Lieut. W. L. Robinson, V.C.

Fermanagh Herald September 9th 1916. ARRESTS IN FERMANAGH. On Monday the police of Roslea, Co., Fermanagh arrested two young men named Patrick Beggan, Eshnadarragh, and Hugh Murphy, Rellan, on a charge of evading military service. Both had been in Scotland. They now expressed their willingness to join an Irish regiment, and accordingly they were taken to Clones and thence to Enniskillen for enlistment. A third house in the district was visited by the police, but the young man they sought had returned to Scotland.

Fermanagh Herald September 9th 1916. PORTOBELLO SHOOTINGS. At the concluding sitting on Thursday of the Portobello Shootings Commission, Lt., Dobbin, who was commander of the guard on the occasion of the shootings gave evidence, having been brought back from the fighting line in France for the purpose, and he stated that Captain Colthurst ordered the prisoners out of the guard room and said; "I am going to shoot them, Dobbin; I think it is the right thing to do." He admitted that a grave irregularity had been committed both in regard to the holding of Mr. Skeffington as a hostage and respecting the shooting of the three men; but was not in a position to say to his superior officer that what he was doing was right or wrong. (Ed. The Royal Irish Rifles company commander Captain Bowen-Colthurst, who ordered the shootings, was controversially adjudged "insane" at the subsequent inquiry and court-martial.)

Fermanagh Herald September 9th 1916. EDUCATION IN FERMANAGH. It will afford our readers genuine gratification to peruse the remarkable list of successes achieved by the pupils of the Presentation Bros., St., Michael's, Enniskillen in the Intermediate examinations. Nearly 30 pupils were successful in these examinations. Parents and guardians residing in Fermanagh and the adjacent counties will receive the news as tokens of the excellent tuition imparted with zealousness and imbued with the spirit of achieving success. But the results, admirable though they may seem, are only in keeping with the hitherto high reputation of this noble, painstaking, and firmly established teaching Order. The Presentation Brothers have not been teaching in Enniskillen for a great many years, yet the methods and reputation had long preceded their advent and is justified by the high estimation in which they are held by the townspeople.

Fermanagh Herald September 9th 1916. AND THEN THIS TRASH. Considering the facts, it was positively sickening to read the hypocritical sub-leader in last week's *Impartial Reporter* which a disgusted reader of that paper was good enough to send me. It was headed: Medical and Other Shirkers. This super-loyal hypocrisy of the writer was only equalled by his blatant ignorance of recruiting in England. Had he seen what I have witnessed one day at Blackpool, last week and in the queues outside the Birmingham and London theatres, he would cease from maligning his countrymen, many of whom served "not wisely but too well." This writer

Blackpool

says he will thank the correspondents who send him a list of eligible Irish men of military age who are shirking their duty. Just imagine it. Does he know that there are English shirkers in Ireland in the very town where his paper is published and who have not come forward to serve England. Is he aware of the fact that there are hundreds of young men knocking around Blackpool in holiday attire whose groups I was informed, had been already called up? Did he see a picture in last Friday's *Daily Sketch*, depicting an incident of which I was actually a witness of a detective questioning English slackers when about to enter a Birmingham music hall and who had evaded conscription, as to why they were not in the army. Furthermore does he know that outside that theatre there were found some 60 eligible who had evaded the order? And, lastly it would be interesting to ascertain whether Mr. Trimble is aware that nightly raids are being made in the English theatres and picture palaces for evaders under the Military Service Act. Let him spend some money and come across here and get his facts. It will educate him, and who knows but it may have the effect of deterring him from labelling his sorely tried and all-forgiving countrymen, who have already done more than their share in this world-wide war, while English slackers attend music halls and indulge in whiskies and sodas. England first.

Fermanagh Herald September 9th 1916. BUNDORAN. NOTES AND NOTIONS. This has been a record season for Bundoran. For the past seven weeks the hotels and boarding houses have been packed, and rooms have had to be booked a month in advance. A fortnight ago there was such a rush of visitors that some of them were not able to procure a bed or even sofas upon which to repose and had to "berug" themselves and sleep in the open in motor cars. Those who could not procure such accommodation were obliged to take rooms in Ballyshannon.

Bundoran

Owing to the curtailment of holidays across the water the number of Scotch visitors was less than in previous years. They came from all parts of Ireland – from Dublin, Belfast and even from Cork, and great numbers came from Tyrone, Fermanagh, Cavan and other Ulster counties. And they came because there is no other seaside resort of Ireland that can be put on a par with that for bracing air, magnificent scenery and splendid sea.

My attention has been directed to some criticisms in a Unionist newspaper and anyone who reads them will agree with me that they are silly and childish. Under the heading of "I Hear" the writer says that Bundoran continues to be crowded, but the visitors complain that bedrooms never seem to be cleaned, and that many boarding establishments are understaffed. What does he want the Urban Council to do for visitors? Does he want them to appoint a Town Sergeant to shine their shoes when they get them wet in the sand or water or supply bathers with drinks of hot milk when they come out of the sea? It is the old story, the perpetual grumbler must grumble, and is only happy when grumbling. Bundoran has been provided, with an inexhaustible supply of pure water, which has been certified to be absolutely free from contamination of any kind. And a drainage scheme has been completed at enormous cost, and the town is splendidly lighted by electricity. The streets and roads are well made and well kept – but I forgot about the bedrooms. The critic says he hears that they never seem to be cleaned.

The hotels and a majority of the boarding houses are up to date and comfortable. A friend from Cork, who was a bit of a poet, and I, had dinner one day in a certain hotel. He was so delighted with the meal that he afterwards wrote in the visitors' book –

"One morning fair I met a chap,
Faint hearted, weak and worn,
He had been indulging in a drop,
Said I, go to Bundoran.
Straight to – Hotel he went,
And now upon my honour,
He'd throw a weight with Flannigan,
Or jump with P. O'Connor.

Fermanagh Herald September 9th 1916. DERRY CONFLAGRATION AS WATT'S DISTILLERY IS BURNED TO THE GROUND. DAMAGE OF £100,000 HAS BEEN CAUSED. THE OUTBREAK IS BELIEVED TO HAVE BEEN CAUSED BY AN EXPLOSION. The most destructive fire that ever occurred in Derry broke out at midnight on Saturday night in the huge distillery of Messrs. David Watt and Co., Ltd. Abbey Street, and unfortunately the great conflagration was attended by loss of life. The fire originated in the wash charge room, where a great explosion, believed to be due to vapour took place, setting a large block of buildings in flames and blowing off the roof and part of the outer wall on Frederick Street. It was at this moment that a baker named Henry Doherty, 35 years of age, residing in Rosemount, was passing and was buried in falling debris. He sustained terrible injuries, especially about the head. He lay under the broken masonry for some time and when he was discovered he was in a dying condition. He was removed to the City Infirmary, but expired before arriving at the institution.

Fermanagh Herald September 9th 1916. ENNISKILLEN SOLDIERS DEATH. Mrs. McCaffrey, Enniskillen widow of the late Private Tom McCaffrey, Royal Inniskilling Fusiliers, has received the following letter:

Dear Mrs. McCaffrey, - I have heard that your poor husband 2848, Pte. Tom McCaffrey, Royal Enniskillen Fusiliers, has died as a result of wounds received in action, and I hastened to assure you of my deepest sympathy. You will, I know, be much consoled when I tell you that the day before he was hit he assisted at Holy Mass and received Holy Communion. And, just as he was going into the battle, I again gave him Absolution and when he was wounded I give him the Last Sacraments. Since his death I have offered up the Holy Sacrifice of the Mass for him. R.I.P. Poor Tom was a grand Catholic and always most attentive to his religious duties. Do not worry too much, but rather rejoice in the happy death which God gave him. Again assuring you of my deepest sympathy, and begging a share in your prayers.
Yours very sincerely Rev. John Coghlan, C. F. Royal Inniskilling Fusiliers, B.E.F., France.

September 14th 1916. ESCAPED LUNATICS JOIN THE ARMY AND WERE THE BETTER FOR IT. On Monday at a meeting of the Cork Lunatic Asylum Committee, the Acting Resident Medical Superintendent reporting the escape of two lunatics from the asylum said it was a much more difficult matter these war times to recover escaped patients than in peacetime as they often joined the army and the next the officials heard of them was that they were seen in uniform. Since the last meeting of the Committee a former patient who escaped some months ago turned up at the asylum in Cork having served six months in France and he was better mentally after six months in the trenches than when he escaped from the institution. I.R.

Cork Lunatic Asylum

Fermanagh Herald September 16th 1916. MOTOR ACCIDENT NEAR CLOGHER. DOCTOR'S DAUGHTER KILLED. A very sad motor accident on Friday evening a short distance outside Clogher, by which Miss Ivy Kathleen Ross, the 13 year old daughter of Dr. Ross, Clogher, lost her life. It appears that Dr. Ross was accompanied by his two daughters on a professional visit in a motor car owned by Mr. John Johnston, Clogher, and when the car was going round a very sharp corner on the road the chauffeur applied the brakes rather quickly and the car overturned. Miss. Ross, Sen., jumped from the car, but the other three occupants were thrown on the road, the car pinning Miss Ivy Ross down and causing serious injuries which ended fatally. Dr. Ross was badly injured about the side and back and the greatest sympathy is felt with him and his family on their terrible tragic bereavement.

Fermanagh Herald September 16th 1916. THE MILITARY SERVICE ACT. VISITS TO FOOTBALL MATCHES AND MUSIC HALLS. Men of apparent military age were stopped after a football match at Hull on Saturday and required to produce registration cards and exemption cards. About 250 who could not do so were marched to the neighbouring police station. At Reading a similar course at a football match resulted in between 50 and 60 being detained. At local music halls in Bermondsey and Rotherhithe only a few were marched off. At Glasgow a number of tea rooms were visited and a number of names and addresses of young men taken.

Fermanagh Herald September 16th 1916. IRISH NATION LEAGUE. GREAT MEETING IN DUBLIN. IMMENSE GATHERING IN PHOENIX PARK. ABLE AND ELOQUENT SPEECHES. PARTITION POLICY DENOUNCED. In the presence of a gathering of considerably over 15,000 people, the Irish Nation League was successfully launched at a great open air meeting in the Nine Acres, Phoenix Park, on Sunday. Considerable enthusiasm prevailed during the proceedings, and the speakers especially those from Ulster received a very cordial welcome.

Fermanagh Herald September 16th 1916. UNIONIST JOURNAL AND LOUGH DERG. (IMPARTIAL REPORTER.) *To the editor of the Fermanagh Herald. Dear Sir, - The following paragraph appeared in the Impartial Reporter of last week: "LOUGH DERG. There were 11,000 pilgrims to Lough Derg, County Donegal this year. This number meant on an average 44,000 shillings to the Railway Company; 11,000 shillings to the car drivers, 11,000 shillings to the owner of the ferry who pays £50 a year to Colonel Sir John Leslie Bart., for the privilege and how many thousands to the Prior of Lough Derg for board and keep only the Prior knows."*

Lough Derg

11,000 Pilgrims did not visit Lough Derg this year. £50 a year is not the amount paid by the ferryman to the landlord; nor does each pilgrim pay one shilling for the ferryman. The contributions of pilgrims for "board and keep" did not benefit the Prior or any other individual to the extent of one penny.
Yours faithfully, Patrick Keown, P. P. Enniskillen.

Fermanagh Herald September 16th 1916. JOTTINGS. Head –Constable McLean, Ballinrobe, has been transferred to Kesh, Co., Fermanagh. At a special Court held in Bundoran police barrack on Saturday a man belonging to the tramp class, named John O'Neill was ordered to be imprisoned for two months on a charge of assault on a constable. At the same court, a woman named Lizzie O'Neill, of no fixed residence, brought up for begging, was ordered to be imprisoned for one month.

Fermanagh Herald September 23rd 1916. And the usual quarter the meeting of the A.O.H. (B.O.E,) Division 455, Mulleek the following resolution was passed unanimously: - "That we, the members of this division, strongly condemned the action of those responsible for the recent disgraceful treatment of the Irish migratory labourers who were brought to England and Scotland for the usual harvest work."

Mrs. Henderson, Cabra, Irvinestown, has passed away at the age of 103 years. Her son, Mr. James Henderson, who predeceased her, was for a number of years Chairman of Irvinestown Guardians.

September 21st 1916. THE DEATH OF SECOND LIEUTENANT C. A. CROWE. The war like a giant octopus has stretched its devastating hands in many directions and claimed its victims by the 1000 but we feel in special measure sympathy with those in our own midst who have fallen prey to its ravages. Today we have to record that this sad affliction as once more fallen upon an Enniskillen family. Second Lieutenant Cecil A. Crowe, son of Mr. and Mrs. Thomas Crowe, Drumclay, Enniskillen on the 9th Inst. made the supreme sacrifice. Having been educated at Portora Royal School where he displayed not only scholastic ability and also splendid athletic prowess, he joined the staff of the Ulster Banking Company and was stationed at Belfast, Derry and Cookstown. In these places, as in his native town, he was most popular. When war broke out he nobly responded to the call and it was not without great difficulty due to infirm sight that he eventually was permitted by the Medical authorities to don khaki. F.T.

September 21st 1916. THE PREMIER'S GREAT LOSS. SON KILLED IN ACTION. It is officially announced that Mr. Asquith has received intimation that his son Lieutenant Raymond Asquith, Grenadier Guards, was killed in action on the 15th. He was the eldest son of the Premier and was born in November 1878. He gained many honours at Baliol and was called to the Bar in 1904. He was a former president of the Oxford Union. Mr. Asquith had three sons of military age, Raymond, Cyril, and Arthur and when the call for men came all promptly volunteered for service. Arthur was one of the first of the country's volunteers to see active service. Joining the Royal Naval Reserve he was with the division which gallantly delayed the Germans capture of Antwerp. F.T.

September 21st 1916. WANTED. Lady (country) requires young Protestant Farmer's daughter as working help; treated as one of the family: man kept. Apply Miss Black, Aughnamoyle, Omagh.

Respectable Protestant help wanted for two people, seaside; comfortable situation. Apply this office. F.T.

On Saturday, 16th of September 1916 at his residence in Townhall Street, Enniskillen, William Ritchie, Fellow and ex Vice President of the Institute of Journalists, editor and proprietor of the Fermanagh Times aged 66 years.

We wish to acknowledge our indebtedness to Mr. P. E. Mulcahy, of the Fermanagh Herald staff for his valuable assistance and kindly sympathy during our recent bereavement.

It is officially announced that Lieutenant T. M. Kettle, Royal Dublin Fusiliers has been killed in action. Deceased, who was in his 36 year, was a Professor of Economics in the National University. He went to Belgium shortly after the declaration of war as a correspondent of the *Daily News*. Subsequently he obtained a commission and prior to being drafted to France he took a prominent part in recruiting activities in Ireland. Lieutenant Kettle who was a native of Swords, County Dublin was a member of the Irish Bar but was best known as a journalist and author. He represented East Tyrone in Parliament from 1906 to 1910 when he retired to embark on professional work. Mrs. Kettle is the daughter of Mr. David Sheehy, M. P. F.T.

September 21st 1916. WAR NOTES AND COMMENTS. If the subject where less grim there would be something decidedly entertaining in the protests of the Germans against such 'unfair methods' of warfare as the use of 'tanks' against them. An Austrian paper has now carried the idea a step further in an impassioned protest against the whole of the Allies scheme of operation on the Somme. 'It is simple butchery. One might suppose that the Anglo-French Governments have made up their minds to kill a fixed number of Germans per week or month.' The people who invented poison gas can cry out against unfair methods in warfare only at the price of making themselves ridiculous.

Mr. Hugh Jones tells an interesting story of a soldier and his comforts. This man was in France and the authorities were surprised at the number of parcels arriving addressed to him. There were in all about 3,000 parcels and it seemed that some special arrangement would be needed to send the lot to him. Enquiries were made and it was learned that all these gifts were sent as a sequel to an advertisement inserted by the soldier in a London paper to the effect that he was a lonely soldier without friends or relatives, and would be glad of correspondence from a lonely girl. F.T.

September 21st 1916. SPLENDID ALLIES SUCCESS. THE NEW ARMED MOTOR IS SPREADING TERROR AMONG THE GERMANS. THE NEW BRITISH ARMED MOTOR CAR MADE ITS NEW APPEARANCE ON SATURDAY. The unexpected appearance of the new British armed car seemed to have been not only effective from a military point of view but also to have created panic among the enemy. A French officer who acts as a link between the British and French armies told Reuters correspondent with huge glee of the consternation which spread among the Germans when these sinister flat footed monsters advanced spouting flames from every side and careless alike of rifle and machine gun fire right up to and over barbed wire entanglements crushing everything before them seeking out machine guns and silencing them. Making the advance of German reinforcements through their communication trenches impossible by enfilading fire and holding up terrified bands of Germans eager to flee. On the Somme front at the precise moment when the bombardment stopped the Germans had the surprise of seeing advance in front of the waves of assaulting troops enormous steel monsters from which spurted a continuous fire of great violence. One would have described them as gigantic infernal machines. Their front which was shaped like a ram smashed down every obstacle. The heavy automobiles bounded across overturned and uneven ground breaking through barbed wire and jumping trenches. In the German ranks there was really a mad terror. The soldiers of the German Emperor fell back in haste abandoning their arms ammunition and equipment. I.R.

British Mark I male tank near Thiepval, 25 September 1916.

(Ed. While researching my first book *Castle Caldwell and its Families* which was published in 1980 I visited the John Rylands Library in Manchester where a large volume of Castle Caldwell material was deposited by a relation of Catherine Caldwell of Castle Caldwell, Belleek who had married a Samuel Bagshawe. While there I met Major Bagshawe and was entertained for tea at Ford Hall, the Bagshawe residence. The Major had fought in tanks in WW1 and told me that the noise inside the tank from the engine and its machine guns was horrendous and greatly added to by the noise of the German machine guns and rifle fire striking the tank. As a result his hearing was greatly impaired and I am afraid he drove rather as if he was still in a tank.)

September 21st 1916. A BAVARIAN COLONEL'S JOY RIDE. ONE CAR HAD A STRANGE ADVENTURE WITH A BAVARIAN REGIMENTAL COMMANDER. In its journey through the village the car suddenly came upon a dug-out. In the language of a man who was there, 'she just sat down on the dug-out, and a colonel, came out to see what the matter was. When he saw the machine he promptly put up his hands. Here was a dilemma. There were no infantry nearby who could take over the prisoner. The commander of the car solved the problem by opening a manhole and hauling his captive inside. He was a tight fit in the hatch and he put him on the floor. Thereafter for some hours this officer of the Crown Prince Rupprecht's army had the novel experience of journeying about watching his captors kill Bavarians in large numbers and hearing the rat-tat-tat of German bullets flick harmlessly against the heavy metal skin of his travelling cage. A climax of his incredible experience came at the finish of the day's fight when he was decanted at the roadside behind the British lines and was received with cheers. I must mention the complaints of some German machine gunners regarding the armoured car that captured them in the Martinpuich. They said that such fighting was bloody butchery, unsportsmanlike, like killing sheep, etc. etc. One of them added bitterly, we fired at them but only saw blue sparks. What could we do but give ourselves up. I.R.

September 21st 1916. LIFE ON A GERMAN SUBMARINE. A German who has been on a German submarine during several expeditions to British waters has given the *Stavanger Aftenblad* an interesting account of his experiences. 'The vessel was a large modern one with a crew of 28 - all strongly built men in their prime. Our expeditions generally lasted two months. The oil and benzene we got from German trawlers. As we had wireless installation on board we were able to keep in communication with Germany and where to go at certain points where we would meet the trawlers. Sometimes we were under the sea for 15 hours at a time but then the air became suffocating. It is very fatiguing to submerge. We used to get quite deaf and had to shout to one another. It affected our nerves dreadfully and two brave strong fellows about 30 years old went mad. I myself had to go to hospital for some months. At the beginning of the war the English captured many of our submarines. I have been told about 30 or 40 but we soon found means of protecting ourselves against the nets.' I.R.

Submarine interior

September 21st 1916. ENNISKILLEN ROYAL SCHOOL FOR GIRLS. GOOD STAFF OF TEACHERS AND THE BEST OF NEW EQUIPMENT. A great local event occurred unostentatiously in Enniskillen on yesterday when the Enniskillen Royal School for girls opened its doors in Darling Street for the reception of pupils and for the first time ladies in college cap and gown conducted school classes here. The Fermanagh Protestant Board of Education has long been impressed with the necessity of supplying a higher class school for girls on the same lines as the Royal School at Portora for boys but it had not the funds at its command and had to first repair and keep in good order the fine pile at Portora and build it up securely before diverting any of its funds to the Royal School for girls. On yesterday the first headmistress of Enniskillen Royal School for girls had her first pupils on her roll. Miss Muriel F. Eccles is a lady of no ordinary attainment for not only is she a graduate of the University of Dublin and a Moderator of Trinity, a rare distinction, but she holds the diploma of teaching from Trinity College showing that she possesses the gift of imparting knowledge as well as acquiring it. The vice principal is Miss May Bradshaw, B. A. who took her course in honours and Miss Read, B. A. who is strong in pure mathematics and in science assists and a number of other assistants will be determined by the number of pupils; for an increased number is promised for next term so that it is just possible that all the people who may like to come there may not find sufficient accommodation and the Board may be obliged to limit the number. It will be a case of those coming first receiving first attention.

There can be no question about the ability and competence of the teaching staff. As to the equipment of the school it is of the best. The senior girls are provided with separate desks and separate chairs; each desk being a lock up desk - the material being pitch pine varnished. This arrangement provides for individuality, prevents crowding, and gives the teachers according to the new system better opportunities of going among the different pupils and gauging their work. In another room provided with dual desks the middle grade girls are provided for; and in another room below tables and tiny chairs of different heights show the provision made for the Kindergarten. A blackboard dado runs round the school for the little ones so that they will not have to hold their heads high up for observation

The original Enniskillen Royal School for Girls, Darling Street.

at the blackboard. A room with hand basins is set apart for cloaks, hats and boots while a lovely playground is in the rear affording a nice ground for the children. The boarders' apartments are well furnished, well lit and very comfortable; and everything that could be devised for the comfort and wellbeing of all concerned has been provided by the Board. Clay for modelling will interest the little ones and up to date maps and accessories are provided for the seniors. The Board expect the school to pay its way. It is for the people of Enniskillen and Fermanagh mainly to say whether they wish to retain this most valuable institution in their midst instead of sending their girls to other places for their education; for unless the school be well supported the Board may withdraw its grant and close the premises, and concentrate all their energies on the Boys School which is steadily growing from term to term. The fees are low commensurate with the quality of the education, the like of which will not be surpassed in schools demanding much higher fees. I.R.

September 21st 1916. THINGS IN GENERAL AND NOTHING IN PARTICULAR. War brings in its trail real sorrow and suffering. Most towns are now towns of mourning. Never before in this district has there been such universal grief as day by day one's dearest friends and school acquaintances are taken away. Take Enniskillen for example. I totted up roughly on my fingers the other day 37 of the principal households in the town that are now in morning. Poor Cecil Crowe! Big strong and fearless, good natured, full of ready wit, an old Rugby three-quarter who played on the Portora 1st; he joined the 12th Inniskillings in May last. Like most soldiers he was a fatalist. He used to say that anyone who shared his room whether at Ballykinlar or Enniskillen, would be killed and it was so. There were three officers who one after another slept in the same room as Lt. Crowe. The name of one I forget but the second was Charlie Crockett and when both these had gone to France and were killed, he told his third old school chum my youngest brother Noel D. Trimble that he would also be killed and his prophecy was unfortunately too true for and as he himself left Enniskillen for the front he said he would never come back alive. And he never will for he was killed in the charge at Quincy on the ninth Inst., leading his Company. Cecil Crowe gave up his post in the Ulster Bank to serve his country, and so keen was he to overcome the dimness of vision that to some extent disqualified him from the army, that like his school fellow, Noel Trimble, he resorted to artifice to overcome the difficulties of the examination. Both these young men who were conscious of their deficiencies in the matter of sight, took means to satisfy the examiners that all was right which was not right. Neither of them was truly physically qualified for the army. But the nobility of spirit was there –the spirit of self-abnegation was there – the sense of duty to help their country was there - and these young men who had been together in Enniskillen Royal School went forth animated by the same spirit and both paid the supreme penalty. I.R.

September 21st 1916. OUR INNISKILLINGS HAVE SUFFERED HEAVILY. Our boys of the 1st, 2nd, 7th, and 8th Inniskillings have taken an active part in the recent Big Push; while the 11th Inniskillings are remaining near the sea and getting the ranks filled up after the heavy losses they have borne. The 7th and 8th Inniskillings have been engaged in the capture of Guillemont and Ginchy and have suffered heavily. The commanding officers of both battalions, Lt. Colonels Young, and H. P. Walton have been killed and the second in command in both cases are wounded. Captain W. P. Kerr, a very capable officer, is at present in command of the 7th battalion which has suffered severely. The 8th battalion has suffered so acutely in officers that only four have been left, one of the officers killed being, Lieutenant T. M. Kettle, a brilliant Irishmen and previously a Member of Parliament, who was in Enniskillen on recruiting duty and made an impressive speech in the County Hall. We take pride and glory and all that our gallant boys have done, - but O, the losses should inspire us all to send out more men to the help those who remain instead of wringing our hands or giving way to tears. I.R.

T. M. Kettle

September 21st 1916. Lough Derg. We much regret that the paragraph published in last week's Impartial Reporter when being pruned was not left clear in its wording as to be beyond misconception. Referring to the Pilgrimage to Lough Derg this year we gave certain figures, supplied to us, and Rev Canon Keown we are given to understand, considered there was some innuendo in the words relating to him. We deeply regret that the meaning intended was not made clear, as we had not the most remote intention of making any references to the Canon's charges to the Pilgrims, nor do we entertain any opinion on the subject.

What was intended was to show the great local circulation of money at Pettigo and Lough Derg not only in the necessary fees charged for cars and at the ferry boat but for the upkeep of the place, - which is in strong contrast to many years ago. Pilgrims used to walk barefoot to Lough Derg; but the railway changed all that; the Sanctuary became better known, and now 20 people come by rail for one that travelled by road formerly; and the outlay of money correspondingly great. Everything is kept, we understand, in good order and there is no one who knows Canon Keown but would be satisfied that anything under his care would be properly administered. I.R.

September 21st 1916. THRIVING CLONES INDUSTRY. Messrs. Noble, Bros. who carry on the chief industry in Clones and who are well known makers of all classes of traps and driving vehicles have now extended their business and have opened up a motoring branch. Some idea of the popularity of Messrs. Noble's rally traps may be learned from their exhibits not only at Clones Show but also at Enniskillen. At the former seven exhibits were on the ground, of which six were sold and at Enniskillen Show six were shown and all sold. Messrs. Noble's enterprise and good workmanship command business. I.R.

September 21st 1916. BY THE DEATH OF MR. WILLIAM RITCHIE, Enniskillen has lost one of its most entertaining after dinner speakers. A fountain of ready wit, genial in his disposition and possessing a rich and cultured flow of language, he was always at social gatherings a welcome guest. He made an exceptionally good Chairman and had a grasp of all subjects under debate and conducted proceedings at meetings in a dignified manner. For three years he was Chairman of the Urban Council and from the founding of the Yacht Club up to his death, he was Chairman of the Yacht Club House and General Committees. At a meeting of the Fermanagh County Council Mr. E. M. Archdale moved that the sympathy of the Council be conveyed to Mrs. Ritchie and family of the late William Ritchie for their sad loss. Mr. Archdale said the late Mr. Ritchie had been editor of one of the best country newspapers, (*Fermanagh Times*) which he had conducted straightforwardly in every way and never did anything to hurt the personal feelings of those politically opposed to him. The people of all politics in the county greatly regretted his death and had been most sympathetic. All seemed to feel that they had lost a personal friend. He certainly did himself. I.R.

Fermanagh Herald September 23rd 1916. LISNASKEA GUARDIANS. THE MASTER'S POSITION. FORCED TO RESIGN. The chairman Mr. J McElgunn said that they all knew that the master had adhered strictly to the rules, and if the "poor woman" had gone into the probationary ward there would not have been another word about it. But she did not, and in his opinion that was her own fault. She went away, and when she again came the gate was locked, but the gate should have been locked at 10.00 according to the regulations and therefore the porter and master were carrying out the orders of the Local Government Board. He thought the action of the Local Government Board extraordinary.

Mr. Rennick – it is too bad to think or say that the man who has spent the best part of his life here should now have to go. It's absurd that the Local Government Board will put a man out for keeping to the rules laid down by themselves. Mr. Maguire said we hear a lot about the Germans, but if they are as bad as the Local Government Board they must be bad enough. The master having considered the advisability of resigning decided to tender his resignation, requesting a month's notice. The Guardians accepted the resignation with regret.

Fermanagh Herald September 23rd 1916. THE NEW TIME. The following has been published: -Local Government Board Dublin 12th of September, 1916. Sir, - I am directed by the Local Government Board for Ireland to draw your attention to the Time Ireland Act 1916 under which Western European time is to be observed throughout Ireland from and after the 1st of October next. Instead, therefore, of clocks been put back 1 hour at 3.00 AM on the night of the 30th of September next, in accordance with the terms of the said circular, they should be put back only 35 minutes.

Fermanagh Herald September 23rd 1916. OBITER DICTA. A FALACIOUS BELIEF. At the Enniskillen Guardians meeting on Tuesday, Mr. E. M. Archdale, DL made a statement that truth of which seems to be held by many people. It was in reference to a soldier's wife who was in receipt of a separation allowance from her husband, and was kept by the Guardians. Mr. Archdale said that there was a good deal of immorality and drinking going on among "these class of women." Such is not true. Cases appear in the courts from time to time but for the one woman who takes to drink in consequence of handling her husband's separation allowance, there are hundreds of mothers who dispose of their allotments in a righteous manner. Mr. Archdale should not condemn thousands of good and faithful wives because of the errings of a few.

Fermanagh Herald September 23rd 1916. ON LAST MONDAY I PAID A FINAL TRIBUTE OF RESPECT TO THE MEMORY OF MY FELLOW JOURNALIST, WILLIAM RITCHIE, and perceived the townspeople of Enniskillen following the remains of one whom they knew and respected as a friend and esteemed and appreciated as a brilliant writer. My personal acquaintance with Mr. Ritchie was full of pleasant memories of delightful literary and musical chats. As a literary man he was never perhaps fitted for newspaper work. He soared far above. It would be safe to think that his proper sphere in journalism would have been at a high class magazine work; for his style was brilliant, his ideas originally and his expression forceful. Cigarette smoking, he indulged in and with avidity. He was never without the inevitable cigarette, and, like many other journalists, he could seldom write or think without the seductive weed between his lips. It was a happy

coincidence that his coffin was covered with flowers, for he was passionately fond of them. The funeral was remarkable, and was a consoling and wonderful tribute to his memory as well as to the esteem in which he was held by all sections of the public.

September 28th 1916. BRITAIN'S NEW WEAPONS AND THEIR REMARKABLE ACHIEVEMENTS. The topic of the moment both with their soldiers and the German prisoners is the new 'Tanks" or mobile turrets which have done such valuable work, wrote Reuter's Correspondent after the last splendid advance. These wonderful new motor cavalry called 'Tanks' are ponderous, they're heavy, they are slow; they move upon caterpillar wheels but they are impossible to knock out except by a direct hit. They move forward undisturbed by the most deadly barrage of fire. They are inevitable like Fate. They are not to be put down. It is really to Mr. Winston Churchill that the credit is due more than to anyone else says Mr. Lloyd George. He took up with enthusiasm the idea of making them a long time ago. The enemy has by no means a monopoly of inventive ingenuity. F.T.

Fermanagh Herald September 30th 1916. JOTTINGS. In the airship raids on Sunday and Monday on England, 74 persons were killed and 152 injured.

Before Mr. T. Gavin presiding, and other magistrates sitting at the Lisnaskea Petty Sessions on Saturday, a large number of persons were summoned for drunkenness. Nominal penalties were inflicted.

Mr. Patrick Daly, son of Mr. Patrick Daly, contractor, West Rock, Ballyshannon who lately passed an examination in wireless telegraphy at the Marconi School, Cahirciveen, County Kerry has been summoned to London to join his ship, for which city he left on Tuesday morning. We wish Mr. Daly success in his new sphere of labour.

Lord Aberconway, presiding at the annual meeting of John Brown and Co., Sheffield, said when the war is over they anticipate a great demand, which they were ready to meet for merchant tonnage. In wages they had paid an average of 10 shillings a week for every man and boy more than ever before. In the collieries absenteeism was largely responsible for the increased cost of coal.

Benjamin Porter, manager of the Hemsworth Gas Works, was fined £2 at Pontefract Petty Sessions Court on Saturday for not having an attendant to receive air raid messages by telephone. The defendant, who was on holiday when the raid took place, at the beginning of the month, left a lad in charge of the telephone. When the call was passed no reply could be obtained, and the police on making an investigation found the lad so sound asleep that they had to go through a window and shake him before he could be wakened.

His life for chestnuts –George Kerns, schoolboy, aged 13 of 490 Oldpark Road, Belfast was fatally injured by falling from a tree when gathering chestnuts. "Accidental death" was the jury's verdict.

At Kerry GAA County Board a letter was read from the Central Council as to the right of police to enter sports fields without payment, and Mr. P. J. O'Connell who presided, said no exception should be made in the matter.

A French Graveyard December 1916.

OCTOBER 1916

October 12th 1916. NOTES. Some compensation has been offered for one public scandal. It will be remembered that when the office of Resident Medical Superintendent of the Ballinasloe Lunatic Asylum became vacant a few years ago, Dr. Mills was passed over on the grounds that he was a Protestant. The vacancy having again occurred on Monday Dr. John Mills was again a candidate. He has been the Acting Medical Superintendent and when he was proposed the other candidates withdrew their applications and he was appointed unanimously and to the great delight of the patients who cheered widely when they heard this news.

The Ulster Gaelic League have refused to pay tax on receipts at football matches, but are holding money in hand to pay up if they cannot obtain redress by questions in Parliament. It is the old story.

An electrical engineer named Theerman, of Manchester had a telephone without a permit and at the city police court he was fined £10 with costs for using it. £10! In Ireland it would have been one shilling.

Trotting Race Meetings have very properly been suppressed in Glasgow by the Munition Authorities. The same prohibition should extend to all races in England and Ireland.

It seems hard to believe that Mr. C. S. Parnell was 25 years dead last week. The funeral was, perhaps the greatest procession which Dublin ever saw.

To have a water famine in summer and to be flooded each winter is the present dilemma in which the Irvinestown people are situated. When heavy rain falls the centre of the town looks like a miniature Venice except that the water makes its way into the houses and rises sometimes to a depth of 2 feet.

The purchase of hay by the military authorities in the Kesh district has created a lot of dissatisfaction because an equal price was not given for all hay bought though the hay was said to be all the same quality. Had all got the same price no demur would have been heard but a few getting a better price has caused the friction. I.R.

Mr. C. S. Parnell.

October 12th 1916. LISNASKEA. THE CLERK OF THE UNION RESIGNS AFTER 46 YEARS OF LOYAL SERVICE. A letter was received at to the Board of Guardians meeting on Saturday from Mr. J. O'R. Hoey, Clerk of the Union who wrote regretting that owing to the state of his health he would be unable to resume duty at the expiration of his leave of absence and therefore begged to tender his resignation. 'I desire' he wrote 'at the same time to return you my most sincere thanks for the unfailing kindness, courtesy and forbearance which I have experienced at your hands. I have held the office for 46 years and nine months during which period I have never, prior to my present illness, put you to a farthings expense for substitutes, disallowances by auditors or otherwise. Tributes were paid to the Clerk and the Board accepted the resignation with regret. I.R.

October 12th 1916. CLONES PETTY SESSIONS. John Higgins, a tramp, was charged under the Defence of the Realm Act with being found wearing military trousers without authority. Defendant said he got the trousers in Strabane and thought it was no harm to wear them. He was fined 10 shillings and costs with the alternative of prison and the trousers to be returned to the military authorities.

John McCloy, Dublin Street, Monaghan, was summoned for driving a motor car on the public street without having affixed to it in front an identification mark and also for failing to produce a driver's licence. On Mr. Knight's representation on his behalf, defendant was let off with a fine of one shilling in each case and costs. I.R.

Fermanagh Herald October 14th 1916. ULSTER'S VIEW OF CONSCRIPTION. WORKERS OPPOSITION. Writing from Belfast, a correspondent of the *Daily News* says "I have ascertained how far the views of the Belfast Unionist workers coincide with those expressed by the Ulster Unionist leader. It was pointed out very emphatically to me that, with the exception of Sir Edward Carson, no one in Ulster had asked for Conscription for Ireland. Of course, Sir Edward would find plenty of support from the commercial and mill owning class above military age. Of a number of unionists men interviewed no one favours the application of the Military Service Act to Ireland. They pointed out, as do the Nationalists in the South and West that Ireland has contributed her fair quota to the Army and held that if all of the Irish-born men in English and Scottish regiments from both North and South were drafted into the Irish regiments the gaps would be filled three times over.

Belfast 1916

A prominent Belfast trade unionist official interviewed, said: "I move amongst the workers, and I know public opinion about military service in Ireland outside the safely badged shipyards and engineering workers and those above military age, and the North is in agreement with the South. Let Sir Edward Carson come to Belfast, hold a meeting advocating Conscription, and find how many men outside the above classes between the age of 18 and 41 he will have in attendance. Let him go to Unionist Northern farmers who this year failed to secure labour even at four times the cost of previous seasons and find whether they are in favour of military service. If the North desires Conscription, how comes it that the recent appeal for men from the trenches to fill up the Ulster Division gaps practically fell on deaf ears?

Fermanagh Herald October 14th 1916. REDMOND'S RECORD. NEVER A NATIONALIST. AN INCOMPETENT AND DISCREDITED PARTY. The corrupt and Anti–National Agreement entered into between the Irish Party Leaders and the Government for the Partition of Ireland was a fitting climax to the policy the Party Leaders have pursued for years past, the policy in every detail loathsome and repulsive to every true Nationalist. The dogged persistence with which the Party Leaders adhered to the Lloyd George Proposals, the deception that they practiced in order to conceal from the people the true nature of these Proposals; meant that that they had entered into, without any a warrant from the people, against the will of the people and in utter defiance of the National sentiment; the trickery that they resorted to at the Belfast Conference in order to get these Proposals a semblance of support, the fact that the conference was packed with personal friends and retainers of Mr. Devlin, and dominated by bullies from the Berry Street Club, all these considerations impressed the Nationalists of the North with the necessity for forming some independent organisation to safeguard the National cause. The agitation that was set on foot in the areas proposed to be excluded, mainly in Fermanagh, Tyrone and Derry City. That culminated in a great meeting in St., Columb's Hall, Derry and was successful in defeating the plot for the dismemberment of Ireland. But there was ample reason to believe, as there are still is, that further attempts would be made to give effect to the Agreement and to carry it into law. In order to deal with this standing peril, and be prepared for any emergency the Anti–Partition League was formed.

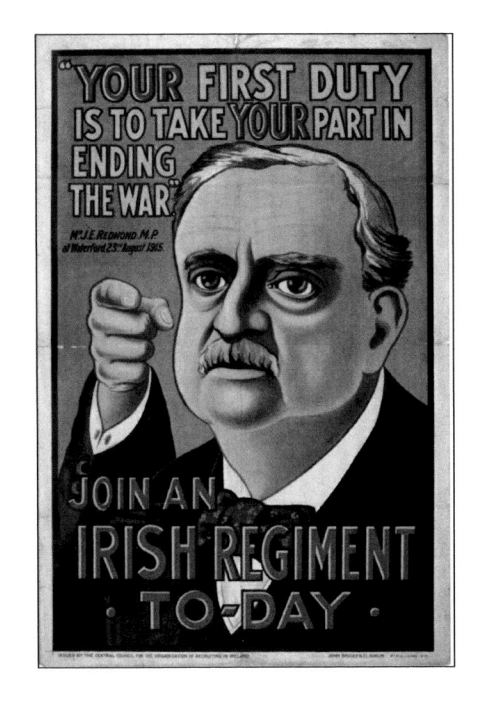

Fermanagh Herald October 14th 1916. JOTTINGS. A great slump was noticeable in the prices offered at the Enniskillen fair on Tuesday. Live pigs showed very considerable decrease in the amounts fetched; this is attributed to the shortage of potatoes, flooding and consequent damage to root crops, which form an important feeding stuff for pigs.

It is known that considerable feeling exists in Maguiresbridge and surrounding districts that there should be a co-operative flax mill started in this county. This would mean that the flax grower would get fair and equitable prices for their flax and tow, and also that they would not be forced to sell their produce to the first buyers in the markets.

In a recent issue of the *Gardiners' Chronicle*, we notice that at the show held near London under the auspices of the Royal Horticultural Society, in the potato class, that the section devoted to "Irish Chieftains," the exhibit of "Lissadell" was very highly commended. This exhibit was raised by Mr. F. J. McKenna, the master of the Manorhamilton Union, who deserves much praise for bringing Manorhamilton into the limelight at such an important show.

Fermanagh Herald October 14th 1916. OBITER DICTA. A WORTHY CAUSE. The Dublin rising has left in its wake a train of dire desolation and sorrow. To us in Enniskillen little knowledge of the privations and sufferings of many families is available. We can only imagine it, but as time goes on many sad and a harrowing accounts reach the sympathetic and philanthropic ears of those residing in the provinces – stories of starving woman, and children, who, prior to Easter were unacquainted with the grim significance of want. Dublin, in it's more fashionable quarters, is again bright. The music in the theatres is still heard, the brilliantly lighted tramcars are again moving around, and business is returning to normal. But away in many parts of the city are destitute families. Some of them are the dependants of those who lost their lives; there are also those who took no part in the rebellion, but the places in which they were employed have been demolished and of course their services are no longer required. It was to relieve in some little way this pitiable situation that it was decided to start a National Aid Association. For this purpose Canon Keown called a meeting in the Gaelic Hall and all agreed that a collection should be taken up through Enniskillen which will appeal to all creeds and classes. It is outside of the domain of politics and religion. It is a charitable and purely philanthropic undertaking, as Dublin Protestants as well as Catholics are benefiting by the National Aid Association. On Sunday evening a committee was appointed, as well as collectors, who will visit the different houses in the parish during the course of the next two weeks. Everybody is expected to contribute something no matter how little.

October 19th 1916. THE SHOOTING OF SHEEHY-SKEFFINGTON AND THE COMMISSION'S STRONG REPORT. THE OFFENCE OF MURDER. The report of the Royal Commission appointed to investigate into the circumstances, the arrest and subsequent treatment of Mr. F. Sheehy-Skeffington, Mister T. Dixon and Mr. P. J. McIntyre was issued on Monday afternoon. It states that it was conceded on all hands that Mr. Skeffington had no connection with the Rebellion; that his views were opposed to the use of physical force and that he was engaged on the afternoon of his arrest in making some public appeal to prevent looting and the like. The Commissioners find that apart from the evidence of insanity there can be no excuse or palliation of the conduct of Captain Bowen-Colthurst at the time he committed the offence of murder in ordering the shooting of the three men. That was frankly recognised by those who appeared before the court on behalf of the Military Authorities.

Dealing with the condition of affairs at Portobello Barracks where the shooting took place the report states: - The Garrison there was insufficient and it was for the purpose of resisting any serious attempt which might have been made, was reinforced by a medley of soldiers from different regiments together with some sailors. It was not to be wondered that state of affairs produced considerable laxity of control and cohesion. The officers in charge of the guard were young men who had left school and of necessity were without military experience. The fact combined with Captain Colthurst's masterful character and superior rank did much to excuse their failure to offer any effective opposition to this treatment of prisoners under their charge. The raid on the house of Mrs. Skeffington subsequent to her husband's death is described by the Commissioners as being discreditable and it was regrettable and surprising that Captain Colthurst found himself free to act as he did on that occasion. The shooting of unarmed or unresisting civilians without trial constituted the offense of murder whether martial law had been proclaimed or not.

A man of courage. Sir Francis Fletcher Vane was an hereditary peer born in Dublin of an Irish mother and English father. A career officer in the British Army, he was sacked from the Army ('relegated to unemployment') for preventing an Army cover-up of a number of military murders in Dublin during the 1916 Insurrection. It was Vane who revealed the murder of the well-known writer and pacifist Francis Sheehy Skeffington, by Captain Bowen-Colthurst. Vane was an extraordinary character. Born in 1861 at 10 Great George's street, Dublin, he died in London in 1934. Although an army officer, he spoke on anti-war platforms, was a democratic aristocrat with socialist and republican sympathies who challenged the jingoism of the empire and the demonising of its enemies. The Vane family had a long tradition of championing human rights. An ancestor, Sir Henry Vane, led the republicans in Parliament during the English Civil War and in 1656 his tract *A Healing Question* affirmed the doctrines of civil and religious liberty. He resigned from politics rather than acknowledges Cromwell as Lord Protector. When the monarchy was restored he was tried for treason and executed in 1662. Sir Francis was sent to Military college in Oxford, was commissioned in the Scots Guards before his appointment as captain in the 26th Middlesex Cyclist Battalion. When Britain invaded the Boer Republics in 1899, he was sent to South Africa, Appointed as a military magistrate in 1902, he was sacked for being "pro-Boer".

Sir Francis Fletcher Vane

He was firmly set against the heavy-handed military repression of the Boer people and wrote *The War and One Year After* (1903) attacking British was methods. *His Pax Britannica* in 1904 amplified his stand and he was put on the "retired" list. However, he had become South African correspondent for the *Daily News* and *Manchester Guardian*. Then in 1906 he stood as a Liberal candidate in the UK General Election. Although unsuccessful he became active in the anti-war and suffragette campaigns. With the outbreak of the 1914-18 War he felt it was his duty to return to army service again. With the rank of Major he was sent to Ireland as a recruiting officer. When the insurrection took place he was ordered to take command at Portobello Barracks, Dublin. There were about 300 soldiers in the garrison mainly from the Royal Irish Rifles and the Ulster Militia

Battalion. Vane went round the area of Rathmines, personally placing observation posts. On Wednesday, April 26, he returned to the barracks.

It was then that he discovered the activities of Captain J.C. Bowen-Colthurst in his absence.

Three "suspicious" persons were being held at the barracks. They were the writer Sheehy Skeffington and two journalists Thomas Dickson and Patrick MacIntyre. Captain Bowen-Colthurst had decided to conduct some raids and on the night of April 25 he had taken the prisoners with his raiding party to act as hostages, human shields, against all rules of war. At Rathmines they came across a 17-year old boy named Coade coming from a church, and, on orders, one of the soldiers smashed the boys jaw with his rifle butt. Then Bowen-Colthurst stood over him and shot the boy, as he lay senseless on the ground. The raiding party then proceeded to the home of Alderman James Kelly, a Unionist, but Bowen-Colthurst had mistakenly identified him as a Sinn Féin councilor. They destroyed his house with grenades. Another Dublin councilor, Richard O'Carroll, was also shot by Bowen-Colthurst. Returning to barracks, Bowen-Colthurst then ordered his sergeant, William Aldridge, to take the prisoners out and shoot them. This he did, in Bowen-Colthurst's presence. Vane returning to barracks and discovering what had happened had Bowen-Colthurst confined to Barracks pending court martial. On reporting to army headquarters, Vane found his superiors justifying Bowen-Colthurst's actions. Royal Engineers arrived and repaired the bullet holes in the barracks walls so they could not be seen. Vane was removed from command and Bowen-Colthurst was released and allowed to conduct a vicious raid on Mrs. Hannah Sheehy Skeffington's house for "incriminating evidence".

On May 2, Vane left for England and, using contacts, managed to secure a meeting with Field Marshal Lord Kitchener and Bonham Carter, private secretary to the Prime Minister. After two weeks of prevarication, in which Vane was "relegated to unemployment", on May 18, Lord Chief justice of England, Lord Reading, accepted a military court martial in private so that the Government would be spared a public hearing. Bowen-Colthurst was quickly found guilty but insane. He was confined to Broadmoor criminally insane hospital for one year, then released and allowed to go to Canada where he died in 1965. The Government then offered Mrs Hannah Sheehy Skeffington £10,000 compensation. She refused and demanded the full facts be made public and even former President Theodore Roosevelt became interested in the case. Thanks to Vane, the horrors of the murders committed by Bowen-Colthurst became public.

In 1917 Vane attempted to publish a book on the 1916 insurrection but the proof copies were seized and prevented from publication by the military censors. The manuscript was subsequently lost. This was the first of Vane's books that was suppressed for he wrote a book recounting incidents from South Africa, the *1914-18 War and the Irish insurrection*, which was also seized and suppressed by the military censor. He took up residence in Italy in 1918. His wife died there in 1924, and he returned to London's Bayswater in 1927, leaving Italy after his political views caused him to fall foul of the Fascist Government of Mussolini.

In 1930 he published his autobiography *Agin The Government - Memories and Adventures of Sir Francis Fletcher Vane*, giving full details of the Bowen-Colthurst affair. British officers like Vane, General F.P. Crozier, and latterly Captain Fred Holroyd and Major Colin Wallace, have demonstrated that there are occasional army officers of great moral courage who find principles a more powerful force than political expediency. We should honour them. Courtesy of Peter Berrisford Ellis and *The Irish Post*. F.T.

October 26th 1916. WAR NOTES AND COMMENTS. A battalion of the Canadian Expeditionary Force which received its camp colours a few days ago from the Duchess of Connaught is unique among the fighting units raised at home or abroad during the war says the *Times*. It is an Irish battalion composed of Catholics and Protestants in equal numbers, commanded by officers, rather more and half of whom are Catholics and attended by a Catholic chaplain and a Protestant chaplain. Officially, it is named the Duchess of Connaught's

Own Irish-Canadian Rangers; unofficially it is likely to be known as the battalion of Orange and Green.

The recruiting campaign was on several of its branches distinctly novel. From first to last it was conducted by regimental officers, with Major Campbell Stuart as chief recruiting officer. The next step was to construct on Dominion Square, Montreal, model field fortifications like those in France and to hold meetings beside them every evening. The greatest asset of the recruiting officer was the active and self-sacrificing cooperation of the clergy, both Catholic and Protestant. The Catholic priests gave the utmost help, both by speech and by influence. Their speeches were printed and distributed at the doors of the churches and with their approval meetings were held outside the churches after Mass on Sunday mornings. The Protestant clergy were not less sympathetic, some of them actually lending their pulpits to the recruiting officers during Sunday evening services. F.T.

October 26th 1916. THE M.P. FOR NORTH FERMANAGH RESIGNS. Mr. William Eames, Secretary Fermanagh Unionist Association has received the following letter dated 17th of October from Mr. Godfrey Fetherstonhaugh M.P. for North Fermanagh. Dear Sir, As I previously intimated to you I have sent in my application for the Chiltern Hundreds in order to vacate my seat for North Fermanagh. I would have done so much sooner but that I wished to be in the House of Commons when the responsibility for the Dardanelles adventure – which proved for fatal to those dear to me – came up for discussion. As the prospect of that seems a very deferred one I think it better to resign now. Through you I thank the electors of North Fermanagh, those who supported me for willing and hearty services and those who voted against me for uniform courtesy even in the heat of three contested elections. Mr. Fetherstonhaugh was elected for the constituent in January 1906 and has contest three elections successfully. His brother Major Fetherstonhaugh, Royal Dublin Fusiliers was killed at the Dardanelles about 12 months ago. F.T.

October 26th 1916. ALLEGED HUGE WASTE IN THE IRISH EGG INDUSTRY CAUSED BY CARELESS PACKING. Questions were asked by Mr. Donovan addressed to the Vice President as to the condition of the egg transport from Ireland. He asked was he aware that hundreds of thousands of pounds worth of eggs are smashed every year in transit from Ireland to London, the damage being attributed to bad packing, inefficient handling and pilfering and whether he is aware that in a recent consignment of 3,500 eggs from Ireland only 1,900 arrived intact. Mr. P.W. Russell replied that the whole question as to the packing and conveyance of Irish eggs was engaging the special attention of the Department. F.T.

NOVEMBER 1916

November 2nd 1916. THE IRISH LANGUAGE REVIVAL. CLASSES FORMED OVER THE COUNTRY. One result of the Easter week disturbance in Ireland and the events which followed has been to direct more attention to the Irish language revival movement. All over the country additional members have flocked into the Gaelic League which was never stronger in the country than at present. In the city of Cork the League was just holding its own. Now, however, there are five branches of the Gaelic League with very large memberships holding Irish language classes. There has been such an influx of students that several additional classes have been arranged for. And lately several private classes have been established for businesses and professional people who do not wish to attend the league classes. What is happening in Cork is happening all over country. I.R.

November 2nd 1916. SUNDAY EVENING IN AN ENNISKILLEN SHOP. AN ACTION AGAINST A WELL-KNOWN MERCHANT. 'HE PUT HIS ARMS AROUND ME AND HELD ME TIGHT.' A case of considerable local interest was heard at Enniskillen Quarter Sessions when Elizabeth Maguire, a domestic servant, sued Joseph Latimer, merchant, Cross Street, Enniskillen for £40 for assault and £10 for breach of contract. The plaintiff said she was in the kitchen when Mr. Latimer called to her to bring up milk to feed cats that were in the shop. She brought up the milk to the shop and as she was putting it down on the counter defendant put his arms around her and held her tight. She screamed and then ran out, and went up to Mrs. Keown's house Cross Street and made a complaint to her and went to a solicitor the next day. Joseph Latimer, defendant, said he was about 70 years of age and was married with a grown up family and was not thinking much nowadays about young girls. He said all he did on this occasion was to put his hand on the girl shoulder to help her up into the window with the milk for the cats. As a rule he read the *Christian Herald* while sitting in the hall on Sunday evenings and he was doing so on this evening. The judge granted a decree for ordinary assault which did take place for £5 and costs. F.T.

November 2nd 1916. DUBLIN METROPOLITAN POLICE. MEMBERS JOIN THE ANCIENT ORDER OF HIBERNIANS. The action of certain members of the D. M. P. – about 700 in number – associating themselves as members with the Ancient Order of Hibernians is a question which must engage the immediate attention of the authorities. By the terms of the oaths which they are obliged to take the members of both the City Force and the Royal Irish Constabulary undertake not to become members of any political or secret society, the Society of Freemasons excepted. The dispute with the City Police arose out of a claim made by them for an increase in their wages of 12 shillings per week and further that the war bonus they receive should be made retrospective to date from the commencement of the war. About 700 of the men have now joined the ranks of the Hibernian organisation. It is understood that their contention is that the Ancient Order of Hibernians is no more a political organisation than the Order of Freemasons and that they have as much right to join the Hibernian as other members of the force have to join the Masonic body. F.T.

A member of the Dublin Metropolitan Police.

November 2nd 1916. A. V. C. FOR CASTLEBLANEY AND THE SECOND FOR COUNTY MONAGHAN. Another addition has been made to the roll of Ulster V. C.s, that coveted decoration having been won by Private Thomas Hughes, Connaught Rangers. The official account of his gallantry reads: - For most conspicuous bravery and determination. He was wounded in an attack, and returned at once to the firing line after having his wounds dressed. Later seeing a hostile machine gun, he dashed out in front of his company, shot the gunner, and single-handedly captured the gun. Although again wounded he brought back three or four prisoners. Private Hughes is one of many Ulsterman serving in the Connaught Rangers. He is a son of Mr. Patrick Hughes, Castleblaney, County Monaghan. He is the second Monaghan man to win the V.C. in the present war the other being Sergeant (now Lieutenant), David Nelson, Royal Horse Artillery who was awarded the Cross for his gallantry at Lery on the 14th of September, 1914 with the famous L Battery. I.R.

Fermanagh Herald November 4th 1916. JOTTINGS. Captain J. Samuel Irvine, Royal Inniskilling Fusiliers, wounded in action, is the younger son of Mr. C. E. R. A. Irvine, Sessional Crown Solicitor, Drumgoom Manor, Maguiresbridge. He joined the army at the outbreak of the war and went through the Gallipoli campaign without a scratch. He contracted typhoid fever, and was in hospital at Mudros, and later in London. His elder brother, Captain C. Samuel Irvine, was badly wounded in France in August 1914, and is a prisoner of war in Germany.

A most successful dance was held in in the Moat Hall, Lisnaskea, on last Sunday evening. The dance was organised for the purpose of futhering the cause for which the National Aid Association was initiated, and this good object drew an extremely large attendance. It was a most enjoyable evening, and the hall, which was nicely decorated for the occasion, was packed. Great credit is due to every member of the committee and also to the ladies who worked so hard to make the dance the great success it undoubtedly was.

Fermanagh Herald November 4th 1916. REDMONDITE RED HERRINGS. In his speech at Sligo Mr. Redmond, the leader of the Irish Tail of the British Liberal Party, spoke of what he called the Constitutional movement, and said that it was doomed if the country did not give unquestioning obedience to those who were elected as the servants of the people. This is a device on Mr. Redmond's part to stampede the country into his Partitionist and "conscription if necessary" camp. He wants to terrify the people with the spectre of red revolution. Truth to say it is no fault of his and his fellow Tailers if the revolt against their slavishness and treachery has not taken a more dreadful shape. But the Nationalist movement as established by Parnell and Davitt (if that is what Mr. Redmond means by the Constitutional movement) is not more in danger than Mr. Redmond is in "danger" of voluntarily throwing off his Whiggery and his patriotic mask. The country is all right and sees its way perfectly before it; it is Mr. Redmond and his colleagues who are all wrong.

November 9th 1916. GREENORE BOAT SUNK IN COLLISION. NEWRY STEAMER DOWN WITH ONLY ONE SURVIVOR AND FEARED LOSS OF 200 LIVES. A very grave shipping disaster took place on Friday night resulting in the sinking of the two steamers involved and the loss it is feared of all passengers and hands except one. The colliding steamers were the outgoing *SS Connemara* of the London and North West Railway Company's Greenore and Holyhead service and the incoming Newry collier, *Retriever*. The disaster is said to be due to a collision between the vessels off the Bar during the height of the fierce gale which raged all around the coast. There is only one survivor, a man named James Boyle of the *Retriever*. I.R.

November 9th 1916. AN ENNISKILLEN HERO WELCOMED IN ENGLAND SERGEANT MAJOR GUY BLEAKLEY a native of Enniskillen and a recent winner of the Military Cross who is married to a daughter of Mrs. O'Hara, Henry Street is a most popular and efficient soldier and his many friends hereabouts will be glad to read of this reception for him in Stourbridge. It is a tribute to the respect and popularity his gallantry and personality have won for him. F.T.

Fermanagh Herald November 11th 1916. MR. REDMOND AND CASEMENT. Mrs. Agnes Newman, sister to Rodger Casement, writing to the American Press on the execution of her brother, says that as a last resource John Redmond was asked to sign a petition for reprieve and he replied, "No, I will not sign it, even if you come to me an hour before the execution. This man has done more harm in Ireland than all the others put together."

Fermanagh Herald November 11th 1916. WANTED. Rabbits – thousands wanted every week. Best trapped or snared and making 8p to 1s each. Highest prices in trade for all classes of game will be paid every Tuesday at the Butter Market, Enniskillen. James Campbell. Head office – 100 Stockwell Street, Glasgow.

WANTED. Working men wanted, with families of boys and girls for work in Woollen Factory; constant employment and good wages. Apply Henderson & Eadie, Ltd., Lisbellaw, Co., Fermanagh.

Fermanagh Herald November 11th 1916. JOTTINGS. Record prices were paid suppliers for last month's milk by the Fivemiletown and Brookeborough Co-operative Dairy Society, as high as 10½d per gallon being paid at Brookeborough, and 9¼d at Fivemiletown. The monthly fair and half-yearly hiring market was held in cold, bleak weather in Fivemiletown on Friday.

Enniskillen has figured in the death roll of the ill-fated *Connemara*. Miss Jenny McElgunn whose father was for many years a member of the Town Commissioners, and who resided at Queen Street, was amongst those who lost their lives. The deceased lady, had, we are informed, had been in America for some years and was in Enniskillen on a holiday when she decided to return on Friday and unfortunately booked her passage to Holyhead on the *Connemara*. Much sympathy will go out to her relatives and friends.

SS Connemara.

Fermanagh Herald November 11th 1916. FERMANAGH COUNTY COUNCIL. THE WATER SUPPLY TO BELLEEK POTTERY. Mr. P. Scott, J.P. made the following statement regarding the water supply to Belleek Pottery, "What keeps the upper and lower lakes from being at the same level? It is because the obstructions were never properly removed, or no attempt was ever made to clean up past Enniskillen? Yet in the supposed interests of the people around the upper lake, the sluices at Belleek are now kept open night and day, and the only industry of its kind in Ireland is been strangled by depriving it of its water power, and the workers left to starve. Is it not plain that the river is not able to carry down as much water as the sluices can vent, and the Lough Erne Drainage Board do nothing only open the sluices, which has just as much effect on emptying Upper Lough Erne as "the lady with a broomstick had of keeping out to the tide." (Laughter.)

Fermanagh Herald November 11th 1916. APPALLING DISASTER OFF THE DOWN COAST. THE GREENORE – HOLYHEAD PASSENGER STEAMER SUNK AND THE COLLIDING CARGO BOAT ALSO FOUNDERS. NEARLY 100 LIVES ARE LOST. During the height of the gale on Friday evening a collision occurred at the mouth of Carlingford Lough between the L. and N. W. Company's twin-screw steamer *Connemara* and the Newry-owned cargo steamer *Retriever*. The former had just left Greenore Quay with passengers, livestock, and cargo for Holyhead on her regular service trip and the latter was inward bound to Newry with a cargo of coal. Both vessels sank within a few minutes of the impact, and of the entire complement, consisting of 93 souls, only one was saved. This was a seaman of the *Retriever* named Boyle, who, clung to an overturned boat and was washed ashore. The disaster took place within sight of land about 8.30 p.m., when the gale was at its height, but efforts to reach the scene from the shore or take to the boats were impossible in the boiling seas, and both vessels went to the bottom sweeping away their human freight with a completeness startling to contemplate. The *Connemara* carried 51 passengers and 31 of a crew, while the Retriever's crew numbered eight and the survivor was a fireman of the collier named James Boyle of Warrenpoint. Most of the *Retriever's* crew belong to Newry district and those of the *Connemara* to Holyhead while the latter's passengers included several Irish cattle salesman and many emigrants from Monaghan, Cavan and Leitrim. Up to Sunday evening 58 bodies had been recovered, many bearing traces of having been dashed against the rocks.

Fermanagh Herald November 11th 1916. MANORHAMILTON GUARDIANS. COST OF MEDICINES. The Local Government Board wrote returning copies of requisition for medicines recently submitted by the medical officer of the Dromahaire dispensary district, pointing out that the supply of the items marked appear to be ordered in great quantity. Mr. McHugh said the doctor should be the best judge but nevertheless an order was made that the doctor be more economical in future. The potato contract was discussed after the contractor wrote requesting the Guardians to increase the price owing to the scarcity of potatoes and their failure in many places, as it was impossible to obtain a supply at anything like his contract price of five shillings five pence per hundredweight. He also pointed out if the Guardians could not see their way to acceded to his request to accept his letter as a 31 days' notice, and relieve him of the contract after that period had expired.

November 16th 1916. NOTES. Owing to the increased cost of food a special Government Committee is considering the desirability of a war standard loaf.

By a small majority Australia has decided not to have conscription.

The *Southern Star*, Skibbereen, has been suppressed by order of the military authorities for publishing an article about the police entitled '*The Mollies and the Masons*'.

Potatoes are said to be making a profit of £57 an acre in England.

Numbers of women are now being trained as carpenters in Surrey for contract work such as the construction of huts.

The German Crown Prince is in disgrace for his failure before Verdun. He has been transferred to Alsace.

The Irish Party last week voted in opposition to the Government and supported Sir Edward Carson's resolution on the question of the sale of properties in Nigeria to only British born subjects.

The British Ministry of Munitions employs directly 1,850,000 men and 400,000 women.

The sum of £110 has been collected in Enniskillen for the relief fund in aid of the relatives of the Dublin Sinn Fein rebels. Few of the subscribers in this list have ever given anything in aid of the starving Inniskilling prisoners of war.

The new vats for pickling eggs at the Enniskillen Scottish Co-Operative Stores are capable of holding over five million eggs!

Nearly 5 miles high is the wonderful record of Flight Lt. Guidi of the Italian army. It makes one feel a little giddy.

The elections in the United States have resulted in the return of the first woman M.P. (Ed. Jeannette Pickering Rankin (June 11, 1880 – May 18, 1973) was the first woman elected to the United States Congress, in 1916 and again in 1940, from the state of Montana. After winning her House seat in 1916 she said, "I may be the first woman member of Congress but I won't be the last." Rankin's two terms in Congress coincided with U.S. entry into both World Wars. A lifelong pacifist, she was one of 56 members of Congress who voted against entry into World War I in

Jeannette Pickering Rankin.

1917, and the only member of Congress to vote against declaring war on Japan after the attack on Pearl Harbour in 1941. In addition, she was the only woman to cast a Congressional vote in favour of the Constitutional Amendment granting women unconditional voting rights. I.R.

November 16th 1916. IRVINESTOWN WORKHOUSE. AN ENGLISH CRITICISM. The Irvinestown Guardians have decided to close their workhouse and fever hospital. The proposal was supported by figures which showed that last year the average number of the inmates under care was 29; and that the cost of maintaining them apart from officials' salaries worked out at one pound a week each. It was also shown that those for whom the Guardians are responsible can be boarded out for seven shillings a week each and that altogether a saving of well over £1,000 a year can be accomplished by the proposed change. A very curious argument was brought forward against the new scheme though it did not avail to cause its rejection. This argument was that the poor paupers would better be put against a wall and shot than sent away to a strange place and perhaps be badly treated. 'It may be hoped that Irish Poor Law administration is not that quite so low an ebb as the speaker appears to believe. Perhaps, and more probably, his vehemently worded plea was merely a piece of Irish exaggeration not meant to be taken seriously. *The Hospital*. F.T.

November 16th 1916. RABBITS FOR THE TROOPS. A Woking Army contractor told the local Military Service Tribunal that he had been asked by the authorities to contract for a regular supply of rabbits for the troops, but being unable to obtain the necessary labour, he was not in a position to do so. This new diet he said was being adopted in order to bring down the price of butcher's meat to the general public. The men welcomed the change. It had been found, he added, that a half pound of rabbit was as good as a pound of butcher's meat. F.T.

November 16th 1916. CHARGE AGAINST A CANADIAN. At Marlboro Police Court Robert Rossborough, a corporal in the Canadian Mounted Rifles was charged as an unauthorised person for being in possession of a quantity of cocaine and also with being an absentee from his regiment since October 15. The police arrested the accused in Old Crompton when showing cocaine in boxes to a female companion. The accused cast down the boxes and struggled. He now has stated that the cocaine did not belong to him. The police said he had been previously arrested as an absentee, but had escaped. The accused was remanded. F.T.

November 16th 1916. RECRUITING IN IRELAND. A Special Correspondent of *The Times* telegraphs from Dublin: - If the state of things in Dublin is any true indication of the state of things in this country generally it may safely be said that recruiting is dead in Ireland. Here a man of military age, even if he be a young man of the cap brigade may loiter at street corners, or about the city, or seat himself in a Picture House or Music Hall in the full confidence that no recruiting sergeant or official will come along to trouble him. There are few people on this side who would pin any hopes to a new recruiting campaign as a means of bringing into the Service the thousands of men of fighting age and fitness who may be seen in Dublin any day of the week. The 'atmosphere' is too unhealthy for any appeal to duty or national honour or patriotism or anything else which in more favourable conditions might lead men to enlist of their own free will. The result is only too plainly clear in the sheer indifference to the war and all its works which is the outstanding feature of the Dublin of today. It is not surprising that those who have to live in an atmosphere so deadly to every patriotic impulse should despair of any fresh effort to recruit Irishmen by voluntarism. F.T.

November 16th 1916. MILITARY FUNERAL AT CLONES. The remains of the late Private Joseph Beatty, Royal Engineers, a native of Clones were conveyed to that town from Liverpool on Sunday morning for internment. The deceased had been wounded in the foot and recovered but contracting pneumonia died in hospital. A guard of honour of the Royal Irish Fusiliers from Armagh attended under Sergeant Quinn and the funeral was carried out with military honours, the coffin being draped in the Union Jack. Men of the R.I.C.

took part in the procession as well as the local post office letter-carriers and other officials and members of the Irish National Foresters. The cortege was the largest seen in Clones for a long period, all classes wishing to do honour to the departed hero who had been in the employment of the Post Office but left to serve his King and country. Rev P. McQuaid, C.C. officiated at the graveside. F.T.

November 16th 1916. WHY POTATOES GO UP. Mr. H. R. Stannard writing from 'Somewhere in Potato Land, Lincolnshire' to the *Weekly Dispatch* says: Before the war the cost of producing an acre of potatoes was from £12 to £16; now it is £15 to £20. But even if you put it as high as £20 – a most generous estimate – what justification is there for prices ranging from £40 to £80 to the merchant? Some weeks ago one of the biggest farmers in the county thought he had made a very smart deal by selling more than 1,000 acres of growing potatoes at £40 an acre (£5 a ton) a profit of £20,000. Those potatoes today have not been moved and the purchaser can sell at £10 a ton - £80,000 - making a profit of £40,000 which amounts means a total profit on the two deals of £60,000. What will the price be by the time the merchant has put those potatoes on the market and made his profit? Fortunes are being made almost every day; farmers and merchants are dazzled by the great gold deposits in potato land. F.T.

November 16th 1916. POLICE REFUSED ADMISSION TO AN IRISH HURLING MATCH. A GAA SECRETARY ARRESTED. In the course of a hurling match at Pallasgreen, County Limerick, two policemen approach the gate and sought admission to the field. The Secretary of the Limerick County Board, G.A.A, Mr. James Ryan, who was present, declined it is stated, to admit them without payment. The two constables thereupon withdrew but subsequently returned with eight other policemen and placed Mr. Ryan under arrest on a charge under the Defence of the Realm Act. Defendant was brought to a local police barrack and detained in custody pending instructions from the military authorities. Bail was refused. F.T.

November 16th 1916. DEALING WITH THE REGISTRAR-GENERAL'S RETURN of the number of men available for military service in Ireland the *Pall Mall Gazette* says: -The Nationalist Party claims that it would be an outrage to make these 160,000 do their part in the defence of the Empire; that it is the inalienable right of young unmarried Irishmen to stay at home and fill their pockets from the high prices of produce and labour, while English, Scottish and a Welsh breadwinners are put in training to protect them. The first act of an Irish Parliament would evidently have to be an alteration of the national emblem to whatever form of parasite the popular taste in zoology happens to prefer. F.T.

November 16th 1916. THE SOMME FILM. Residents of Enniskillen and the surrounding neighbourhood will have an opportunity next week of witnessing the film of the Battle of the Somme in Enniskillen Townhall. This film is a wonderful production; it is in five parts and takes 2 hours to show. It has been said that such gruesome sights should not be shown to the public in all their reality and gruesomeness but they bring home to us in some small degree the fearful havoc of battle, the trials of our brave soldiers, their undying heroism and pluck and that despite all the frightfulness of war, their spirits are cheery and bright. The pictures are thrilling and awe inspiring and as it is expected that large crowds will wish to see them, they will be shown twice nightly at 7 and 9.00 for three nights in succession from Monday next the 20th until Wednesday the 22nd. Visitors from the country who wish to see this film should be present at the 7.00 p.m. house as the later house is more crowded than the first. The prices of admission will be one shilling 2 pence and 7 pence. There will be three matinees on Monday, Tuesday and Wednesday at 3.30. I.R.

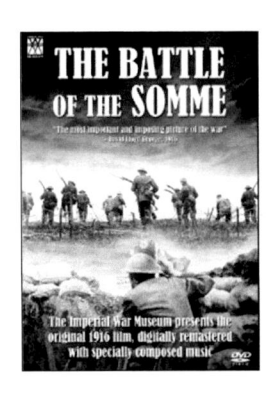

Fermanagh Herald November 18th 1916. DON'T FORGET THAT THE FAMOUS BATTLE OF THE SOMME IS BEING SCREENED IN THE TOWN HALL on next Monday, Tuesday and Wednesday evenings, with matinees on the three days. Those who are constant readers of the war news, and are following up the events of the great Somme struggle will derive great interest from this extraordinary film, while it will also give an accurate idea of what life at the Front is like. The picture, taken under fire, is regarded as the greatest achievement yet accomplished in cinematography. That is certainly saying a great deal for it. In

England and Dublin, it was wondered at, and the picture palaces in which it was exhibited were always crowded to overflowing. It may be interesting to state that the film was obtained by a Mr. Malins at the request of the Government and during the operation a shell exploded close to where Mr. Malins was "turning the wheel" and took clean away one of the legs of the tripod on which the camera rested. Its vividness is extraordinary. Special music, I understand, will be played, and the attraction being a big one the hall should be crowded each evening. The enterprise of the Picture Company is indeed to be commended, and it is to be hoped that the townspeople will respond to show their appreciation for the efforts which are being made, and the expense gone to for their delectation

Geoffrey Malins' How I Filmed the War.

November 23rd 1916. BEFORE THE BATTLE. LAST MOMENTS IN A BRITISH DUG-OUT. The *Petite Journal* correspondent relates that after having traversed part of the battlefield he entered the dug-out where he found British soldiers who he says in another moment would be dashing in a wave of assault upon one of the trenches which the Germans still hold near Beaucourt. 'I look at these soldiers,' he continues. 'It must not be said that a soldier before rushing to death does not think of death. No. See these young British soldiers. Their faces reveal their seriousness. They are contemplating the probable fate which awaits them. They think of it resolutely and coldly. Thus are tragedies beautiful. These men are talking very low to one another with the intonation of the confessional, with slow, very infrequent gesture. Mingling with those who are about to leave for the charge are others who tomorrow will be returning to the rear. The former are entrusting the latter with their final commissions. One says: 'You will send that letter to mother' another 'You will write and tell my wife so and so.' What magnificent sang froid. All think they may be going to their death; all are making their last will and testament.

The hour of departure approaches. An officer makes a sign, the men gather under their officers who explain the ground which the assailants have to cross. Now they are ready in Indian file. Slowly they ascend to the communications trench. The dugout empties. That is how British soldiers leave for battle. I.R.

November 23rd 1916. THE PAYMENT OF NATIONAL SCHOOL TEACHER. Rev. Father Humphreys, P.P., who lives in County Tipperary is a very virile Nationalist who speaks out his mind plainly. Strong and exaggerated language may be forgiven in politics, but when Fr. Humphreys enters the arena of domestic discussion, on such a simple question as to the payment of National School Teachers, he is equally outspoken – if not more so. Here is a sample of his language in this purely domestic controversy: - Sir – In your issue of today appears a letter on the above subject signed 'A Catholic Manager.' Who is that Catholic manager? I deny your right as Editor to allow a cowardly sneak and snake to spew his venom in your columns with the impunity of anonymity. Your correspondent is evidently a bad bastard cross between a ghoul and a spectre. (Ed. Not hard to work out who the bad bastard is.) I.R.

November 23rd 1916. THE PRICE OF CATTLE. We have heard and give the statement for what it is worth that the government intend to include beef among the articles on which the maximum price will be fixed. Milk in England is now regulated in price, potatoes will follow and it is expected that butchers will be prohibited from selling beef beyond a certain figure. I.R.

November 23rd 1916. NOTES. The death took place at 9.00 p.m. on Tuesday night of the Emperor of Austria after a reign of close on 68 years. He was aged 86 years.

There will be no more white bread after the New Year. 'Standard bread' or our new war bread will then be the only bread available.

A boiled egg in a London restaurant now costs 3½ d and two boiled eggs on toast 11d.

In the fourth Irish egg laying competition a white Wyandotte pullet made a world's record laying 306 eggs in the year.

Franz Joseph in c. 1905 Emperor of Austria

A big government scheme is about to purchase some 200 Glasgow public houses at almost six years purchase.

A nurse in a hospital in France says that she has been attending our wounded Tommies for four months in operating theatre and has not once heard a man swear. The great tanks at the front are estimated to have saved our army in France 20,000 casualties. I.R.

November 23rd 1916. THE ENEMY'S VIEW OF THE WAR. REVELATIONS OF PRISONERS LETTERS MAKE CLEAR THAT GERMANY IS LOSING. Here are some extracts from the personal papers of German prisoners written during recent weeks. The trenches are quite fallen in, writes a member of the 14th Bavarian Regiment in his diary. Plenty of dead and unburied. On the way to the sixth company we lost our way and dead and buried were to be seen in masses in and out of the trenches. Heads were sticking out in the middle of the trenches. Six or eight men were lying piled on top of one another - we saw some terrible sights. The English aviators and artillery are greatly to be feared. One often thinks their gunners get no food or pay if they don't shoot continuously. What have we to eat? 15 g of cheese, 25 g of butter and coffee in service bottles not fit to drink – water would have been better. The day before yesterday we had tinned meat that stank. The English have been sending over heavy shells day and night without pause. The dugout shakes, creaks and trembles. Now the entrance has just again been destroyed. Always this nerve racking anxiety. Now you are going to be buried under the wreck of the dugout. Up to now it has been all right but 'how long' is the dreadful the question.

The war is a low scoundrel affair writes a member of the 3rd Ersatz Regiment. The German government deceives the people. One sees it very clearly in this wholesale murder. One can hardly help being ashamed of being a German since we put up with this. We must turn our rifles around and destroy the whole Government. That gang have caused us to be killed. Remember this if I don't come back dear Greta. It is already quite clear that Germany is losing and getting into a horrible state. F.T.

November 23rd 1916. MAGUIRESBRIDGE MAN WINS MILITARY CROSS. Lieutenant S. P. Lough, of the Canadian Infantry, son of Mrs. Lough of Maguiresbridge has been awarded the Military Cross for conspicuous gallantry in the field at the Somme front on 15th September. The official account says: - 'He was in command of a stretcher party and personally superintended the work of rescuing the wounded which was carried out under intense fire for 10 hours. He was a splendid example of courage and initiative throughout.' Lieutenant Lough was wounded at the battle of St. Eloi in May last. His brother Robert is also with the Canadians. F.T.

November 23rd 1916. MAGHERACULMONEY PARISH NATIONAL EGG COLLECTION. The following contributions have been received for November. – Mrs. T. Phillips 12, Miss M. Walmsley eight, collected by Miss M. A. Beacom – Mrs. McDonagh 12, Mr. John Birney six, Mrs. E. Humphreys one shilling; Mr. William Humphries one shilling, Mrs. Jack Birney one shilling, Mrs. William Brimstone 6d, Sergeant Noble eight pence, Mrs. Robinson 4d, Mrs. E. McDonagh six pence collected by Miss Gibson – Miss Aiken 12, Miss Gibson six, Miss Elliot three, Miss Elms one shilling, Mrs. McAnerin one shilling. – Alice C. Robinson, Hon. Sec., Ardess. November 28 1916. F.T.

November 23rd 1916. WANTED. Two steady young men, at once as Flagmen on Rollers, with prospect of becoming Drivers. County Surveyor, Enniskillen. F.T.

November 23rd 1916. BRITANNIC SUNK. LARGEST LINER AFLOAT. 50 PERSONS PERISH. The Secretary of the Admiralty makes the following announcement: - The British Hospital Ship *Britannic* was sunk by mine or torpedo on Tuesday morning 21st Inst., in the Zea Channel, Aegean Sea. There are 1,106 survivors, 28 of whom are injured and it is estimated that 50 are lost. The *Britannic* was a 50,000 ton liner being the largest afloat. It was launched at Belfast in February 1914 and was a sister ship to the ill-fated *Titanic* and also to the *Olympic*. (Ed. RMS *Olympic* was a transatlantic ocean liner, the lead ship of the White Star Line's trio of Olympic-class liners. Unlike her younger sister ships, the *Olympic* enjoyed a long and illustrious career, spanning 24 years from 1911 to 1935. This included service as a troopship during the First World War, which gained her the nickname "Old Reliable". *Olympic* returned to civilian service after the war and served successfully as an ocean liner throughout the 1920s and into the first half of the 1930s, although increased competition, and the slump in trade during the Great Depression after 1930, made her operation increasingly unprofitable. She was the largest ocean liner in the world for two periods during 1911–13, interrupted only by the brief tenure of the slightly larger *Titanic* (which had the same dimensions but higher gross tonnage due to revised interior configurations), and then outsized by the SS *Imperator*. *Olympic* also retained the title of the largest British-built liner until the RMS *Queen Mary* was launched in 1934, interrupted only by the short careers of her slightly larger sister ships. F.T.

HMHS Britannic.

November 23rd 1916. A SPECIAL NIGHT AT THE PICTURES. AN ENTERTAINMENT TO SUPPORT THE MILITARY RECREATION ROOMS IN THE TOWNHALL. The soldiers stationed in Enniskillen can spend the long winter evenings writing letters home and can have a game of Bagatelle, Draughts, Ludo, Dominos etc. or read the daily newspapers and magazines and also have refreshments such as tea, coffee, cocoa, porridge etc. at almost nominal charges in the Townhall. The fact that the rooms are crowded nearly every night is the most convincing proof that they serve a useful purpose and are thoroughly appreciated by the men. Such an undertaking however cannot be carried on without expense and consequently a special entertainment at the Pictures has been organized for next Thursday evening to raise funds. Special films are being engaged for the occasion and these will be varied by musical and other items. A thoroughly enjoyable evening is anticipated so that those who purchase tickets – which have been fixed at the extremely moderate prices of 1 shilling eight pence and 1 shilling 2 pence respectively, including tax, will get splendid value for their money in addition to assisting a good cause. The soldiers stationed here are all preparing to take their place in the trenches and it is as little as our townspeople can do to make their stay in our town as pleasant as possible. Whether they really appreciate the military amongst them, or whether, after all, they only want the soldiers for the profit they can make out of them in business, will be, in some measure at least, gauged by the attendance in the Townhall next Thursday evening. The Enniskillen String Band, with a number of new selections, will accompany the pictures, and there will be a sketch by military officers and songs by talented artistes. F.T.

November 23rd 1916. LOCAL TRAGEDIES. Fate or as some would term it ill luck falls with a heavy hand on some families and in a strange way. I read of a Roscommon woman whose six sons were all killed in the war. On Saturday evening last the remains of Miss Jeannie McElgunn, daughter of the late Mr. H McElgunn, Ann Street, Enniskillen were brought home to her birthplace. She was drowned on the *Connemara* which went down in the Irish Sea three weeks ago. Miss McElgunn's remains were buried by lantern light and in the same grave had been buried her brother Robert Hugh and her sister Annie. Death by drowning seems to have been the fate that had dogged the footsteps of the McElgunn family as both Robert and Annie were drowned in the year 1886. Robert was aged only 4 ½ years and was hurling a hoop at the old brewery premises when he fell into the water. Annie McElgunn I believe was drowned in one of the Leitrim lakes.

CAPTAIN J. M. REGAN,
Royal Irish Rifles. Was stationed for some time as District Inspector R.I.C. at Limerick from which place he joined the Army and where he made many friends.

The female body of another *Connemara* victim was recovered late at night at Cranfield. She had been apparently about 20 years of age and wearing a deep blue skirt, brown short jacket, laced Derby boots with toecaps. The features were undistinguishable. A letter was found on her person with part of the address on the envelope undecipherable. The following was made out – Miss Lizzy C….. Bally….. – County Fermanagh. Inside the letter advice was given when she would get to London to ask no questions of anyone except a policeman. This makes over 80 bodies recovered from the disaster. The remains of Miss Lizzy Collins, Ballycassidy, Ballinamallard, County Fermanagh aged 18 years one of the victims of the *Connemara* disaster whose body was recovered on Friday night were interred on Monday in the old Churchyard, Kilkeel.

Another sad incident in connection with this sea catastrophe was witnessed in Enniskillen on Saturday night. An old man of about 60 years of age from Cashel, County Leitrim had lost two of his daughters and the remains of one came to Enniskillen by the same train as Miss McElgunn's. There was no train to bring him home. He wept bitterly and was in dire distress as he could not get a car nor had the money to pay for one. A good hearted fellow –Mr. Alex Lavelle of Cornagrade Terrace, I believe, took care of the old man, procured a motor car and send him home with the coffin that contained his daughter's body.

Mr. and Mrs. Thomas Dane of Shankill, near Lisbellaw, have received notification from France that their son Private William Dane was killed in action on the 20th of November. I.R.

Fermanagh Herald November 25th 1916. JOTTINGS. An interesting addition to the series of Notable English Trials, published by Messrs. Hodge & Company will be a volume soon to be issued dealing with the trial of Sir Rodger Casement.

The ceilidh organised by the committee of the Lisnaskea Catholic Dancing Class, and which came off on Sunday night was very successful. Subscriptions amounting to £4-10-0 were handed in, and the secretaries were instructed to hand same to the Rev. Fr. Carragher for the Irish National Aid Association.

An American explanation of why bread is dear is that there is a 25 per cent world deficiency, delay in threshing in Canada, due to shortage of labour, and continuance of drought in Argentina, the locking up of the Russian supplies, and unfavourable yields in France and Italy. India and Australia alone have promising crops.

DEATH OF PRIVATE DANE.

TESTIMONIES TO HIS WORK.

Mr. and Mrs. Thomas Dane, of Shanco, near Lisbellaw, have received notification from France that their son, Private William Dane, No. 26085, 11th Battalion, Royal Inniskilling Fusiliers, was killed in action on 20th November, 1916.

Before enlisting Private Dane was a member of Cornafanog half Company, U.V.F. and also a very highly esteemed member of Cronafanog L.O.L. No. 1333. His death at the early age of 27 years is deeply regretted by a large circle of friends and acquaintances in the district, where he was beloved by all who knew him.

The following letters were received from his Captain and the Chaplain:—

11th Battalion, R. Innisk.
Fusiliers, B.E.F., France,
21-11-'16.

Dear Mr. Dane,—I regret very much to have to inform you that your son, No. 26085 Private W. Dane was killed in action on the evening of the 20th ult. He was a very fine soldier and I thought a lot of him and will miss him. He had made himself very popular with his comrades and everyone is sorry to lose him. The officers of A Company and men of the company offer you their very sincere sympathy in your sudden bereavement and ask you to find consolation (if there can be any) in the fact that he died so gloriously and with good heart in the service of his King and country. We will lay him to rest this afternoon at three o'clock, in the presence of most of the company and all his chums in a nice little cemetery behind our lines. The exact location of the grave will be notified you later, and a cross will be erected with inscription in his memory.

With my sincere sympathy,—I remain yours truly, T. C. SWEENY, Capt Commanding A Company.

11th Royal Inniskilling Fus.

Fermanagh Herald November 25th 1916. STATE AND FOOD CONTROL. The Government proposal as to food production and control of prices occupied the attention of the House of Commons again on Thursday. The Food Controller will have drastic powers, which briefly will mean – No more "corners"; No more potato – profiteering; No more wilful waste; No more all-white bread; Restrictions on confectionery; Maximum price for milk; and a scheme of national stocktaking, compelling merchants, etc., to furnish returns of all stocks, contracts, and prices. Dealing with the question of Irish production, Mr. Runciman promised to consult the Department in Ireland and Irish opinion in regard to the application of the scheme to this country.

Fermanagh Herald November 25th 1916. STANDARD BREAD. Standard bread will become universal in England on January 1st says the *Daily Mail*. Up to the last day of 1916 bakers will be allowed to use what stocks of white flour they have in hand. There are not many bakers who have stocks of white flour equal to more than three weeks supply of wheat bread. Millers are to be given only seven days in which to begin milling Standard flour in place of white. The seven days will begin from the date of publication of the Order in Council by which the new regulations will be enforced.

Fermanagh Herald November 25th 1916. POTATO SUPPLIES. IMMENSE ULSTER SHIPMENTS. The Belfast correspondent of the *London Star* states that, convinced that the export of Irish potatoes would be prohibited at an early date, Ulster farmers and produce merchants are busy shipping across the Channel immense quantities in anticipation of an embargo. The railway companies' stores are congested by the abnormal rush of consignments, and special steamers from Belfast, Derry, Larne and, Coleraine, and the Co., Down ports have been chartered to carry cargoes. Prices have further slumped £3 a ton in the local markets. Potatoes were 10 shillings cheaper in London on Thursday. Potatoes, says the London correspondent of the *Liverpool Post* will certainly drop still further in view of Mr. Runciman's threat that profits will be limited.

Fermanagh Herald November 25th 1916. IMPORTANT TO FARMERS. £15 -- £500. There is no need to sacrifice your stock when by holding on to them you can probably double your price. Now is your time to buy cattle and make money. We will advance you cash without security on reasonable terms. We complete Loans within 48 hours from receiving application. For particulars, apply SECRETARY, DUBLIN ADVANCE, Co., Ltd, 99 DONEGAL ROAD BELFAST.

November 30th 1916. LOUGH ERNE DRAINAGE BOARD AND THE BELLEEK POTTERY. A special meeting of the Lough and River Erne Drainage Navigation Districts was held on the 24th Inst., to consider a letter read by the Secretary from the Fermanagh County Council suggesting that a conference might be held between representatives of the Belleek Pottery Company and the Board and two members of the County Council and the Chairman as it was represented by Mr. Scott, a member of the Council, that it was quite possible to reduce the floods without interfering with the Pottery Company. It was agreed that the Board would be pleased to meet the deputation at the next meeting on the 11th of December. F.T.

November 30th 1916. CHRISTMAS POULTRY. TURKEYS AND GEESE. We shall commence buying on a Monday the 11th inst and continue each day up until and including the 20th Inst. Our arrangements are on a large scale and we expect to pay good prices for fat, straight breasted birds. All birds should be properly fasted before selling so as to enable us to ship in good condition. Parties coming a distance of 10 miles and over will get an allowance towards expenses. D. Donaldson and Son, Derrygonnelly. F.T.

November 30th 1916. VISCOUNT CRICHTON'S WILL. PERSONAL PROPERTY TO THE VALUE OF £55,769. Lieutenant Colonel Viscount Crichton, M.V.O., D.S.O., Royal Horse Guards, of Crom Castle, Co., Fermanagh, extra equerry to the King and who was with the Sir George White in the defence of Ladysmith, was killed in France on the 31st of October 1914 leaving personal property in the United Kingdom of the value of £55,769 – 3s – 4d. F.T.

Fermanagh Herald December 2nd 1916. JOTTINGS. Lieut.-Col. Viscount Crichton, eldest son of the Earl of Erne, Crom Castle County., Fermanagh, who was killed in France left £55,769. He directed that articles given him on his marriage and on his reaching the age of 21 are to be held as heirlooms. They include a silver cup presented to him by the King, four silver flower dishes from the Prince and Princess of Wales, a cup from the Household of the Prince and Princess of Wales and a cup from the Horse Guards.

On Friday's casualty list appeared under the heading of killed the names of Private P. Henderson, Inniskillings, Enniskillen, Private P. Owens, Dublin's, Lisbellaw, and Private G Rafferty, Enniskillen who resided at Fivemiletown.

It is stated that Lieutenant Dominic Mervyn Archdale, of the King's African Rifles, was killed in action on the 13th of November. Lieutenant Archdale who was aged 24 years is the son of Mr. E. M. Archdale, M. P., Ballinamallard, who has one other son in the Army and two in the Royal Navy. At the Enniskillen Guardians meeting on Tuesday, a vote of sympathy to Mr. and Mrs. Archdale was proposed by Mr. F. R. Carson. In seconding, Mr. E. Corrigan regretted Mr. Archdale's loss. He had never seen Mr. Archdale say or do anything that was not charitable and kind, and he thought that the county had not got a more Christian gentleman as a public man. The Chairman, Mister J. Crozier, J. P. endorsed what had been said adding that he did not know a more genial gentleman in the Enniskillen union than Mr. Archdale. The motion was passed in silence.

CAPT. C. W. D'ARCY IRVINE, 6th Leinsters, wounded and missing, believed killed, is the elder son of Major C. C. D'Arcy Irvine, J.P., of Castle Irvine, Irvinestown, and of Fanny Kathleen, daughter of Lieut.-Colonel Jesse Lloyd, of Ballyleck, Co. Monaghan. He was formerly in the 3rd Irish Rifles. His father was an officer of the 3rd Royal Inniskilling Fusiliers and of the North of Ireland Imperial Yeomanry.

French soldiers attending Mass 1916.

DECEMBER 1916

December 7th 1916. A POLITICAL BOMBSHELL. BIG CABINET CRISIS. MR. ASQUITH RESIGNS. THE KING'S SENDS FOR BONAR LAW AND A GENERAL ELECTION PROBABLE. A political crisis of the first magnitude arose last weekend. Mr. Bonar Law has declined to form a cabinet. It is possible that the King will now send for Lloyd George. For a long time Mr. Lloyd George is known to have been gravely dissatisfied with the dilatory and irresolute manner in which the Cabinet and the War Committee have directed the war. On Friday he informed the Prime Minister and he could not continue to remain a member of the Government unless the machinery for directing the war was drastically overhauled. I.R.

December 7th 1916. A POLITICAL BOMBSHELL AS MR. ASQUITH RESIGNS. On Tuesday night Mr. Asquith motored to Buckingham Palace and tendered his resignation to the King who immediately sent for Mr. Bonar Law. So in dramatic fashion ends the political uncertainty of the last few days and Mr. Asquith lays down a position which he had held since April 8th 1908 when he succeeded the late Sir H. Campbell Bannerman – a Premiership of record length. F.T.

December 7th 1916. MILITARY NOTES. ITEMS OF LOCAL INTEREST. Particulars are now to hand of the death already reported of Sergeant A. W. Galbraith, Royal Inniskilling Fusiliers and U.V.F. of the Mall, Ballyshannon. Rev Jackson Wright, in a letter to Mrs. Galbraith says: - He went out with a party to examine wire in front of the German trenches and with his usual accuracy of detail he and his officer were last to return. All the others got safely back but your husband and the officer had to take refuge in a shell hole just outside our wire, where, with the aid of rockets they were seen and exposed to rifle fire. Your husband was struck by a bullet on the side of the temple and so shattered the side bone of the head that his condition was hopeless. He was quickly conveyed to a hospital and notwithstanding the fine skill of a clever surgeon never recovered consciousness and died next afternoon. It may be some consolation to know that he was considered the bravest man in the battalion and his courage and fine character won the respect of all. F.T.

Fermanagh Herald December 9th 1916. MAGUIRESBRIDGE NATIONAL VOLUNTEER KILLED. Mrs. Graham of Maguiresbridge, on Saturday received intimation from the Commanding–officer of the battalion, that her son Lance-Corporal James Graham, Royal Enniskillen Fusiliers had been killed by a German sniper on the 24th of November last in France. Deceased formerly belonged to the Maguiresbridge Company of the National Volunteers, and had been in the Army Reserve prior to the war.

December 14th 1916. NOTES. The oil wells in Romania were destroyed before the Germans reached them so that they could be of no service to the enemy.

The women porters on railways in Germany have been reprimanded by the Railway Director at Danzig for not taking their work earnestly enough and they are ordered to salute their superiors in military fashion.

An early primrose was pulled at Castle Caldwell on 9th December by Mr. George Johnston, Tawnagorm and sent forward to this newspaper office.

CORPORAL H. V. A. MERCER, North Irish Horse, who was home on short leave from the front about a fortnight ago, is younger son of Mr. T. A. Mercer, Jeweller, High Street, Enniskillen, and is the well-known amateur International footballer. He holds the important position of divisional sniper, and has had some exciting and interesting experiences at the front.

It has been found absolutely necessary to restrict hampers and perishable goods by passenger trains in England to a hundredweight. Woman porters cannot handle the heavy weights. Poultry dealers on this side of the Channel complain of the new restriction on weight as injurious to Irish exporters. The regulation however is undeniably necessary and the only trouble will be to pack more hampers than before. About 306,254 cwt of poultry of a value of £1,071,839 were sent from Ireland to England last year and about £50,000 worth of rabbits so that the trade is considerable. The necessities of the hour caused by the war overcomes all other things and there is no possibility of the weight provided for being reduced as there are not porters to handle the heavy baskets or hampers. I.R.

December 14th 1916. POLICE MATTERS. 'Swear the police' is now the commonplace and undignified phrase at the opening of most Petty Sessions courts. One does expect to find some 'tone' in the lowest court in the land and magistrates might follow the example of the Pettigo Court for their clerk, Mr. Robinson declares the court open in as dignified a manner as the High Court in Dublin. When the magistrates take their seats on the bench, Mr. Robinson stands up and announces: 'This court of Petty Sessions is now open. God save the King.

Recently some visitors arriving in Enniskillen from Dublin received a rude shock. Coming into the town, they saw the words 'Victoria Hotel' in large letters and pulling up at the front door of what they thought was an up to date hotel were surprised when they found that the building was not a hotel but the No.1 Police Barracks. Surely the Crown can afford even a bucket of whitewash to colour the walls for they are badly in need of recolouring as is the case of the Ballinamallard Barracks to which I recently referred where the signboard over the barrack door bears the words 'Coulter Bros.' I.R.

December 14th 1916. THE HOARDING OF PROVISIONS. Sir, I have heard the farmers of the country or a good many of them are buying flour and storing it up for fear of the coming year. Surely there should be a stop put to it. What is the poor man and the labouring man going to do with large families: they cannot buy provisions and store them up for the coming year. They will call in with their week's pay and do not get half of what they formerly got for the same amount of money. Is it fair then for the farmers to be let buy and store up and raise the markets on the poor and working man. The farmer has had prosperous years for all he had to dispose of. The poor working man was not able to lay by anything. Hundreds of farmers have not sent one of their sons to fight for the homestead or country: the poor working man has done so in thousands. Are those men going to be let store up the provisions that God has sent for all until the poor die of hunger? Are the clergy of all religions going to stand by and not raise their voices against unscrupulous hoarding of God's provisions the same way as the past – no look to the humble and only for the humble and their manhood, the gentry, the farmer and clergy would be in the humble boat with the poor. What encouragement will this act of the farmers have on the young men and boys of the country in going forward to enlist? Surely the local Government Board should take steps and have every hoarding in the country taken from those unscrupulous men and given to those entitled their fair share of what they are justly entitled to and must have. They are also hoarding up tons of potatoes for famine prices. A.E.

(Ed. Impartial Reporter.) The government has botched this matter as they have botched other things. There should not have been any time allowed for selfish people to store up goods. The government have stimulated the hoarding of goods and the raising of prices.

PATRIOTIC BROOKEBORO' FAMILY.
This photograph shows Sergt. Orr (standing in centre), of Brookeboro,' and his four soldier sons. They are all serving in the Inniskilling Dragoons. On the right of the father is Thomas and on the left is John, while those seated are Harry and William. Sergt. Orr served through the South African War, and was commended for his services.

December 21st 1916. THE REBELLION PRISONERS RELEASED ON FRIDAY. All interned Irish Rebellion prisoners were released on Friday last. It was officially announced in Parliament on Thursday night in reply to Mr. T. P. O'Connor, Mr. Duke saying he had given the case the most anxious consideration since he assumed office and had come to the conclusion that in view of all the facts the time had come when the advantages of releasing these men far outweighed the risk and he had so advised the government. Steps had, however he added, amidst cheers, been taken that day to proceed with as little delay as possible to return prisoners to their homes. I.R.

December 21st 1916. DEATH. Sergeant Arthur, James Balfour Moffitt, Australian Imperial Force, killed in action, was the eldest son of the late Mr. William Moffitt and Mrs. Moffitt, Barnalacken, Ederney, County Fermanagh and a nephew of Miss Moffitt, 29 Essex Street, Belfast. He enlisted in Sydney, New South Wales on 22 August 1914. He emigrated from County Fermanagh six years ago and was twice wounded in the Gallipoli campaign. F.T.

December 21st 1916. LISNASKEA ELECT A NEW CLERK OF THE UNION AND MASTER OF THE WORKHOUSE. Mr. Robert Irvine, who has been acting clerk, since his temporary appointment has given entire satisfaction to the Board and was elected by a majority of four votes. There were three candidates for Master of the Workhouse and Mr. Martin (acting master) was appointed with a clear majority over the two other candidates Mr. Swift and Mr. Reihill. F.T.

December 21st 1916. BALLINAMALLARD. FOWL PLUCKERS ON STRIKE AND THE POLICE CALLED. An exceptionally large turkey market was held this year at the Ballinamallard Creamery. For a good number of years the Dairy Society has been trading in poultry during the Christmas season. The prices were good and everything was carried out satisfactorily and good returns are expected. A rather exciting incident occurred during the market, the pluckers, to the number of 30, going out on strike for an increase of wages. They became so threatening that the police had to be called to disperse them. F.T.

Fermanagh Herald December 23rd 1916. IRISH RAILWAY DISASTER. FIVE MEN KILLED IN MAYO. Five railway workmen belonging to Castleconnell, and Oola were killed in a railway collision at Kiltimagh (G. S. and W. Railway), on Tuesday evening. The disaster occurred about 5.00 p.m. when in foggy weather a train of empty wagons from Sligo collided with a ballast train from Tuam, in one of the vans of which there was a large number of workmen. The impact was so terrific that the van was telescoped, three of the occupants being instantly killed while two others sustained such serious injuries that they died shortly afterwards. Several men were also severely injured. Both engines were derailed and badly damaged and the permanent way was much cut up. Dr. Maguire, Claremorris; Dr. Mulligan, Swinford, and Dr. Madden, Kiltimagh, were quickly in attendance and rendered all possible assistance. Dr. Maguire described all the killed and injured as fine young men. A special ambulance train subsequently conveyed the injured to Tuam. The names of the killed are; -Thomas Murphy, Patrick Godfrey, William Patterson, Martin Burns and Martin Raineford.

MANY OF THE BIG STARS OF THE MUSIC HALLS were active in their support of the fighting man and raised thousands of pounds for various Armed Forces charities. The famous Harry Lauder established his eponymous Million-Pound Fund for Maimed Scottish Soldiers and Sailors, and went to France to entertain the troops, writing a memoir of his experiences. Lauder's only son, Captain John Lauder, 8th Battalion, Argyll and Sutherland

Highlanders, was killed on 28th December 1916 at Poiziers, and the song *Keep right on to the end of the Road* was written by his grieving father. One of the most enduring songs of the conflict, the chorus epitomises the sacrifice and stoicism of a nation confronted with the calamity of The Great War:

Keep right on to the end of the road
Keep right on to the end
Tho' the way be long, let your heart be strong
Keep right on to the end
Tho' you're tired and weary still journey on,
Till you come to your happy abode
Where all you love, you've been dreaming of
Will be there, at the end of the road.

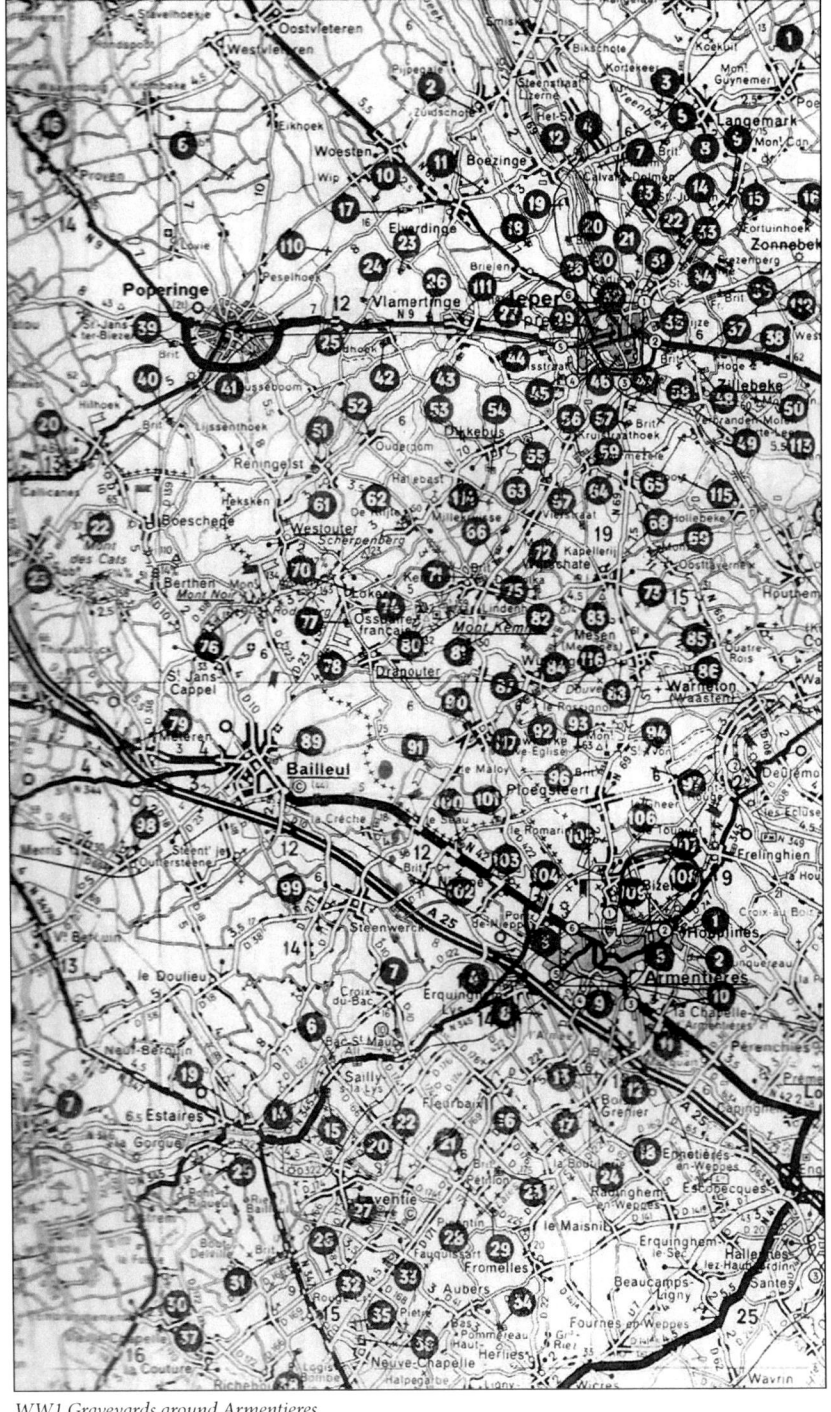

WW1 Graveyards around Armentieres.

INDEX

10th Royal Hussars 83.
11th Royal Inniskillings 97.
12th Inniskillings 20, 51, 63, 77, 91,107.
14th Bavarian Regiment 105, 124.
16th Irish Division 60.
186th Regiment, Prussian Infantry 84.
19th Regiment
1st Dragoon Guards 21.
1st Royal Inniskillings 99.
26th Middlesex Cyclist Battalion 115.
2nd Batt. Hampshire Regiment 21.
2nd Batt. Irish Guards, B.E.F. 23, 25, 26, 83.
3rd Batt. Royal Irish Rifles 3, 17, 19, 21, 76, 77, 82, 85, 93, 100, 115, 118, 121.
3rd Cameron Highlanders 41.
3rd Ersatz Regiment 124.
5th Inniskillings 97.
5th Royal Irish Rifles
67th Regiment 21.
6th Service Battalion, Leinster Regiment 13, 20, 21.
7th Royal Inniskilling Fusiliers 77.
8th Battalion Argyll and Sutherland Highlanders 131.
8th Battalion Inniskilling Fusiliers 77.
8th Highland Light Infantry 20.
8th Inniskillings 30, 36, 107.
9th Lancers 88.

Abbey Street, Derry 102.
Abbey Street, Enniskillen 14, 15, 77.
Aberconway Lord 110.
Aberdeen 91.
Aberdeen, Lord 60.
Aberdeenshire 30.
Achill 25.
Act of Union 90.
Adams Joseph 19.
Adams Robert 19.
Aegean Sea 124.
Africa 35.
Aghnablaney. Fermanagh 29.
Aherne, Rev. D. 17.
Aherne, Sergeant 33.
Aiken, Miss 124.
Aixles-Bains 86.
Alberta 24.
Aldridge, William 115.
Alexandria 23, 86.
Allen, Second Lieutenant 20.
Aloysius, Rev Father 69, 78.
Alsace 120.
Altrincham, Cheshire 71.
Ann Street 30, 125.
Annagarvey bog 79.
Antrim 47.
Antwerp 104.
Arbour Hill Barracks 78.
Archdale Estate 2, 89.
Archdale, Dominic Mervyn 35, 128.
Archdale, John 89.
Archdale, Miss Angel 80
Archdale, Mr. E. M. 12, 35, 70, 128.
Archdale, Mr. W. 109.

Archdale, Mrs. 128.
Archdale, Right Hon E.
Archdall, H. L. St. George.
Archdall, Major M. J. M. 41.
Archdall, Mr. E. Hugh, 37.
Archdall, Mr. Mervyn 90.
Ardent 78.
Ardess 124.
Ardrossan 57.
Argentina 126.
Arigna coal 17.
Arkansas 24.
Armagh 2, 57, 70, 98, 121.
Armagh Jail 98.
Armstrong, Mr. Edward 15.
Armstrong, Sergeant Frank 16.
Army Service Corps 8, 31.
Arney 17.
Ashbourne Police Barracks 55.
Ashton-on-Ribble 67.
Ashwoods 63.
Asquith Mr. 42, 43, 52, 59, 60, 78, 104, 129.
Asquith, Arthur 104.
Asquith, Cyril 104.
Asquith, Lt. Raymond 104.
Asquith, Miss Elizabeth 32.
Asquith, Mrs 32.
Athy 70.
Atkinson, Bro. Joseph 27.
Aughnamoyle, Omagh 104.
Austin, Admiral Sir Horatio 86.
Australia 42, 120, 126, 131.
Australian Imperial Force 131.
Austria, Emperor of 123.
Austria/Austrian 68, 77, 90, 104.
Ayr. 27.

Bachelors Walk 51.
Bagshawe, Major 105.
Bagshawe, Samuel 105.
Bairley, Aberdeen 91.
Baker, Second Lieutenant 20.
Balaclava 19.
Baliol 104.
Balkans 14.
Ballinamallard 12, 35, 91, 125, 128, 130, 131.
Ballinasloe 37, 111.
Ballinrobe 103.
Ballintra 17.
Ballybay 36, 40.
Ballycassidy 125.
Ballyconnell 98.
Ballyhenry 47.
Ballykissane 56.
Ballyleck, Monaghan 21.
Ballymakenny 63.
Ballyshannon 3, 7, 8, 17, 25, 27, 69, 71, 83, 91, 98, 101, 110, 129.
Baltic Sea 86.
Bank of Ireland 51, 53, 54.
Barlinnie Prison 74.
Barnalacken 131.
Barrett, Inspector 38.
Barton, Mr. Justice 8.
Battle of the Somme film 122.
Bavaria 84, 105, 124.

Bawnboy 40, 50.
Bayswater 116.
Beacom, Miss M. A. 124
Beatty, Mr. George 50.
Beatty, Private Joseph 121.
Beatty, Sir David 80.
Beggan, Patrick 100.
Beggars Bush Barracks 67.
Belcoo 8, 64.
Belfast 2, 7, 25, 28, 33, 40, 47, 52, 53, 57, 59, 66, 68, 80, 82, 83, 87, 90, 94, 101, 104, 110, 112, 113, 124, 126, 127, 131.
Belleek 22, 71, 82, 105.
Belleek Pottery 8, 71, 120, 127.
Belmore Mountain 7.
Belmore, Earl of 90.
Belturbet 2.
Benaughlin 7.
Bennison, Mr. J. A. J.P. 98.
Benson, Mr J. 25.
Benson, Mr S. 25.
Beresford, Mr. Peck 97.
Berlin 21, 29, 38, 42, 47, 80.
Bermondsey 103.
Berry Street Club 113.
Birdwood, General 9.
Birmingham 67, 100.
Birney, Mr. John 124.
Birney, Mrs. Jack 124.
Birrell Land Act 12.
Birrell, Mr. Augustine 40, 42, 50, 60, 61, 73, 76.
Black Prince 78.
Black Sea 86.
Black Watch 53.
Black, Miss 104.
Blackbog, Parish of 72.
Blacklion 50.
Blackpool 100.
Blatchford, Mr. Robert 32, 38.
Bleakley, Sergeant Major Guy 119.
Boer Republics 115.
Boer War 16, 77.
Boho A. O.H. 92.
Boulogne 53.
Bowen-Colthurst, Captain 100, 114, 115, 116.
Boyle, James of the Retriever 119, 120.
Boyle, Rose Ann 37, 38.
Boyne, Battle of 84, 85, 87.
Bradley, Sergeant 28.
Bradshaw, Miss May 106.
Brakespeare, Nicholas (Adrian 1V) 69.
Brennan, Mr. Terence 68.
Brentwood 26.
Bril, Louis 21.
Brimstone, Mrs. William 124.
Britannic, British Hospital Ship 124, 125.
Broadmoor Insane Hospital 116.
Brockagh Bridge 7.
Brooke, Captain H. Bryan 91.
Brooke, Captain H.V. 91
Brooke, Captain Sir Basil S. 83.
Brooke, Mrs 91.
Brookeborough 33, 59, 71, 92, 120.
Brown, John and Co., 110
Brown, Miss Annie 95.
Brown, Mr. F. R. 12, 77.
Brown, Mr. P. R. 12
Brown, Mr. W. J. 14.

Buchanan Street Station 74.
Buckingham Palace 3, 83, 93, 129.
Bulgarians 5, 68.
Bundoran 77, 91, 98, 101, 103.
Bunting, Edward 47.
Bunting, James 47.
Burke, ex-sergeant, Lurgan 23.
Burke, Sergeant T. E. 23.
Burkett, James Parsons 69, 70.
Burns, Martin 131.
Burns, Mr. 63.
Butler, Captain H. H.G. 91.
Butter Market, Enniskillen 120.
Byrne, Brigadier General John A. 93.
Byrne, Miss 78.
Byrne, Mr. Dublin 69.
Byrne, Thomas 33.

Caddick, Lance Corporal 15.
Cahirciveen 7, 110.
Calais 25.
Caldwell, Catherine 105.
Caldwell, Thomas E. 40.
Callowhill, Derrylin 60.
Cameron Highlanders 37, 41.
Cameron, Colonel D. W. 41
Campbell Bannerman, Sir H. 129.
Campbell, James 120.
Campbell, Major Stuart 116.
Canada 15, 24, 29, 53, 91, 116, 126.
Canadian Expeditionary Force 116.
Canadian General Hospital 53.
Canadian Infantry 53, 124.
Canadian Militia Department 83.
Captain W. 21.
Carlingford Lough 120.
Carlisle 40, 81.
Carn, Irvinestown 91.
Carnarvon 12.
Carney, Mr. Edward 14.
Carney, Mrs. Abbey St. 77.
Carney, Ptk. Nugent's Entry 63.
Carney, Sergeant James 14.
Carragher, Rev. Fr. 126.
Carrickmacross 4.
Carrickmore 56.
Carrigodrohid House 93.
Carron, Mr. Peter 40.
Carruthers, Alex. 92.
Carson, 80.
Carson, Frederick 30.
Carson, Mr. F. R. 128.
Carson, Sir Edward 7, 48, 59, 64, 66, 74, 81, 112, 113, 120..
Carter, Bonham 116.
Casement, Sir Roger 24, 42, 50, 52, 64, 96, 120, 126.
Cashel, County Leitrim 126.
Cashel, near Derrygonnelly 28.
Cassidy, Thomas 77.
Castle Archdale 83, 84, 89.
Castle Caldwell 105, 129.
Castle Irvine 7, 11, 21, 36, 86.
Castleblaney 4, 118, 119.
Castleconnell 131.
Castlederg 40.
Cathcart, Mr. John, Monea. 28.

Caulfield, Rev. Mr.
Caulfield, Sir St. George.
Cavan 2, 50, 101, 120.
Cavell, Nurse 21.
Cavendish Butler, Hon. Henry 91.
Celtic Football Club, Enniskillen. 65.
Chamberlain, Sir Neville 76, 93.
Champagne 25.
Cheevers, Private John 2.
Chicago 12.
China 23, 71.
Christian Brothers 68.
Christian Herald 118.
Churchill, Colonel Winston 29, 68, 79, 109.
Civilian Army 57.
Clancy, Mr. F. J. 98.
Clan-na-Gael 52.
Clanrickarde Estate 12.
Clanrickarde, Marquis of. 46, 47.
Claremont Mission 19.
Claremorris 25, 131.
Clark, Captain Wingfield 83.
Clark, Mrs. Elizabeth 83.
Clark, P. J. 65.
Cleary Sergeant 17, 18, 19, 38.
Cleary, Mrs. 15.
Cleary's, Messrs. 51.
Cleenish, parish of. 64.
Clegg, Mr. 71.
Clements, Mr. Mercier 47.
Clogher 79, 102.
Clogher Guardians 97.
Clogher, Bishop of. 89, 98.
Clogher, Dean of. 30.
Clones 30, 35, 40, 47, 89, 95, 100, 108, 111, 121, 122.
Clonkeelan, Clones 95.
Clyde Revolt 38.
Coade, J. J. 115.
Coghlan, Rev. John C. F. 102.
Coldstream Guards Regiment 19.
Colenso, battle of. 14.
Coleraine 94, 127.
Collins, Cornelius 55.
Collins, Miss Lizzy 125.
Colorado 24.
Compulsory Service Bill 61.
Connaught Rangers 118, 119.
Connaught's, Duchess of. 116.
Connemara, SS. 119, 120, 125.
Connolly, James 52, 57, 65, 68, 70, 74.
Connolly, Mrs. 98.
Conscription 7, 28, 56, 59, 77, 100, 112, 113, 119, 120.
Consistorial Congregation 20.
Consolidated Districts Board 49.
Constantinople 7, 9, 48.
Convery, Mr. J. P. 72.
Cookstown 2, 21, 104.
Coote, Mr. 40.
Coppard, George 89.
Cordite 81.
Cork 19, 25, 28, 57, 71, 73, 80, 93, 101, 118.
Cork Hill 51.
Cork Lunatic Asylum 102.
Cornagrade Terrace 126.
Coronal 80.
Corrigan, Alderman 37.
Corrigan, Mr. E.

Corscadden, Mr. P. 82,
Corscadden, Second Lt. 82.
Cosgrove, Councillor 43.
Costello, Peter 70.
Coulter Bros 130.
Coulter, Mr. Jason 7.
Cranfield.
Crawley-Boevey, Captain C. 31.
Creighton, Mr. 92.
Creighton, Tommy, 35.
Crete 71.
Crimea 19, 23, 86.
Crockett, Charlie 107.
Crockett, Lieutenant 51.
Crocknacrieve 15.
Crom 127.
Cromwell, Lord Protector 37, 115.
Crowe, Mr. and Mrs. T. 104.
Crowe, Second Lt. Cecil A. 107.
Crozier, General F.P. 116
Crozier, Mister J. J. P. 128.
Crudden, Patrick 50.
Crumley, Mr. Patrick, M.P. 7, 14, 63.
Crystal Palace 47.
Cuffley.
Cullen, Constable J. 80
Cullen, Gunner John J. 80.
Cullentra 47.
Curragh 51, 59, 69.
Curran, Sergeant 63.
Custom House 52.

D.M.P. 59.
D'Arcy Irvine, Admiral St. George. 23, 86.
D'Arcy Irvine, Captain C. W. 21.
D'Arcy Irvine, Captain W. 21.
D'Arcy Irvine, Commander J. 23.
D'Arcy Irvine, Major C. C. 7, 21, 36, 70.
D'Arcy Irvine, Mr. W. 21.
D'Arcy Irvine, Mrs, Castle Irvine, 11.
D'Arcy, Lance Corporal J. 97
D'Arcy, Mrs. Toneyloman 97.
Daily Chronicle
Daily Express 33, 51, 88.
Daily News 7, 112, 115.
Dalton 66.
Daly, Edward, (shot) 61.
Daly, Mister P. Ballyshannon 7.
Daly, Mr. Patrick 7, 110.
Daly, Mr. Robert 77.
Dame Street 55.
Dane, Mr. and Mrs. Thomas 126.
Dane, Private William 126.
Danzig 129.
Dardanelles 6, 9, 17, 20, 21, 25, 32, 86, 97, 116, 117.
Darling Street 99, 106.
David Watt and Co., Ltd 102.
Davies, General 9.
Davies, Mr. War Office 22.
Davitt, M. 72, 119.
Day, Rev Godfrey 98.
Day, Right Rev. Morris 89.
De Robeck, Admiral 9.
De Valera, Edward 71.
Deeping St. Nicholas 96.

Defence 78.
Defence of the Realm Act 27, 50, 92, 111, 122.
Delvin, County Westmeath 97, 98.
Denmark 80.
Derry 28, 60, 63, 67, 74, 81, 82, 83, 90, 93, 102, 104, 113, 127.
Derry City 63, 81, 83, 94, 113.
Derry dockers 67.
Derry Jail 40.
Derrygonnelly 28 127.
Derrylin 7 60.
Devenish, Parish of 92.
Devlin, Mr. 78, 94, 113.
Distinguished Conduct Medal 79.
Distinguished Stranger's Gallery 38.
Dixon, Mister T. 78, 114.
Dobbin, Lt. 100.
Doherty, Henry 102.
Dominion Parliament Buildings 18.
Dominion Square, Montreal 116.
Donaghmoyne 4.
Donaldson, D. and Son 127.
Donegal Board of Guardians 25.
Donegal town 17.
Donegal 25, 40, 53, 86, 91, 98, 99, 103, 127.
Donnelly, Mr. A. E. solicitor 58.
Donnelly, Private Francis 77.
Donnelly, Thomas, Market St. 63.
Donnington Hall 32.
Donoghue 57.
Donovan, Mr. 117.
Doris 86.
Dornock / Eastriggs 81.
Douaumont 47.
Dover 24, 34.
Doyle, Sir Arthur Conan 81.
Drapers Association 17.
Dresden 38.
Drogheda, History of. 66.
Dromahaire Dispensary District 120.
Dromore, Lord Bishop of. 20, 25, 98.
Drum, Lance Corporal P. 63.
Drumany 60.
Drumbad 27.
Drumclay, Enniskillen 28, 104.
Drumcoo 37.
Drumee 86.
Drumeer 37, 40.
Drumgorn Manor 119.
Drummee.
Drumpeen 91.
Drumskinny 17.
Dublin 2, 4, 13, 15, 17, 19, 25, 27, 34, 37, 41, 43, 47, 48, 50-71, 73, 75-77, 80, 82, 89, 93, 99, 101, 103, 104, 106, 109, 111, 114, 115, 117, 120. 121, 123, 127, 130.
Dublin Chamber of Commerce 62.
Dublin Corporation 48, 61, 61.
Dublin Metropolitan Police 60, 118.
Dublin Shipping Company 27.
Dublin slums 70.
Dublin Street, Monaghan 25, 111.
Dublin, County 66.
Duke, Mr. 32, 97, 131.
Dumfries and Galloway 81.
Dungannon 56, 57, 94.
Dunkirk 72.
Dunville, Lieutenant R. L. 53.

Eames, Mr. William 116.
Earls, Bro. Jas. 27,
East Tyrone 104.
Easter Monday 51, 57, 60, 67.
Eccles, Miss Muriel F. 106.
Eden Street, Enniskillen 19.
Ederney 20, 38, 72, 91, 92, 131.
Edinaclaw 38.
Edwards, John 91.
Edwards, Mr. John R. 91.
Egypt 14.
Elliot, Miss 124.
Elliott, Mr. William 36.
Ellis, Harry, Ederney 91.
Ellis, John, Ederney 91.
Ellis, Peter Beresford 116.
Ellis, the executioner 96.
Elmes, Lilly, Kesh 26.
Ely O'Carroll Territory.
Emerson, Private James 91.
Emerson, William, Mill St. 91.
Emmet, Robert 29.
England 4, 15, 18, 19, 25, 26, 28, 29, 30, 34, 37, 40, 43, 50, 51, 53, 54, 57, 59, 61, 63, 64, 68-71, 80, 90, 93, 96, 97, 99, 100, 101, 103, 110, 111, 116, 119, 120, 123, 126, 129.
Enniskillen Barracks 53, 66.
Enniskillen Catholic Ladies 7.
Enniskillen Post Office 8.
Enniskillen String Band 125.
Enniskillen Union 97, 128.
Enniskillen Workhouse 7, 14, 19.
Enniskillen Yacht Club 8.
Enniskillen - too numerous to enumerate.
Eshnadarragh 100.
Essex Street, Belfast 131.
Euston Station 50, 57.
Evicted Tenants Bill 49.

Fagan, James 37, 40.
Falcarragh 53.
Falkland Islands 80.
Falls, Cyril 43.
Falls, Major C. F. M.A. 8, 91.
Farnham Wood 29.
Farrell, Mr. 47
Farrell, Mr. C. Photographer, Clones.47
Farrell, Private Reuben 47.
Fartagh, Monea 63.
Faugh-a-Ballagh 50.
Faussett, Mr. 77
Feely, Michael 47.
Fermanagh 222 matches.
Fermanagh and Donegal Regiment 86.
Fermanagh County Board A. O. H. 92.
Fermanagh Herald 25, 103.
Fermanagh Times 8, 60, 104.
Fermanagh Unionist Association 116.
Fetherstonhaugh, Major 116, 117.
Fetherstonhaugh, Mr. Godfrey 117.
Finnegan, Sergeant Major 63.
Finnegan, Sergeant P. P. 64.
Fitzpatrick, Mr. 17
Fivemiletown 47, 120, 127.

Flanagan, Father 73.
Flanders 2, 6, 79.
Flannigan, Constable 28.
Florencecourt Station 77.
Flowers, Rev. Ed. Belleek 99.
Flowers, Second Lt. J. J. 99
Foch, General 88.
Fokker14.
Fortune 43.
Foster, Mr. 95.
Four Courts 51, 59.
Fox, Mrs. 36, 47.
Fox, Sergeant James. 63
Frankfurt 36.
Frauenlob 80.
Frederick Street 102.
Freemasons 118.
French, Captain B St. G. 91.
French, Field Marshall Viscount. 3, 37.
Fricourt 84, 88.
Fyffe, Sergeant 19.

Gaelic Athletic Association 76.
Gaelic League 14, 51, 66, 111, 118.
Galbraith, Mrs. 129.
Galbraith, Sergeant A. W. 129.
Gallacher, Lieutenant E. 64
Gallacher, Mrs. 82
Gallipoli 1, 9, 22, 68, 71, 119, 131.
Galtrim, Baron of. 67.
Galway 61.
Galway Estates 49.
Garrison 22, 27, 47, 80.
Gartside –Tipping, Commander 24, 25.
Gavin, Mr. T. J.P. 40, 110.
Geddes, George 86.
General Post Office, Dublin 51.
General Synod 52.
George 1V. 10.
German Battle Fleet 78.
German Commander-in-Chief 80.
Gibson, Miss 124.
Gibson, Mr. Justice 47.
Gifford, Miss Grace 66.
Gillis, District Inspector 40.
Ginchy 107.
Ginnell, Mr 69, 92.
Glancy, Mrs. 98.
Glasgow 4, 29, 57, 59, 68, 74, 79, 80, 90, 98, 103, 111, 120, 124.
Glasnevin Cemetery 61, 65, 96.
Gleeson, Father 24.
Glenade 77.
Glenfarne 50, 77, 80.
Godfrey, Patrick 131.
Goldney, Captain Bennett 24.
Good Templars 27.
Goodwin, John 30.
Gordon Highlanders 91.
Gordon. Lieutenant H. C. 8.
Gore, Captain 54, 80.
Gorman, Mary 21.
Gormley, Rev D. C.C. 93.
Gortmore Terrace, Omagh 71.
Graan, Enniskillen 43.

Grafton Street 37.
Graham, Lance-Corporal James 91.
Graham, Mr. George Drumpeen 91.
Graham, Mrs. Maguiresbridge 129.
Graham, Robert 129..
Granard 21.
Grand Lodge of Ireland 90.
Grant, Admiral C. S. G. 23.
Gray, County Inspector 55.
Gray, Major 30.
Great George's Street, Dublin 115.
Greenore 119, 120.
Grenadier Guards 53, 104.
Gresham Hotel 57.
Gretna 81.
Griffin, Gerald 67.
Griffith, Arthur 51.
Grome, Lance Corporal F. 63.
Grosvenor Place 72.
Gubrawooly, Swanlinbar 83.
Guidi, Flight Lt. 120.
Guillemont 107.

Haig, Sir Douglas 84, 87, 88.
Hall, James 63.
Hall, Lance-Corporal Frank 71.
Hamburg 38.
Hamilton Mrs. 17
Hamilton, General Sir Ian 6, 9, 21.
Hampshire, H.M.S. 53
Hanover Square 13
Hardie, Keir. 72
Harland and Wolff. 3
Harland, Sir Edward. 80
Harwood, Nicholas, 83
Haskin. 56
Healing Question, A. 115
Heaney, Archie. 92
Hegarty, Mrs. L Ballyshannon. 17
Hegarty, Private J. 17
Hemsworth Gas Works. 110
Henderson and Eadie 120
Henderson, Mr. James. 103
Henderson, Mrs. Cabra. 103
Henderson, Private P. 127
Henry, Mr. Denis S. K.C. 74
Hessey, Major. 14
Hibernian Bank 70
Hibernian Rifles 57
Hibernians, Ancient Order of. 82, 98, 118.
Higgins, John, a tramp. 111
Hindenburg. 25
Hiscocks, Mr. S. W. 31.
Hobson, Bulmer 68
Hoey, O'R. Greenhill. 59, 111.
Holroyd, Captain Fred 116.
Holyhead.56, 119, 120.
Home Rule 12, 56, 65, 70, 74, 80, 81, 83, 90, 92, 94.
Home Rule Act. 65, 83.
Hooge 23.
Hope, Private T. 13.
House of Commons 7, 38, 60, 61, 90, 92, 94, 116, 126.
Hoy, Anne of Scandally 28.
Hughes, Mr. Patrick, Castleblaney 119.
Hughes, Private Thomas.118

Hughes, Sir Sam, C-in-C. 29,
Hull 18, 103.
Humphreys, Father P.P. 123
Humphreys, Mrs. E. 124
Humphries Midshipman 35
Humphries, Mr. John 77.
Humphries, Mr. William 124.
Huntley District of 30.
Hussey, Mr. 67.
Hynes, Pte. W. Gas Lane 63.
Indefatigable 78.
India 3, 71, 93, 126.
Inishmore Hall 77, 91.
Innis Rath, Lisnaskea 91.
Inspector General RIC. 76, 93.
Invincible, H.M.S. 78, 80.
IRB 51.
Irish Boy Scouts 76.
Irish Land Purchase Act 1904 89.
Irish Liquor Trade. 92
Irish National Foresters 122.
Irish News 47, 59.
Irish Post 92, 116.
Irish Republican Brotherhood 51.
Irish Times 50, 51.
Irish Volunteers 33, 42, 55, 56, 57, 74.
Irish-Canadian Rangers 116.
Irvine Mrs 11.
Irvine, Admiral 23, 86.
Irvine, Captain C. 20, 21.
Irvine, Captain J. S. 119.
Irvine, Commander John 23.
Irvine, John 88.
Irvine, Major George M. 10, 21, 36.
Irvine, Mr. C. E. R. A. 119.
Irvine, Mr. Robert 131.
Irvine, Mr. William 63.
Irvine, Rev George M. 86.
Irvinestown 2, 10, 11, 36, 40, 77, 77, 91, 92, 94, 103, 111, 121, 131..
Isle of Man 3.
Isle of Wight 90.
Italy 116, 126.

Jacobs Biscuit Factory 55.
Japan 121.
Jellicoe, Admiral 80.
Jenkins, Rev. Mr. A. J. 66.
Johnson, Tommy 86.
Johnston William 18, 63.
Johnston, Granard 21.
Johnston, Jack 33.
Johnston, Judge 67, 68.
Johnston, Matthew 19.
Johnston, Mr. George 129.
Johnston, Mr. John 102.
Johnston, Mr. Robert 94.
Johnston, Thomas 92.
Johnstone, Sarah, Lack. 18.
Jones, Mr. Hugh 105.
Jones, Pte. J. 63.
Jordan, Jeremiah M.P. 8.
Jutland, Battle of. 78, 80.

Kelly, Alderman James 115.
Kelly, Mrs 36.Kemmell-Wytschaete
Kelly, Private T. Townhall St. 30.
Kenny, Mr. Justice 48.
Kent 2, 31.
Kent, Thomas 71.
Kent, William 71.
Keown Mr. 17.Kerns, George.
Keown, Mrs. Cross St. 118
Keown, Patrick P. P. 103, 108, 114.
Kerr, Captain W. P. 107.
Kerry 19, 76, 110.
Kesh 12, 26, 91, 103, 110.
Kettle, Lieutenant T. M. 104, 107.
Kettle, Mrs. 104
Kildallen Rectory, Belturbet 2.
Kilkeel old Churchyard 126.
Killarney 76.
Killduff, Constable.
Killorglin 56.
Killybegs 91.
Killybuggy 19.
Killyhevlin 50.
Kilmainham Prison 72, 78.
Kilmorey, Earl of. 29.
Kiltimagh 131.
King, Captain E. J. 2.
King, Rev. E. J. 2.
King's African Rifles 35, 128.
King's Bench Division, Dublin 47.
King's Liverpool Regiment 82.
King's Medal 14.
Kingsbridge 69.
Kingstown 67.
Kirkpatrick, Mr. 14
Kitchener, Lord 78, 79, 88, 116.
Kitchener's Volunteer Army 87.
Knight, Mr. M. E. 95, 112.
Knott, Captain J. E. 63, 65.
Knox, Dr. 7, 95.
Knox, Mrs. 95.
Knox, Private. 51.

La Boiselle 88.
Labouchere, Mr. 49.
Ladysmith 127.
Lambert, Mr. G. 68.
Lancashire Fusiliers 99.
Lanesborough, Earl of. 91.
Lansdowne Road 67.
Larkin, Jim 54.
Larne 66, 76, 127.
Latimer, Joseph, Cross St. 118.
Lauder, Captain John 131.
Lauder, Harry 131.
Lavelle, Mr. Alex 126.
Law, Mr. Bonar 7, 18, 129.
Law, Sergeant R. 91.
Leclerc, Maurice 21.
Leicestershire Regiment 83.
Leonard, Corp. Jim, Market St. 63, 65.
Leonard, Lt. F. P. M. 63
Leonard, Mrs. Head St. 47.
Leslie, Colonel Sir John 50, 63, 99, 103.

Levinson, David 40, 47.
Liberty Hall, Dublin 23, 51, 54, 70.
Liddle, Flight Sub-Lt. T. R. 63.
Liddle, Mr. Hugh 63.
Lilio, Luigi 84.
Limburg 24.
Limerick 56, 73, 122.
Limerick County Board, G.A.A. 122
Lincolnshire 96, 122.
Lion.
Lipsett, Brigadier General L. J. 3, 83.
Liquor Control Board 29, 81..
Lisbellaw 12, 15, 23, 74, 77, 91, 120, 126, 127.
Lisnarick 2, 91.
Lisnaskea 7, 10, 13-15, 23, 24, 33, 36, 40, 50, 63, 69, 90-92, 95, 98, 108, 110, 111, 119, 126, 131.
Lissadell 54, 113.
Little, John, Manoo, Kesh 91.
Little, Mrs. Irvinestown 92.
Liverpool 30, 40, 47, 82, 121.
Liverpool Echo 36.
Liverpool Post 127.
Lloyd, Fannie Kathleen 21.
Lloyd, Lt. Colonel Jesse 21.
Local Government Board 33, 62, 95, 108, 109, 120, 130.
Lochiel 41.
London 18, 27, 34-36, 48-50, 58, 64,78, 88, 96, 99, 100, 105, 110, 113, 115-117, 119, 123, 125, 127.
London and N. W. railway 47.
London Police Force 65.
Londonderry 51.
Lonsdale, Sir John 59.
Lothian farmers 98.
Lough Derg 99, 103, 108.
Lough Erne Drainage 8, 71, 120, 127.
Lough, Lieutenant S. P. 124.
Lough, Mrs. Maguiresbridge 124.
Lough, Robert 124.
Lower Abbey Street 51.
Lowry, Admiral Sir Robert 29.
Lowry, George, wounded 92.
Lowry, Lt. General Robert 29.
Loyal Volunteers 60.
Lunny, Mr. 95.

MacDonagh, Thomas 65, 66.
MacManus, Mr. Seamus 25.
MacManus, Seamus 25, 42
Madden, Colonel 56.
Madden, Dr.131.
Madden, Mr. Justice 42.
Magee, Constable 53.
Magee, Daniel, Garrison 80.
Magee, James 80.
Magee, Joseph28.
Magheraculmoney 89, 124.
Magherafelt 94.
Maguire, Bro. 92.
Maguire, County Inspector 30.
Maguire, Dr. 131.
Maguire, Elizabeth 118.
Maguire, Mr. J. 108
Maguire, Mr. Michael 8.
Maguire, Mr. Moses 28.
Maguire, Mr. William J.P. 72

Maguire, Mrs. Annie 28.
Maguire, Sargent C. 85.
Maguiresbridge 15, 37, 40, 77, 80, 90, 92, 95, 113, 119, 124, 129..
Mahaffey, Dr.51.
Makeny 91.
Malahide 66, 67.
Malins, Mr. 123.
Mallon, Inspector NSPCC 13.
Malta 71.
Mametz 88.
Manchester 105, 111.
Manchester Guardian 79, 115.
Manorhamilton 19, 82, 113, 120.
Mansion House, Dublin 37.
Markievicz, Countess 13, 28, 54, 56, 61, 76.
Marlboro Police Court 121.
Marshall Law 66.
Martin, Gerald 63.
Martin, Joseph 4.
Martin, Mr. (acting master) 131.
Martinpuich 105.
Maxwell, Sir John l 93.
Mayo 25, 131.
McAleer, Billy 92.
McAnerin, Mrs. 124.
McArdle, Mr. Peter 4.
McBride, Major 61.
McBrien, Mrs. 82
McBrien, Mrs. David 22.
McBrien, Private David 22.
McCaffrey, Mrs. 102
McCaffrey, Private Tom 102.
McCanny, Owen 19.
McCarroll, Rev. Fr. 96.
McClintock, Robert 91.
McCloy, John 111.
McCormick, Patrick 14.
McCullagh, Mr. 40.
McDermott, John 68.
McDonagh, Mrs 124.
McDonagh, Mrs. E. 124
McElgun, Mister J. 14, 69, 108.
McElgunn, Annie 125.
McElgunn, Miss Jeannie 120, 125, 126.
McElgunn, Mr. H, Ann St. 125.
McElgunn, Robert Hugh 125.
McGahey, Robert 92.
McGahey, Sergeant Major 63
McGlade, Sergeant 63.
McGrath, Ambrose O.S., C.F.I.G. 26
McGuinn, Sgt J. S. 26.
McGurn, Mrs. 99.
McHugh, Dr. of Derry 82.
McHugh, Mr. Pettigo 97.
McIntyre, Mr. P. J. 78, 114.
McKeown, Mr. 17.
McKiernan, James 98.
McKinley, Second Lieutenant 20.
McLean, Constable 103.
McMahon, Father 82.
McManus, Corporal Bernard 99.
McManus, Miss 99.
McManus, Mr. James J.P. 71,
McManus, Mr. John 25.
McManus, Mr. Matthew 83.
McManus, Mrs. Strand St. 99
McManus, Private James 71.

McManus, Private Patrick 83.
McManus, Private Thomas 83.
McMeekin, Second Lt.77
McMillan Mr 22.
McNiff, Sargent 65.
McNulty, Mister P. 69.
McQuaid, Rev P. C.C. 122.
McRae, George 91.
Meath, County 55, 56, 77, 80.
Mercer, Major General 83.
Mercer, Sophia 17.
Methodist 8.
Metz 25.
Meux, Admiral Sir H. 29.
Meyer, Lieutenant 32.
Milan 36.
Mildina 42.
Miles, Trooper Harold J. 22.
Military Cross 77, 79, 83, 119, 124.
Military Service Act 22, 25, 35, 96, 98, 101, 103, 112.
Milligan, Miss Alice 36.
Milligan, Mr. Seton F. 36
Milligan, Second-Lieutenant 63.
Millihan, Mr. G. A. 82.
Mills, Dr. John, 111.
Mitchell, Freddie 92.
Moan, Mr. Charlie 98.
Moat Hall, Lisnaskea 119.
Moat School 24.
Moffitt, Miss 131.
Moffitt, Mr. William 131.
Moffitt, Mrs. 131
Moffitt, Sergeant Arthur J. B. 131
Molloy, Constable 38.
Molloy, Mary 13.
Monaghan County of, 20, 21, 25, 111, 118, 119, 120.
Monaghan, Mrs. 17.
Monroe, General Sir C. 9.
Montana 120.
Moohan, Mr. John 68.
Moohan, Mrs. 68.
Moore, George T. 92
Moore, Mrs. Margaret M. 41, 42.
Moraghy, near Castleblaney 4.
Morris, Captain W. A 82
Morris, Joseph 32.
Morris, Second Lt. W. 82
Morrison, James 30.
Morrison, Mr. James 77.
Mossband near Longtown 81.
Mount Argus 43.
Mount Jerome Cemetery 61.
Mountcharles 25.
Mudros 119.
Mulcahy, Mr. P. E. 104
Mulhern, Rev Dr. 20, 25, 98.
Mullaghdun 7.
Mulleek 103.
Mulligan, Dr. 131
Mulligan, Mr James 40.
Munitions 2, 22, 25, 28, 38, 47, 48, 62, 77, 81, 97, 120.
Murphy, Hugh 100.
Murphy, Mr. Judge 65.
Murphy, Thomas 131.
Mussolini 116.
Myles, Captain J. S. 91
Myles, Mr. John, Ballyshannon 91.

Nahan, Mr Matthew 73.
National Aid Association 114, 119, 126.
National School Teachers 123.
Navan 4, 55.
Neale, Mr. 69.
Nelson Monument 68.
Nelson, Mrs. East Bridge S. 86
Nelson, Sergeant, David 119.
Nelson, William 86.
Nenagh 24.
Neville, Mr. 52.
Nevin, Rev. Father Eugene 43.
New York Sun 68.
New Zealander 81.
Newbridge 69.
Newcastle-on-Tyne 67.
Newman, Mrs. Agnes 120.
Newry 29, 119, 120.
Newtownbutler
Nicaragua 23, 86.
Nicholson, James, Constable 17, 19.
Nigeria 120.
Nine Acres, Phoenix Park 103.
Nivarre, Sub Lieutenant 72.
Noble, Andrew 19.
Noble, Bro. J. W. 27.
Noble, Bros. Clones 108.
Noble, Sergeant 124.
Noblett's toffee shop 59.
Norfolk 89, 90.
North Wall, Dublin 25, 93.
North Westmeath 92.
Northampton 58.
Northern Bank 10.
NSPCC 13.
Nugent, Major General 84.

O'Carroll, Richard 115.
O'Connell Street 59.
O'Connell, Mr. P. J. 110
O'Connell, Sir Morgan 76.
O'Connor, Mr. T. P. 131.
O'Doherty, Rev. Monsignor 81.
O'Duffy, Kevin 57.
O'Dwyer, Dr. Bishop 73.
O'Hanrahan, Henry 61.
O'Hanrahan, Michael 61.
O'Hara, Mrs. Henry St. 120.
O'Keefe, Mrs. Garrison 22.
O'Keeffe, Rev. G. E. 22
O'Neill, Alderman C. D.L. 94.
O'Neill, Eoin 57.
O'Neill, Lizzie 103.
O'Neill, Rev. Dr. 20.
O'Neill, Right Rev Monsignor. 30.
O'Rahilly, The 61.
O'Tooles 67.
Old Age Pensions Act 40.
Old Crompton 121.
Oldpark Road, Belfast 110.
Olympic 124, 125.
Omagh 20, 21, 36, 58, 71, 81, 85, 94, 104.

Omeath 29.
Oola 131.
Orange and Green, Battalion of 116.
Orangemen 90.
Oranmore 61.
Orkneys 78.
Ottawa 8.
Owens, Private P., Lisbellaw 127.
Oxford Union 104.
Oxfordshire, Hospital ship 25.

Pall Mall Gazette 122.
Pallasgreen 122.
Parker, Andrew, Ann St. 30.
Parnell, Mr. C. S. 111, 119.
Patten Dr. 9.
Patten, Mr. John 91.
Patten, William, gassed 91.
Patterson, William 131.
Peace Preservation Act 76.
Pearce, Margaret 69.
Pearce, P. H. 56, 57, 65, 69, 78.
Pearce, William 61, 69.
Pearl Harbour 121.
Pelly, Captain W.S.H. 91.
Pelly, Rev. C.H. M.A. 91.
Pembroke, H.M. Dockyard 83.
Penelope 86.
Percy Place 58.
Perth 40, 47, 74.
Petite Journal 123.
Petrograd 78.
Pettigo 27, 29, 50, 53, 92, 97, 108.
Pettigo Court 130.
Phillips, Captain 93.
Phillips, Mrs. T. 124
Pilgrim Sect 15.
Pim, Mr. Justice 80.
Plunkett, Honourable Maud 67.
Plunkett, Joseph 61, 66.
Poison Gas 104.
Poiziers 132.
Pontefract Petty Sessions 110.
Pope Gregory XIII 84.
Portadown 56.
Porter Porter, Mr. J. Belleisle 23, 71.
Porter, Benjamin 110.
Porter, Captain J. G. 23.
Porter, Second-Lieutenant H. A. 23.
Portobello Barracks 61, 65, 72, 78, 100, 114, 115.
Portobello Bridge 72.
Portobello Shootings 65, 100.
Portora Royal School 60, 79, 97, 104, 106, 107.
Portrush 98.
Portsmouth 27.
Powis, Lord 68.
Presbyterian minister 66.
Presentation Bros. 100.
Presley, George 8.
Presley, John 8.
Press Association 7, 57, 58.
Preston magistrates 67.
Prince of Wales 86.
Princess Mary, H.R.H. 15.
Princess Patricia's 53.

Pullnaranny, Ballintra 17.

Queen Mary, RMS.78, 81, 125.
Queen Street 63, 120.
Queen's Medal 14.
Queenstown Hospital 25.
Quigley, Father 77.
Quigley, Mr. James 77.
Quincy 107.
Quinn Willie, the Diamond 19.
Quinn, Corporal J. R.I.R. 85.
Quinn, Mr. Thomas, the Diamond 85.
Quinn, Mr. William 2.
Quinn, Sergeant 121.

Rafferty, Private G. 127
Raineford, Martin 131.
Rankin, Jeannette Pickering 120.
Rathgate 55.
Rathkeeland 71.
Rathmines 13, 52, 115.
Rathmullan 23.
Rawlinson, General H. 88.
Read, Alexander 53.
Read, Bro. W. 27
Read, Fred 53.
Read, Jennie 53.
Read, Mr. Robert 53.
Read, Private S. T. 53.
Reading 103.
Reading, Lord 116.
Reagan, Constable 50.
Red Cross 8, 55, 97.
Redmond, Mr John 7, 28, 29, 56, 57, 59, 61, 65, 66, 77, 92, 94, 99, 113, 119, 120.
Redmond, Mr. William 90.
Reid, Mr., Warden 80.
Reid, Seaman Gunner 80.
Reid, Second Lt. 20
Reihill, Mr. 131.
Rellan 100.
Rennick, Mr. 108.
Retriever 119, 120.
Reuters 105.
Rialto Bridge 61.
Richardson, General Sir G. 84.
Richardson, Mr. H. S. 36.
Richardson, William 10.
Ring, Rev. Dean 96.
Ritchie, William 104, 108, 109.
Ritty, Captain J. 63.
River Laune 56.
River San Juan Expedition 86.
Riversdale 35, 80, 82.
Robertson, Sir William 87.
Robinson Mr. David 79.
Robinson, Alice C. Ardess 124.
Robinson, Lt. W. L. 99.
Robinson, Mr. 130.
Robinson, Mr., Inspector 95.
Robinson, Mrs. 124.
Robinson, Rev. C D.D. 89.
Roche, Corporal Frank, Mary Street 63.

Rogers, Mr. Deputy Coroner 28.
Roman Catholic Church 76, 96, 98.
Romania 129.
Roosevelt, President Theodore 116.
Roscommon 90, 125.
Rosemount 102.
Ross, Dr., Clogher 102.
Ross, Miss Ivy Kathleen 102
Rossborough, Robert 121.
Rossnowlagh 98.
Rotherhithe 103.
Rowe, Head Constable 71.
Royal Army Medical Corps 22.
Royal College of Music, London 36.
Royal Dublin Fusiliers 60, 65, 104, 117.
Royal Engineers 116, 121.
Royal Flying Corps 10, 90.
Royal Horse Artillery 119.
Royal Horticultural Society 113.
Royal Irish Constabulary 17, 76, 93, 118.
Royal Irish Fusiliers 85, 121.
Royal Irish Rifles.
Royal Munster Fusiliers 83.
Royal School for Girls 99, 106.
Ruddell, Rev Canon 89.
Runciman, Mr. 126, 127.
Rupprecht, Prince 105.
Russell, Charles, 32.
Russell, Mr. P.W. 117.
Russia 13, 23, 25, 78, 86, 126.
Russian Military Cross 77.
Ryan, Mr. James 122.
Rylands, John, Library 105.

Sackville Street 51, 54, 76.
Saint Aloysius, Garnethill 68.
Salonika 60.
Sandra, armoured yacht 24, 25.
Saskatchewan 24.
Saskatoon 53.
Scheere, Herr. 80.
Scollan, Irvinestown 94.
Scotland 30, 34, 40, 50, 61, 74, 90, 98, 100, 103.
Scots Guards 115.
Scotshouse 95.
Scott, Mr. P. J.P. 120, 127.
Scottish Corporative Society 30.
Sebastopol 19, 23.
Seraing 80.
Serbia 2, 4..
Sewell, Captain W. T. 91.
Shanagher, Sergeant John 55.
Shankill 126.
Shannon, Second Lieutenant 20.
Shark 80.
Shaughnessy, Lord 29.
Sheehy, Mr. David M. P. 104.
Sheehy-Skeffington, Mr. 65, 72, 78, 114, 115.
Sheehy-Skeffington, Mrs. 116.
Shelburne Hotel 76.
Shelburne Road 67.
Shell Crisis of 1915 81.
Shureys, Mrs. Angus 31.
Simpson, Henry 67.
Simpson, Joseph, Private 91.

Simpson, Mr. T. 97.
Simpson, Mrs. Castlecoole. 97.
Simpson, Private, Castlecoole 97.
Simpson, Robert, Private 97.
Sinn Fein 28, 32,33, 37, 43, 48, 50-56, 59, 61, 62, 64-66, 68, 69, 73, 74,76, 77, 80,90, 92, 93, 120.
Skibbereen 120.
Sligo 16, 50, 54, 60, 119, 131.
Slushill 50.
Smith, Kate 95.
Smith, Lance Corporal F. 63.
Smith, Maggie Ellen 95.
Smith, Mr. Patrick, Tullyalt 95.
Smith, Mrs. 95
Smith, Sergeant J. 65.
Smith, Sir F. E. 64.
Smyth, D. I., Henry.
Snitterton Hall 105.
Solway Firth 81.
Somers, Mrs. Ann 30.
Somme 84, 87, 88, 89, 90, 99, 104, 105, 122, 124.
South Africa 14, 20, 93, 115, 116.
South Derry 74.
Southampton 25.
Southern Star 120.
Spalding 96.
Spanish Armada 12.
Sparrowhawk 78.
St. Eloi 124.
St. Enda's 78.
St. Macartan's Seminary 20.
St., Columb's Hall, Derry 113.
St., Michael's, Enniskillen 100.
Stack, Mr. Austin 55.
Stackpole, H de Vere 32.
Stannard, Mr. H. R. 122.
Stavanger Aftenblad 106.
Steven's Green 52, 57.
Stewart, Colonel H. St. George 41.
Stewart, missing 92.
Stobcross Quay 74.
Stockwell Street, Glasgow 120.
Stourbridge 120.
Strabane 85, 94, 111.
Strong, Sir James H. Bart. 90
Studdert's Bog 95.
Surrey 2, 120.
Sutherland, Duke of. 97.
Suvla Bay 2, 6, 21, 36.
Swan, Mr. William 60.
Swinford 131.
Swords 104.
Sydare School 15.
Sydney, New South Wales 131.

Talbot, Sir Richard 67.
Tawnagorm 129.
Temperance Council 28.
Temple, Sir William, Knight 89.
Templemaghery 89.
Tennant, Mr. 13, 24, 69.
The Hospital 121.
The Mollies and the Masons 120.
The War and One Year After 115.
Thomas, Captain 53.

Thomas, Mr. J. H. MP 58.
Thompson, Private John A. 60.
Tierney Rev. John 66.
Tierney, Rev. Jas. 66.
Time Ireland Act 1916
Tipperary 78.
Tipperary Volunteers 57.
Tipperary, County of 123.
Titanic 124, 125.
Tottenham, Captain C.G.L. 80.
Tottenham, Midshipman D. 80.
Tottenham, Mr. P. M. 80.
Toughy, Constable 28.
Townhall Street 30, 36, 104.
Tracy, Bro. D. C. 92.
Tralee 55.
Trimble, Alwyn 60.
Trimble, Mr. W Copeland 16, 60, 101.
Trimble, Reginald 60.
Trimble, Second Lt. Noel D. 60, 63, 107.
Trinity College 51, 53, 60, 89, 106.
Tuam 131.
Tudenham Park 80.
Tullamore 32, 33, 69.
Tullycreevy 28.
Turbulent 78.
Turnbull, Dr. 74.
Turnbull, Lieut. R.A.M.C. 38.
Tynan Abbey, Armagh 90.
Tyrone County Council 58.

U.S. Congress 120, 121.
Ulster 7, 8, 40, 66, 81-83, 85, 87, 90-93, 101, 103, 111, 112, 118, 126.
Ulster Bank 10, 104, 107.
Ulster Division 19, 63, 84, 85, 87, 91, 113.
Ulster Militia Battalion 115.
Ulster Volunteer 76.
United Kingdom 7, 22.
UVF 84.

Vance, Mr. J. G. S. 80.
Vance, Sub lieutenant P. J. 80.
Vane, Sir Francis Fletcher 114, 115, 116.
Vane, Sir Henry 115.
Verdun 25, 38, 72, 80, 87, 120.
Victoria Cross 89, 91.
Victoria Hotel 130.
Victoria, Australia 42.
Vimy Ridge 72.
Virginia 23, 24.
Virtue Mrs. 19.
Von Hacteler 25.

Walker, Mr. R.M. 13, 16.
Wallace, Major Colin 116.
Walmsley, Miss M. 124.
Walsh, Archbishop 76.
Walton, Colonel H. P. killed 107.
Walton, H. W. Dalzell Lt. Col. 94.
War Savings, Committee 29.

Wardley 26.
Warrenpoint 120.
Warrior 78, 80.
Waterloo 21.
Waternerry, Enniskillen 65.
Watson, Rev. R. 89.
Weekly Dispatch 4, 38, 122.
Weights and Measures Act 30.
Weir, Mr. 91.
Weir, William 91.
West, Mr. John 15.
West, W. H. 12, 15.
Westmeath 80, 92, 97.
Westmoreland Chambers 72.
Wheeler, Mrs. 36.
White Bros, Messrs Omagh 20.
White, Second-Lieutenant E. 77.
White, Sir George 127.
Whitehaven 30.
Wicklow 52, 67.
Wilson Robert 19.
Wilson, U.S. President 42.
Winnipeg Telegram 83.
Woaghternerry 63.
Wolverhampton 67.
Woods, Mr. Robert 47.
Worcester Regiment, R.F.C. 99.
Wray, Mr. John F. LL.B. 94.
Wray, Second Lieutenant C. 94.
Wright, Rev Jackson 129.
Wurttemberg, Duke of 84.
Wyndham Land Act 83.

Yacht Club 8.
Young, Lt. Colonel Lt. Colonel, killed 107.
Young, Mr. D. 20.
Young, S. H. Private, 20.
Ypres 5, 25, 83, 84.

Zeppelins 18, 29, 40.
Zingg, Miss Dolly 42.
Zingg, Mr. and Mrs 42.